Theology and Poetry in Early Byzantium

Theology and Poetry in Early Byzantium examines the *kontakia* and thought-world of Romanos the Melodist, the sixth-century hymnographer whose vibrant and engaging compositions had a far-reaching influence in the history of Byzantine liturgy. His compositions bring biblical narratives to life through dialogue, encourage a level of participation unparalleled in homiletics and push the boundaries of liturgical expression of theology. This book provides an original analysis of Romanos' poetry, drawing attention to the coherence of his theology and the performative nature of his rhetoric. The main theological themes which emerge encourage the congregation to enact the life of Christ and anticipate the new creation: restoration of humanity to God, recreation in the incarnation and life of Christ, and liturgical participation and transformation in that life. By analysing the rhetorical performance of theology in the *kontakia*, the book provides new insights into religious practice in late antiquity.

SARAH GADOR-WHYTE is a Research Fellow of the Australian Catholic University in the Institute for Religion and Critical Inquiry, based at St Patrick's Campus in Melbourne. She is a scholar of late antiquity and Byzantium and has published widely on Romanos, the cult of the Virgin, late antique historiography and religious conflict in late antiquity.

Theology and Poetry in Early Byzantium

The *Kontakia* of Romanos the Melodist

SARAH GADOR-WHYTE

CAMBRIDGE
UNIVERSITY PRESS

CAMBRIDGE
UNIVERSITY PRESS

University Printing House, Cambridge CB2 8BS, United Kingdom

One Liberty Plaza, 20th Floor, New York, NY 10006, USA

477 Williamstown Road, Port Melbourne, VIC 3207, Australia

314-321, 3rd Floor, Plot 3, Splendor Forum, Jasola District Centre, New Delhi - 110025, India

103 Penang Road, #05-06/07, Visioncrest Commercial, Singapore 238467

Cambridge University Press is part of the University of Cambridge.

It furthers the University's mission by disseminating knowledge in the pursuit of
education, learning and research at the highest international levels of excellence.

www.cambridge.org
Information on this title: www.cambridge.org/9781316505618
DOI: 10.1017/9781316492512

First published 2017
First paperback edition 2021

A catalogue record for this publication is available from the British Library

ISBN 978-1-107-14013-4 Hardback
ISBN 978-1-316-50561-8 Paperback

For Michael

Contents

Preface

This book examines Romanos the Melodist's vibrant theological poetry, which until recently has received too little attention in its own right. Thankfully there now appears to be a resurgence of interest in Romanos and so, as one of my colleagues suggested, perhaps we are now in the midst of a 'Romanos renaissance'. In my own contribution, I examine theological ideas and their rhetorical vehicles, focusing on Romanos' theology of salvation and the performative techniques he employs. The key concepts which help to construct Romanos' coherent vision are God's correction and perfection of humanity, the inauguration of a new creation, participation in that creation and anticipation of its final consummation. Romanos' *kontakia* were liturgical texts and, through clever use of rhetorical devices including metaphor, paradox, typology and characterization, Romanos educates his audience and engages them in a performance of their own salvation.

Romanos' thought-world is important for understanding his ideas and to this end I endeavour to consider the inspiration of earlier Greek and Syriac preachers and poets on Romanos' *kontakia*, the deep influence of scripture and its typological significance, the centrality of liturgical performance and sensory perception, the impact of rhetoric and its embodiment, and the effects of different cultural interactions. The *kontakia* enact a lived theology in a time of complex doctrinal controversy and intercultural contact and give us insights into sixth-century lay practice and the communication of theology to a wide audience.

I started work on Romanos as a PhD candidate at the University of Melbourne, under the supervision of Roger Scott, to whom I owe a great deal. Roger's careful reading has been extremely helpful, as have been his encouragement to publish, his generous introductions to other scholars and his continued interest in the project. My thanks go also to Ruth Webb and Mary Cunningham, who generously gave up their time to guide me through the PhD while I was in London and afterwards.

The book has undergone many changes since the dissertation, and I would like to thank all those who helped me to reshape the manuscript. I thank my PhD examiners, Pauline Allen and Niki Tsironis, for their suggestions for transforming the dissertation into a book, and the readers of

Cambridge University Press for their critical analysis of my manuscript at varying stages of development. I am particularly grateful to Derek Krueger for his detailed and insightful criticism of my work, which challenged my thinking and spurred me to make radical revisions, resulting in a book of, I hope, much more depth and wider interest. I also thank Michael Sharp at Cambridge University Press for seeing the potential in the manuscript and for patiently allowing me to recraft it.

I am very grateful to Mich, Peter, Gaye, Neil, Pip, Jean, Tom, Andrew, Matthew, Miranda, Benita and Callum who at different times entertained our son Samuel while I worked, encouraged me to finish it and generally supported me through the process. I thank Matthew and Miranda particularly for their determination to look after Samuel and give me time to work while we were in Cambridge, enabling me to make the most significant revisions.

My especial thanks go to Michael, to whom I dedicate this book, for puzzling with me for so long about Romanos and for his constant love and support; and to Samuel, for whom Romanos is a bit of a mystery, but who has an insatiable love of books and may one day read this one.

Introduction

Hymn, hymn this man, Adam. Worship the one coming to you.
For he appeared for you, as you went forward to observe him,

　　　　　　　　　　　　　to grope for and receive him.
This man whom you feared, when you were deceived,

　　　　　　　　　　　　　because of you became like you.
He came down to the earth so that he might take you up.
He became mortal so that you might become god
and might put on the foremost dignity.
Wishing to open Eden again he lived in Nazareth.
So because of these things sing, man, and chanting rejoice
in the one who appears and illuminates everything.

Ὕμνησον, ὕμνησον τοῦτον, Ἀδάμ·

　　　　　　　προσκύνησον τὸν ἐλθόντα πρὸς σέ·
ἐφάνη γάρ σοι, ὡς ἐχώρεις, 　θεωρῆσαι αὐτόν,

　　　　　　　　　ψηλαφῆσαι καὶ δέξασθαι·
οὗτος ὃν ἐφοβήθης, 　ὅτε ἐξηπατήθης, 　διὰ σὲ ὡμοιώθη σοι·
κατέβη ἐπὶ γῆς, 　ἵνα λάβῃ σε ἄνω·
ἐγένετο θνητός, 　ἵνα σὺ θεὸς γένῃ
καὶ ἐνδύσῃ 　τὴν πρώτην εὐπρέπειαν·
θέλων ἀνοῖξαι πάλιν τὴν Ἐδὲμ 　ᾤκησε τὴν Ναζαρέτ·
διὰ ταῦτα οὖν ᾆσον, 　ἄνθρωπε, καὶ ψάλλων τέρπε
τὸν φανέντα 　καὶ φωτίσαντα πάντα.[1]

On the Epiphany (VI.3)

Singing and worship were intricately intertwined for Romanos the Melodist.
His sung verse sermons (*kontakia*) express a vibrant and optimistic theology about the present reign of Christ and the approaching end time and encourage listeners to partake in that optimism as they worship. Romanos addresses Adam, both as a figure for all humanity and as a type for Christ,

---

[1] The text of the *kontakia* throughout is taken from, and laid out according to, the Oxford edition: Maas and Trypanis (1963). I have also consulted the Sources chrétiennes edition: Grosdidier de Matons (1964–81). All translations are mine unless otherwise stated, but my translations have been informed by the work of Bandy (1975), (1976), Carpenter (1970), Grosdidier de Matons (1964–81), Lash (1995), Schork (1995). I have also consulted Koder (2005), Maisano (2002).

the second Adam. Rhetorical repetition ('Hymn, hymn', line 1) creates a sense of urgency, reflecting Adam's indebtedness to God, who willingly took on human form for his salvation (3). This is the great exchange (5): the second Adam corrects the sins of the first and restores him to perfection. So begins a new creation, a reopening of paradise (7), and one which God freely wills out of love for his first creation. God's actions not only call for worship, in song, but also for expectation of his second advent ('the one *coming* to you', 1).

This passage, from Romanos' *kontakion On the Epiphany*, gives a foretaste of the theological ideas which will be the focus of this book: Christ as the second Adam, who corrects the sins of the first and restores him to perfection; the new creation Christ inaugurates at the incarnation; and how Christians are called to live in that new creation and in preparation for its final consummation in the eschaton. These themes already had a long history in Christian literature and ideas. Reading Romanos' hymns provides evidence for the spread of earlier Christian doctrines presented to a wide audience, largely of lay people, in vibrant poetry and arresting images. Romanos' hymns do not attempt startling theological novelty but he does argue for the truth of a coherent theological vision and seeks to demonstrate its vital importance for Christians living in the sixth century. As preacher, Romanos aims to draw his listeners into deep communion with Christ so that they may anticipate the perfections of heaven in their daily lives.

Romanos' poetics – his clever use of rhetorical techniques and literary devices, his careful choice of vocabulary and the abundant excess of imagery – makes his preaching vivid and emotionally engaging. We have seen Romanos' use of repetition to create a sense of urgency, and his direct address to Adam which transforms Adam, whose plight reflects that of all humanity, into a contemporary figure. Assonance strengthens the link between singing and worship, and the diversity of singing words (lines 1 and 8: 'hymn', 'sing', 'chant') emphasizes the importance of song with deft rhetorical variation. Romanos personalizes God's actions for the life of each member of the congregation by repeating the singular pronoun 'you' ('This man whom *you* feared, when *you* were deceived, because of *you* became like *you*'). In this way, he encourages his audience to identify with Adam. Repeated rhetorical antitheses emphasize the salvific exchange between God and humanity ('He came down to the earth so that he might take you up: He became mortal so that you might become god'). Moreover, alliteration of compounds denoting light and revelation in the final line strengthens the link between Christ's appearance and his dramatic reversal of human darkness. Romanos' use of language is playful and creative, vibrant and captivating.

We will see throughout the corpus Romanos' skilful elaboration of scripture, his vivid language and abundant use of imagery. Take, for example, the *kontakion On the Entry into Jerusalem* (XVI.12):

For was I not dissatisfied with angels? I loved you, the beggar,
                                        I hid my glory
and I, the rich one, have willingly became poor. For I long for you very much.
I hungered, I thirsted and I suffered toils because of you.
Among mountains, cliffs and woodland vales I went about, seeking you,
                                        the wandering one.
I was called lamb, so that, having somehow enchanted you with my voice,
                                        I might lead you.
[I was called] shepherd, and for you I wish to lay down my life,
so that I might pull you up out of the grasp of the wolf.
I suffer everything, wishing that you might cry,
'You are blessed who comes to call up Adam.'

> Μὴ γὰρ ἀγγέλους ἔστερξα;   σὲ τὸν πτωχὸν ἐφίλησα,
>   τὴν δόξαν μου ἔκρυψα
> καὶ πένης ὁ πλούσιος   ἑκὼν γέγονα·   πολὺ γὰρ σὲ ποθῶ·
> ἐπείνασα, ἐδίψησα   διὰ σὲ καὶ ἐμόχθησα·
> ἐν ὄρεσι, κρημνοῖς   καὶ νάπαις διῆλθον   σὲ τὸν πλανώμενον ζητῶν·
>   ἀμνὸς ὠνομάσθην,   ἵν' ὅπως τῇ φωνῇ μου σὲ θέλξας ἄξω·
> ποιμήν, καὶ διὰ σὲ   ψυχὴν θέλω θεῖναι,
>   ἵνά σε τῆς χειρὸς   ἐκσπάσω τοῦ λύκου·
>   πάντα πάσχω θέλων σε βοᾶν·
>   'εὐλογημένος εἶ ὁ ἐρχόμενος   τὸν Ἀδὰμ ἀνακαλέσασθαι.'

Romanos contrasts Adam and Christ through images of wealth (made more prominent by 'p' alliteration in words for poverty and riches, line 2) and of shepherding. Here, as elsewhere, biblical images are juxtaposed with Romanos' own creations as he expands and reframes biblical stories in their re-performance. The tireless shepherd of the Gospels who seeks out his lost sheep (Matt. 18:12; John 10:11–17) has a more specific and varied journey than in those biblical accounts, creating a visual picture in the minds of listeners.[2] By placing the (biblical) images of Christ as lamb and as shepherd in close proximity, Romanos emphasizes the varied roles God plays in human salvation.

---

[2] This was the purpose of the rhetorical device *ekphrasis*, which we will investigate in more detail shortly. See Webb (2007), 16.

Human images for Christ abound. The rich and poor images suggest a descent in social status: from lord to beggar. Christ has human-like desire and experiences a tricolon of human physicality: hunger, thirst, hardship. The physicality of Christ is both central to human experience of him and the paradox of Christianity: through Christ's humanity Christians come to know (and ultimately partake in) divinity.

Romanos often uses overflowing imagery to describe the incarnation and virgin birth, as a symbol of the incomprehensible miracle of God becoming human and perhaps also an expression of Romanos' own abundant joy which he wants the congregation to share. So, in *On the Annunciation II* Mary is the blossom, the rod and the ark all in the one line (XXXVII.6.3), and throughout that *kontakion* Romanos uses multiple images for Mary and the marvel of her virginal conception. These images are usually biblical and the convergence of such different symbols also signifies the fulfilment of history in the incarnation.

In his creative re-presentation of biblical narratives, Romanos is a master of dialogue and characterization. He portrays emotional states with sensitivity as well as vividness. The *pathos* which permeates his *kontakia* enables his audience to feel the characters' emotions, to identify and sympathize with them.[3] This both makes the *kontakia* engaging and is one rhetorical strategy by which Romanos' liturgically performed text aims to shape its listeners' lives. In *On Mary at the Cross*, for example, Romanos characterizes Mary as mother by giving her the reproaches any mother would make to her son's absent friends (XIX.3). Listeners are encouraged to see Mary as a suffering and uncomprehending ordinary mother, human and possible to emulate, who is nevertheless holy and faithful.[4] Christians are called into imitation of Christ and Christ-like models as they live out the new creation in preparation for its consummation and Christ's second coming. Dialogue and characterization enable Romanos to draw his listeners into these desired patterns of behaviour.

Just as characterization enables identification with biblical characters (and therefore emulation of them), imagery in the *kontakia* often gives the audience a personal link to the narrative by drawing on the memory (or imagination) of physical sensations. Taste and scent images may conjure up the sensations associated with the eucharist, and water imagery sometimes

---

[3] Kustas (1973), 55.

[4] For the most recent contribution to the study of Mary in Romanos, see Arentzen (2014). For my own take on Romanos' characterization of Mary, see Gador-Whyte (2013a), 77–92. On Mary's grief in Romanos and the Greek fathers, see Alexiou (1974), Dobrov (1994), 385–405.

makes the congregation recall their baptism.[5] Imagery from everyday life brings biblical narratives close to the everyday lives of Romanos' congregation. Romanos draws on legal terminology, using images of legal justice and judgement to investigate the realm of divine judgement.[6] Imperial imagery depicts Christ as King and his forgiveness of human sin is depicted as imperial pardon;[7] medical imagery makes Christ into a healer and associates physical health with spiritual well-being.[8] Sin is sometimes figured by financial imagery: Romanos employs the language of debts to explore concepts of sin and human failings. Soldiers and athletes provide models of strength and endurance for those fighting against sin and temptation.[9]

Thus, Romanos' rhetorical and literary techniques are constituent elements of the ideas which they communicate. In this Romanos is firmly situated within earlier traditions of Christian literature. The embodiment of language in the divine Logos brought with it a new conceptualization of rhetoric: a means of understanding humanity and the divine economy.[10] The different rhetorical devices reveal elements of this divine economy and contribute to human understanding of it in varied ways: vivid description (*ekphrasis*) unveils personal experience of the divine; typology interprets history christologically; characterization (*ethopoeia*) enables human participation in the divine, and so on.[11] As we will see in subsequent chapters, Romanos' employment of rhetorical techniques is part of his attempt to elucidate and present God's message as he understands it.

Romanos' *kontakia* have been called 'poetry as proclamation'.[12] While the *kontakion* is not strictly a homily, and some take issue with calling it a homily in verse,[13] it does perform some homiletic functions.[14] It was performed in a liturgical setting (on which, see further below) and Romanos uses his compositions to expound the scriptures and educate his listeners about the demands of the Christian life. As proclamation, then, the *kontakion* had a

---

[5] On this use of the senses in Romanos, see Frank (2005), especially 166–8. On similar uses of the senses in wider homiletics (and Romanos), see Frank (2001), (2013b).

[6] See, for example, Romanos' use of συγχώρησις in XVIII.6: Krueger (2004), 161.

[7] For imperial imagery in Romanos, see Barkhuizen (1991b), 1–15.

[8] See, for example, XXI.1–2. On medical imagery in the *kontakia*, see Krueger (2010), Schork (1960).

[9] Romanos describes Joseph as an athlete as he triumphs over passion and temptation: XLIV.22.1–2. See Schork (1995), 23–5.

[10] Kustas (1973), 56.

[11] Kustas (1973), 54–8.

[12] Louth uses this phrase to contrast the *kontakion* ('poetry as proclamation') and the canon ('poetry as meditation'): Louth (2005), 200.

[13] Arentzen (2014), 48–9.

[14] Cunningham (1990), 36–7.

broader reach than other forms of theological composition, whether poetry or learned treatises. As a form of homiletics, and performed in a popular vigil setting, the *kontakion* reached a wide lay audience and was thus an effective means of theological instruction across different social groups. The *kontakion* was also more interactive than ordinary preaching, which had no refrain in which the congregation could take part. Its participatory nature, as well as other devices, such as dialogue and characterization, make the *kontakion* potentially more involving and more effective in its communication than other forms of homiletics. By studying Romanos' ideas, as expressed in the *kontakia*, we can therefore infer more about lay piety and theological understanding, giving us a broader appreciation of Christian faith in this period.

Romanos takes his listeners on journeys through biblical stories, shaping their understanding of the text in often subtle and emotive ways. He forms their faith by making them participate in the biblical narratives: he introduces them to characters and draws them into conversation to help them identify with those characters; he creates visual images of events and positions his listeners as eyewitnesses. Such emotional engagement with characters and events draws listeners into deeper understanding and faith. Romanos and his *kontakia* played an important role in theological education and shaping popular theology and piety in sixth-century Constantinople.

This book is an attempt to explore the theology of the most celebrated Byzantine hymnographer, whose ideas have nevertheless been little studied, and to demonstrate the interconnectedness of these theological ideas and the rhetorical forms used to communicate them. To this latter end, in Chapter 1 I analyse one *kontakion*, *On the Passion of Christ*, to illustrate how the form of the hymn and its rhetorical techniques allow Romanos to explore numerous ideas in a single *kontakion*. All of the theological concepts which will be the focus of subsequent chapters are present (to a greater or lesser extent) in this one *kontakion*.

Chapters 2 to 4 focus on Romanos' theology. It is a theology of salvation, of the recapitulation of human life by God in the person of Jesus Christ: the correction of human sin and perfection of humanity, the inauguration of a new reality in Christ and the anticipation of the second coming and final consummation of that new creation. Humanity is a fallen race, suffering since Adam, sinful in its separation from God. In order to restore humans to relationship with God, God himself took on human form in the person of Jesus Christ: he became the second Adam. In Chapter 2, I explore Romanos' conceptualization of the second Adam and how he corrects the sins of the first Adam and restores humanity to perfection. This renewed perfection, the subject of Chapter 3, begins a new reality, a second creation, in which the norms of the previous creation are dramatically challenged and Old Testament prophecies are fulfilled. This second creation calls for a change of life for Christians. Romanos works hard, as we will see in Chapter 4, to encourage his congregation towards Christ-like living. He sees the responsibility of Christians as one of participation in anticipation: participation in the life of Christ now, in anticipation of the future advent of Christ. Romanos' *kontakia* are marked by optimism. They look forward with great hope and joy towards the second coming of Christ. This book thus moves through Romanos' theology from correction of human sin to apprehension of divine glory.

Like many other great preachers, Romanos made use of the tradition to teach his congregation about theological concepts which he believed were vitally important for their salvation. Therefore, each chapter seeks to situate Romanos' thought within wider themes in Christian thinking through introductory sections which identify resonances with earlier strands of the tradition. These sections enable an evaluation of Romanos' distinctive contributions and aim to outline key aspects of his thought-world, but do not seek to pin down direct influence. The chapters then go on to analyse how Romanos employed earlier ideas in his own synthesis. These investigations of the tradition with which Romanos could have been familiar are by no means exhaustive but are aimed at illuminating the distinctive characteristics of Romanos' own ideas and rhetorical practices. By thus setting Romanos in his wider intellectual context, I hope to show which ideas were strange for the time, which were common and which ideas were controversial and stemmed from contemporary debates. Similarly, I will seek to contextualize Romanos' ideas within his wider society as the book progresses, to help to identify his reasons for emphasizing a particular idea.

Romanos

What little we know about Romanos, apart from his writings, comes from the *Synaxaria*.[15] According to these documents, the earliest of which dates to the tenth century, Romanos was born in Emesa, modern Homs, in Syria. He became a deacon in Berytus (modern Beirut), in the Church of the Resurrection, and then moved to Constantinople some time during the

---

[15] The relevant sections of the *Synaxaria* are reproduced in Grosdidier de Matons (1977), 162.

reign of Anastasius.[16] In Constantinople he was attached to the Church of the Theotokos in the Kyros district. According to legend, the Virgin Mary inspired him to compose his most famous hymn, *On the Nativity I*, after which he composed about one thousand *kontakia* before he died.[17] He is a saint in the Orthodox Church and his feast day is celebrated on 1 October.

This is the hagiographical story we are given of Romanos' life, from which we can infer a few things. First, his birth in Emesa suggests that he was bilingual and 'bi-cultural'.[18] He would have been able to speak and read both Syriac and Greek and was familiar with the literature and culture of these linguistic communities. There are clear congruencies between Romanos' thought and compositions and those of fourth- to sixth-century Syriac theologians, preachers and poets, and the overlap of ideas and images will be significant for the investigation and reconstruction of Romanos' ideas.

Second, if he became a deacon in Berytus he may have been educated there, if not previously educated in Greek grammar and rhetoric in Emesa.[19] Berytus was a centre for education in late antiquity and, although primarily associated with a legal education in the Latin language and in Roman law, may have provided Romanos with the opportunity to study rhetoric.[20] Some have argued that Romanos was a converted Jew,[21] and it may be that he went to Berytus as a Jew (or even a pagan), intending to study law, and converted to Christianity while a student there. We know that groups like the *philoponoi* operated in Berytus, aiming in part to expose and convert pagan and Jewish students.[22] Zacharias Scholasticus, for example, vividly describes student life in the period and records several such attempts.[23] In his *Life of Severus*, we learn that the future bishop of Antioch was converted to Christianity while a law student in Berytus.[24]

---

[16] The current consensus is that Anastasius I is meant. For the debate about which Anastasius, see Petersen (1985b), 2–3. Aslanov suggests that Romanos chose Constantinople because of the power and prestige it offered: Aslanov (2011), 614.

[17] For various interpretations of the legend, see Arentzen (2014), 43–4, Carpenter (1932), 3–22, Maisano (2002), 25.

[18] Brock (1994), 154.

[19] Eva Topping suggests that Romanos would have been trained in the classics in Emesa. See Topping (1976), 239.

[20] See, for example, Libanius' letter to Domninus, epistle 163 in Bradbury's numbering, in which Libanius introduces a student of his who, having studied rhetoric, is now turning to the law: Bradbury (2004), 201–2. See also Hall (2004), 192–3.

[21] Grosdidier de Matons cites an anonymous *kontakion* which celebrates St Romanos as saying that Romanos was the child of Jews: Grosdidier de Matons (1977), 169. Cf. also Yahalom (1987), 122. And see further in Chapter 3 below.

[22] On the *philoponoi*, see Haas (1997), 238–40, Watts (2006), 213–16.

[23] Hall (2004), 163.

[24] Hall (2004), 159.

Yet Romanos' putative conversion is mere conjecture. Most likely he was born into a Christian family and went to Berytus to study law or simply rhetoric and while there became interested in a career in the church. He may even have been connected with Christian schools in Berytus, or have been drawn there by stories of ascetic monks. Whatever Romanos' connection with Berytus may have been, it will be clear from analysis of his *kontakia* that he was rhetorically trained and familiar with earlier homiletics and poetry in Greek and Syriac.

Finally, the image of Mary as Romanos' muse echoes the importance of Mary in Romanos' work and thought, the high esteem given to Romanos' hymns after his death – to the extent that he was considered divinely inspired – and the theological importance given to Mary, as an active intercessor and means of divine revelation, both in the sixth century and subsequently.[25] Although Mary is not the central focus of this book, we will see that Romanos envisaged Mary's role in salvation as a significant one, not least as the new Eve, the near-perfect woman who redeems fallen womankind. The prominence of Mary in the *kontakia* may also reflect Romanos' position as deacon at the Church of the Theotokos.

The *Kontakion*

The word *kontakion* is of ninth-century origin and probably comes from the rod or stick (*kontax* or *kontos*) around which the hymns were wound.[26] Romanos did not use this word to describe his own compositions; a variety of names for the *kontakion* appear in the acrostics, including 'hymn', 'word', 'story', 'psalm', 'poem', 'song', 'entreaty' and 'prayer'.[27] It seems that there was not a definitive term for the *kontakia* at the time. Romanos' compositions differ from other (both earlier and later) *kontakia*, tending more towards homiletics than hymns of praise,[28] justifying the description of the *kontakia* as 'verse sermons' or 'sung sermons'.[29] Classifying the genre of this

---

[25] On Mary in Romanos, see Arentzen (2013), 125–32, (2014).

[26] See Grosdidier de Matons (1977), 37–8; Rosenqvist (2007), 24–5.

[27] ΥΜΝΟΣ, ΕΠΟΣ, ΑΙΝΟΣ, ΨΑΛΜΟΣ, ΠΟΙΗΜΑ, ΩΔΗ, ΔΕΗΣΙΣ, ΠΡΟΣΕΥΧΗ. 'Hymn' occurs four times (I, XXXVII, XLI, LI), 'word' six (IV, VII, XXIII, XXXIV, XXXIX, XLIV), 'story' nine (IX, XVIII, XXI, XXIV, XXV, XXVIII, XL, LIII, LIX), 'psalm' eight (XI, XII, XX, XXIX, XXXI, XLVI, LIV, LV), 'poem' four (XIII, XVII, XLVII, L), 'song' twice (XXVI, XXXV), 'entreaty' once (XLIX), and 'prayer' once (LVI).

[28] Grosdidier de Matons (1977), 3.

[29] See, for example, Grosdidier de Matons (1977), 3. There is no evidence, however, that it replaced a spoken prose sermon. See Cunningham (1996), 176. Against the use of 'sermon' to describe the *kontakion*, see Arentzen (2014), 48.

hymn has therefore posed some problems for scholars. Romanos seems to have been conversant in both Greek and Syriac culture and thus his compositions bridge various genres to form a new, combined genre which, for the sake of simplicity and in keeping with tradition, we will continue to call 'the *kontakion*'.

Romanos' *kontakia* were divided into strophes (or 'stanzas', *oikoi*) and open with one or more proems (*prooimia* or *koukoulia*).[30] The *kontakia* have accentual metres; each strophe has the same metrical form within one hymn, but the metres vary between *kontakia*.[31] The proems differ in metre and may be later additions, or it may be that Romanos himself wrote new proems whenever the *kontakia* were used a second time or in a different context. The first letters of all the strophes make up an acrostic, which usually includes Romanos' name. It often takes the form 'Of the Humble Romanos' or 'The Poem of the Humble Romanos'.[32] Once, Romanos uses an alphabetic acrostic, but it still includes his name.[33] The acrostic would have been hidden to audiences who heard the *kontakia* being sung, but Romanos' mark is clear when one looks at the written text: Romanos has inscribed his ownership of the *kontakia* into them. The acrostic may have functioned as a mnemonic device, enabling easier memorization of the *kontakion* for himself and other cantors.[34] But such devices were also employed in late antique spiritual exercises, and, as such, it may have been part of an ascetic discipline for Romanos, in which he focused on his own humility as he wrote and sung his compositions.[35]

The *kontakia* usually have biblical themes, and are often dominated by dialogue between biblical characters. The narrative generally expands on the biblical one by including more dialogue and sections of exegesis,

---

[30]   The number of strophes varies between eleven and forty, but most of the *kontakia* have about twenty strophes. For example, *On Joseph I* has forty strophes, whereas *On the Resurrection II* has eleven. The frequency of the acrostic 'of the humble Romanos' (ΤΟΥ ΤΑΠΕΙΝΟΥ ΡΩΜΑΝΟΥ) means many of the *kontakia* have eighteen strophes.

[31]   On the metrical structure of the different *kontakia*, see the Metrical Appendix in Maas and Trypanis (1963), 510–38.

[32]   'Humble' is spelt three different ways in the acrostics: *tapeinou* (ΤΑΠΕΙΝΟΥ) (e.g. in *kontakion* 8), *tapinou* (ΤΑΠΙΝΟΥ) (e.g. in *kontakion* 9) and *tapeeinou* (ΤΑΠΕΕΙΝΟΥ) (e.g. in *kontakion* 7). In some cases, variations like this are taken as evidence that a stanza was added (or removed) later.

[33]   The acrostic of *On Joseph I* is ΑΒΓΔΕΖΗΘΙΚΛΜΝΞΟΠΡΣΤΥΦΧΨΩ ΑΛΦΑΒΗΤΟΝ ΡΩΜΑΝΟΥ. That is, all the letters of the alphabet followed by the words 'The Alphabet of Romanos'.

[34]   Grosdidier de Matons (1980–1), 41. This is a very common interpretation of alphabetic acrostics in biblical poetry, according to Assis (2007), 712.

[35]   On the acrostic as ownership and self-imposed discipline, see Krueger (2003), 19–24, (2004), 170–4.

although some *kontakia* develop stories not found in the Bible.[36] He makes a short conversation between John the Baptist and Jesus (Matt. 3:14–15), for example, into a whole *kontakion* – and creates new dialogues for biblical characters or between biblical and non-biblical characters. The expansions and augmentations of biblical material, however, mean that the line between biblical and non-biblical stories is blurred. The process of augmentation of biblical themes may be said to create new versions of the original, while biblical imagery and narratives support the non-biblical material, for example, in the *kontakion On the Victory of the Cross.*

The congregation takes on different roles in the *kontakion* because of the extensive use of dialogue. Dialogue is a central part of the *kontakion* and a major way in which Romanos explained his theology. Through such dialogues, Romanos explores motivations of different characters, presents models of behaviour (and anti-models) and enlivens the biblical narratives of events which recur in the liturgical cycle: dialogues bring the Bible to life.

Another characteristic feature which actively involves the congregation in the *kontakion* is the refrain. At the end of each strophe there is a line (or sometimes two) which the congregation probably sang with the cantor.[37] Romanos' refrains are well integrated into the sense of each strophe.[38] The different characters in one *kontakion* lead the refrain at different points in the hymn, making the congregation take on various different roles. As we will see in Chapter 4, this is one way in which Romanos enacts his participatory theology.

The History of the *Kontakion*

These constituent parts of the *kontakion* set it apart from other forms of literature: there are no obvious Greek antecedents to the genre of the *kontakion*. Rather, the *kontakion* creatively combines three Syriac genres (*memra*, *madrasha*, *sogitha*), and incorporates elements from Greek *kata stichon* hymns and homiletics. Romanos was certainly well placed to draw

---

[36] For example, *On the Victory of the Cross*, which involves a lengthy dialogue between Hades and Satan.

[37] Lingas (2008), 919. Alternatively, there may have been a choir which sang the refrain on behalf of the congregation. See Wellesz (1949), 180.

[38] Unlike the Syriac refrain, often cited as evidence of Syriac influence on the *kontakion* form. Maas is clear that the Greek refrain is an improvement on the Syriac one. See Maas (1910a), 296–7.

on these different traditions but, even supposing other *kontakion* writers were not bilingual, Greek- and Syriac-speaking cultures were far from discrete in this period. Even outside the numerous bilingual communities there was much travel and translation of literature between the two linguistic groups.[39] I do not intend to trace the influence of different genres upon the *kontakion*, since this has been amply covered by others.[40] It seems clear, however, that Romanos drew on these Syriac genres and knew the work of Ephrem the Syrian and Jacob of Serug, among others, and that he was also well-versed in the Greek hymnographic and homiletic traditions.

All three Syriac genres are metrical: each stanza or couplet has the same metrical form, but different homilies/hymns use different metrical patterns. The *memra* is a metrical sermon, set in verse but not sung, and consists of couplets with an equal number of syllables in each line (isosyllabism).[41] Ephrem's *memre* are narrative, often following and developing the narrative possibilities of a biblical text. The *madrasha* and the *sogitha* are both sung hymns. They usually have acrostics, either alphabetical or spelling out a title or a name.[42] *Madrashe* have refrains, and often use dialogue, but they tend to be theological reflections rather than narratives.[43] The *sogitha*, really a subset of the *madrasha*, is distinguished by its dramatic use of dialogue.[44] As well as general influence, Romanos clearly drew upon particular texts – Romanos' *kontakion On the Sinful Woman*

---

[39] Alexiou (2002), 24, Brock (1982b), 17–18, (1994), 150, 152 and passim. On Greek–Syriac bilingualism in late antiquity, see also Lee (2012), 163–73, Millar (2009), 92–103, Taylor (2002), 298–331.

[40] My own contribution to the debate can be found in Gador-Whyte (2013b). The consensus is now a fluid picture of influence from both traditions on each other. It is difficult to assign particular aspects to one or the other tradition. For example, the use of isosyllabism could be evidence for the influence of either tradition: Brock (1989), 141. In general, for the influence of Syriac literature on Romanos and the Syriac origin of the *kontakion*, see Baumstark (1905), Maas (1910a), 290ff., Papoutsakis (2007), 29–75, Petersen (1985a), 174–5, (1985b). These scholars do not focus on Greek debts, but do not discount them entirely. Ševčenko argues for very limited Greek influence on the *kontakion*: Ševčenko (1980), 63. Grosdidier de Matons originally doubted that Romanos was bilingual or was influenced by Syriac literature: Grosdidier de Matons (1977), 286. He later revised his opinion, e.g. Grosdidier de Matons (1980–1), 36. This revision was probably partly in response to de Halleux's review of Grosdidier de Matons' book: de Halleux (1978), 632–41, esp. 641. Cameron argues for the influence of Greek rhetoric and Greek homiletics as well as elements of the Syriac tradition: Cameron (1991b), 92–7. Brock likewise argues for a combined culture of influence. See, for example, Brock (1989), 151.

[41] Ephrem favoured 7+7 syllables, but later Syriac writers used different metres. See Brock and Kiraz (2006), xiii.

[42] Brock (1985), 78.

[43] Maas (1910a), 290.

[44] Petersen (1985b), 13, Schirmann (1953), 158. See also Brock (1983), 35–45.

has strong resonances with a *memra* of the same title attributed to Ephrem (CSCO 311, Scriptores Syri 134).[45]

Many of the techniques and devices found in these Syriac texts also occur in Greek literature, and, as we have said, the two were hardly discrete and non-interacting cultures. Greek had long since moved away from classical accent-based metrics and there are many earlier uses of isosyllabism in Greek texts. The *kata stichon* hymns are likely to have influenced Romanos. Dialogue and question and answer literature were common in classical and later Christian and Neoplatonic philosophical texts written by Romanos' contemporaries.[46] But dramatic dialogue was also deployed in non-philosophical texts in the Greek Christian tradition in texts like Methodius' *Parthenion* and Proclus of Constantinople's *Homily 27*, an acrostic dialogue on baptism.[47] Romanos was also familiar with the corpus of Greek texts under the name of Ephrem, usually called Greek Ephrem (*Ephraem Graecus*). Some of these texts are clearly translations or adaptations of Syriac works by Ephrem, but for the majority no Syriac version survives and their authorship is therefore disputed.[48] Finally, Romanos' *kontakia* are verse, but they deploy many themes, images and techniques found in Greek prose homilies. Once again, as well as the general influence, in some cases we can find a single homily which shows clear resonances with one *kontakion* – for example, the homily on the man possessed attributed to Basil of Seleucia (*Or. 23*, PG 85.269–77) seems to have influenced Romanos' composition of his *kontakion On the Man Possessed with Devils*.[49]

I have used Romanos' *kontakia* as examples here, and yet Romanos was not the only *kontakion* writer and did not himself invent the genre.[50] Names of other *kontakion* writers survive (e.g. Anastasios, Kyriakos, Kosmas), but we know little about them or the extent of their original output.[51] There are

[45] If this homily was not written by Ephrem, it was still roughly contemporary with him and greatly influenced the Syriac homiletic tradition. Cf. Harvey (2002), 72. For the Greek version of this homily, from the *Ephraem Graecus* corpus, see CPG 3:3952.

[46] *Contra* Goldhill (2008), 1–11, esp. 5. Against Goldhill, see Cameron (2014), 8–21 and passim. On late antique dialogue, see Cameron (2014) and, for example, Champion's treatment of dialogue texts on the eternity of the world in fifth- and sixth-century Gaza: M.W. Champion (2014).

[47] Maas (1910b), 12. On the dramatic use of dialogue in homiletics, see, for example, Cameron (1991b), 91–108.

[48] Petersen (1985b), 11.

[49] Matthew 8:28–34; Mark 5:1–16; Luke 8:27–39. Cf. Maas (1910a), 300–2. Maisano also mentions this connection between Romanos and Basil's treatments of the possessed man: Maisano (2010), 265.

[50] Petersen calls Romanos the 'perfector' rather than the inventor of the *kontakion*: Petersen (1985b).

[51] Few of their *kontakia* survive. One *kontakion* by each of these three authors, along with several other anonymous ones, is edited in Trypanis (1968).

few *kontakia* which are clearly earlier than those of Romanos: Grosdidier de Matons counted only four.[52] There may well be more, but problems with dating the *kontakia* make it difficult to trace the history of this genre. These earlier *kontakia* have a similar structure to those of Romanos: they have an acrostic, one or more proems and are written in stanzas with a refrain at the end of each one. But the metrical systems are less complex and in some cases the refrain does not fit logically with the preceding line. These, and the use of an alphabetic rather than titular acrostic in some, we may take as markers of a genre still in development.[53] Romanos thus seems to have written metrically more sophisticated *kontakia*, and to have developed the use of the refrain and dialogue in his compositions. After Romanos, there were many imitators of his work, perhaps even his students,[54] and in some cases we find Romanos' name in their acrostics.[55] Wherever Romanos fitted in the naissance of this genre, such imitation attests to his skill and fame as a hymnographer. *Kontakia* were no longer composed after the ninth century,[56] but remained in use for centuries afterwards, despite this lack of composition.

The Setting of the *Kontakion*

The *kontakia* themselves give us some idea about their liturgical setting. The opening strophe of *On the Man Possessed with Devils* begins thus (XI.1):

The people, faithful in their love of Christ,
coming together at a night vigil in psalms and songs,
unceasingly keep up hymns to God.
Then after the psalm has been sung,
and we have rejoiced at the well-ordered reading of the scriptures,
again we celebrate Christ in song and denounce the enemies.
For this is the lyre of knowledge
and of this knowledge Christ is the guide and the teacher,
the Lord of all.

---

[52] Grosdidier de Matons (1977), 28. Maas likewise argues that Romanos' *kontakia* are the earliest which can be fairly securely dated, but that the primitive nature of some other *kontakia* suggests they might be earlier than Romanos': Maas (1910b), 12.

[53] Grosdidier de Matons (1977), 28, 30. See also Schork (1995), 43. By the same token, Maas and Trypanis suggest that *kontakion* 41, *On Isaac*, is an early experiment by Romanos, since it has no refrain: Maas and Trypanis (1963), xx.

[54] Domitios, for example: Grosdidier de Matons (1977), 56.

[55] For example, Domitios' *kontakion On the Nativity of Saint John the Baptist* has Romanos' name in the acrostic. It is possible that the *kontakion* was altered later to include Romanos' name. See Grosdidier de Matons (1977), 56.

[56] Lingas (1995), 53, Louth (2005), 199.

Ὁ λαὸς ὁ πιστὸς   ἐν ἀγάπῃ Χριστοῦ

  συνελθὼν ἀγρυπνεῖ ἐν ψαλμοῖς καὶ ᾠδαῖς,

  ἀκορέστως δὲ ἔχει τοὺς ὕμνους θεῷ·

ἐπειδὴ οὖν Δαβὶδ ἐμελῴδησε,

  καὶ ἀναγνώσει εὐτάκτῳ γραφῶν ἐπευφράνθημεν,

αὖθις Χριστὸν ἀνυμνήσωμεν   καὶ τοὺς ἐχθροὺς στηλιτεύσωμεν·

  αὕτη γὰρ γνώσεως κιθάρα·

  τῆς δὲ γνώσεως ταύτης Χριστὸς ὁδηγὸς καὶ διδάσκαλος,

ὁ πάντων δεσπότης.

This passage suggests that the *kontakion* was part of (and perhaps con-cluded) a sung night vigil service, for the laity rather than monastics, which comprised singing hymns and psalms and listening to the scriptures.[57] Based partly on this passage from *On the Man Possessed*, the general schol-arly consensus now is that the *kontakion* formed part of a vigil service in the cathedral rite, the *asmatike akolouthia*.[58] The *asmatike akolouthia* was a sung service, which, according to the liturgical ordinal (*typikon*) of the Great Church, incorporated vespers and the morning office (*orthros*) and sometimes an all-night vigil (*pannychis*) or other solemn vigil (e.g. *par-amone*).[59] It therefore involved the singing of psalms and hymns and the reading of scriptural passages.

Two manuscripts of the *typikon* of the Great Church mention the *kontakion* explicitly:[60] manuscript P, a ninth- to tenth-century manu-script, refers to the singing of the *kontakion* at Blachernae after *pan-nychis* in the middle of Lent;[61] and according to a later manuscript (Ox, 1329) the *kontakion* was sung after *pannychis* on 1 September, in honour of Symeon the Stylite.[62] On these occasions therefore, and, we presume, at other times of the year, the *kontakion* formed part of a night vigil.

Elsewhere, Romanos uses the *kontakia* to prepare his listeners for receiv-ing the eucharist. *On the Prodigal Son* can be interpreted as an elaborate

---

[57] The vigil was always designed for the laity and was probably originally instituted by John Chrysostom, in competition with the Arians whose own night-time vigils Chrysostom feared would attract non-Arians. See Baldovin (1987), 182–4, Taft (2006), 32–3.

[58] Lingas (1995), 50–2, Louth (2005), 199–200. See also Frank (2006b), 59–78, Koder (2005), 21, Krueger (2005), 297, McGuckin (2008), 649–50.

[59] See Taft (1991). Mateos gives an explanation of the different uses of *akolouthia* in the *typikon* at Mateos (1963), 279–80.

[60] For Mateos' note on the *kontakion*, see Mateos (1963), 301. For his introduction to the different manuscripts of the *typikon* and their dates, see Mateos (1962), iv–viii.

[61] Mateos (1963), 52[27].

[62] Mateos (1962), 4[12]. Cf. Maisano (2002), 20.

eucharistic metaphor,[63] and in the second stanza Romanos calls for the congregation to take part in this meal (XLIX.2.1–5):

So let us now hurry and partake of the meal,
if we have been thought worthy to rejoice with the Father,
let us feast with the King of the angels.
He provides bread which gives happiness,
and as drink he gives holy blood …

Ἔνθεν σπουδάσωμεν νυνὶ   καὶ μετασχῶμεν τοῦ δείπνου·
    ἐὰν ἀξιωθῶμεν   τῷ πατρὶ συνευφρανθῆναι,
    συνεστιαθῶμεν   τῷ βασιλεῖ τῶν ἀγγέλων·
ἄρτους παρέχει   τοὺς διδόντας μακαριότητα,
    πόμα δὲ δωρεῖται   ἅγιον αἷμα …

The successive hortatory subjunctives in this passage ('let us hurry', 'let us partake', 'let us feast') suggest that celebration of the eucharist followed the singing of the *kontakion*. Although the *asmatike akolouthia* was not itself a eucharistic service, in some cases it led up to the Sunday or feast day mass.[64] Since the story of the Prodigal Son (Luke 15:11–32) was not the Gospel lection for any of the major feasts, I suggest that this *kontakion* was sung towards the end of a Saturday night vigil and was used to prepare communicants both to hear the Gospel and to receive the eucharist at the Sunday service immediately following the lengthy vigil.

Placing the *kontakion* in its probable liturgical setting gives us some idea about his audience, and perhaps also their expectations of his compositions. The vigil service formed part of the cathedral rite, so Romanos' listeners would have been lay people, and not predominantly monks, nuns or ordained clergy. Since the vigil was long and sometimes lasted all night, we can assume that it was the more devout believers who attended, perhaps including recent converts or catechumens. We can assume that Romanos would have been addressing both men and women: legislative (and homiletic) attempts to ban women from attending the vigils attest to their popularity with women.[65] Romanos preached to educate, engage and illumine lay Christians in the cathedral community.

Romanos' *kontakia* quickly became both popular for use in wider liturgical settings and influential in a range of genres. Their early dissemination is attested by four fragments (three papyrus, one parchment) which contain short parts of Romanos' *kontakia* and which all date to between

[63] Barkhuizen (1996), 39–54.
[64] Louth (2005), 199.
[65] Frank (2006b), 62, Taft (1998), 72–4.

the late sixth and the early seventh century.[66] The three papyrus fragments may have formed part of a text for liturgical use,[67] which would support arguments that Romanos' work was quickly employed in liturgical contexts beyond his Constantinopolitan congregation.[68] The seventh-century *Life of Mary of Egypt* contains a phrase 'the filth of my deeds' (ὁ βόρβορος τῶν ἔργων μου) (23), which is the refrain of Romanos' *kontakion On the Sinful Woman*.[69] There is insufficient evidence to claim this as a direct borrowing, but there would be good reasons for the writer of the *Life* to want to associate Mary both with the harlot of the Gospels and with Romanos' presentation of her as the ultimate penitent. These near-contemporary glimpses of Romanos' work are indicators of the early status of his compositions in liturgical settings and beyond them.

As well as these witnesses, we have those which attest to Romanos' continuing importance over several centuries. The vigil service in which the *kontakia* were performed continued in Constantinople until the Latin invasion of 1204 and, although no new *kontakia* were being composed, the *kontakion* probably retained its place in that service.[70] The preservation of some of Romanos' *kontakia* in their complete form in eleventh-century *kontakaria*, such as the Patmos manuscripts 212 and 213, attests to the continuing performance of the *kontakion* in its complete form into this later period.[71] This gives Romanos an extensive reach in the history of homiletics, hymnography and popular religious belief in Byzantium.

The Liturgical Cycle

Having situated the *kontakion* in a liturgical rite, I turn now to the question of the liturgical cycle. We know the shape of the liturgical year in the sixth century, and Jerusalem lectionaries survive from this period,[72] but no sixth-century documentation of the Constantinopolitan liturgical cycle of

---

[66] Koder (2005), 36–7, Krueger (2014), 65.

[67] Koder (2005), 37.

[68] Krueger also mentions the *Miracles of Artemios* (18), which refers to a cantor who sang Romanos' *kontakia*: Krueger (2014), 65. For the text, see Crisafulli and Nesbitt (1997), 114–15.

[69] Krueger (2014), 233 n. 80. For the *Life of Mary of Egypt*, see PG 87:3697–3726. See also Kouli's translation: Kouli (1996), 65–93.

[70] Louth (2005), 199. And possibly the *kontakion* was still being performed even later in Thessaloniki, since according to Symeon of Thessaloniki (PG 155: 553D, 624D–625B) the vigil continued there until the fifteenth century. However, there is a decline in the number of complete *kontakia* in the *kontakaria* after the twelfth century. See Lingas (1995), 56.

[71] Grosdidier de Matons (1977), 69, Lingas (1995), 56.

[72] Krueger (2014), 25.

readings survives. For feast days, the Jerusalem lectionary is a good indicator of the readings but, especially for non-festal days, we must rely on material from the ninth and tenth centuries at the earliest.[73] We cannot assume that these later documents accurately reflect sixth-century practice,[74] especially given the liturgical changes we know to have taken place in the intervening centuries, including the impact of the iconoclast controversy on the liturgy.[75]

However, it remains possible and productive to consider the place of the *kontakia* in the liturgical year. The *kontakaria*, the later collections in which most *kontakia* survive, assign the *kontakia* to particular days in the church's year. Some recent scholarship has argued that these collections do indeed preserve the original position of the *kontakion* and therefore the readings used on those days in the sixth century.[76] Often Romanos' *kontakia* clearly fit the days assigned and this may give us an important insight into the readings which would have been read, both on that day and in the week before. Sometimes Romanos draws on recent readings to explore the reading for the day, presumably assuming his listeners will remember what they heard only a few days before. My purpose is not to determine how accurately the *kontakaria* reflect sixth-century practice, but rather to read Romanos' texts with the liturgical cycle and biblical texts in mind and to focus on the biblical lections and feasts to which particular *kontakia* clearly respond. So throughout I analyse Romanos' texts as performed liturgical texts, living out the cycle of feasts as a way of living the life of Christ, and as part of that I will show how the *kontakia* engage with biblical readings. In some cases these will be the readings apparently set down for the day, but in others the position given in the *kontakaria* will seem inaccurate. This may also tell us more, both about Romanos and about the liturgical life of sixth-century Constantinople.

---

[73] Krueger (2014), 25.
[74] According to Gy, the system of readings which survives for festal days is certainly not older than the seventh century, and most likely dates to the ninth century: Gy (1967), 256.
[75] Kazhdan and Constable (1982), 88, Marinis (2010), 285–6.
[76] See, for example, Koder (2005), 35, 39. Maisano has produced a helpful table of the liturgical cycle and the corresponding *kontakia*: Maisano (2002), 99–100.

1 | *On the Passion of Christ*

In this chapter I analyse a single *kontakion*, *On the Passion of Christ*, focusing on Romanos' different rhetorical techniques. In the course of this tour through his rhetoric, I paint a more detailed picture of Romanos' *kontakia* and the *kontakion* genre. I demonstrate Romanos' proficiency in rhetoric and the wide range of figures he uses to communicate his ideas and make his poetry engaging, vivid and dramatic. We will see how Romanos uses, appropriates and transforms biblical and homiletic material, and the ways in which rhetoric embodies and communicates the central ideas of correction and perfection ('the second Adam'), new creation ('the second creation') and preparation for its consummation in the eschaton ('the second coming'). In seeing these rhetorical figures and theological ideas as they are presented in one *kontakion*, the rhetorical and conceptual coherence of these central ideas begins to emerge. The following chapters will take up individual ideas in more detail and we will be inevitably drawn back into Romanos' use of rhetoric and imagery.

This hymn was probably sung on Good Friday,[1] the day which commemorates the crucifixion of Jesus. It narrates Christ's appearance before the high priest Caiaphas and Pontius Pilate: the events leading up to his crucifixion. Romanos creates a lengthy debate between Jesus and the Jewish crowd about healing on the Sabbath, and explores Jesus' interactions with Caiaphas and Pilate, in order to demonstrate the significance of the crucifixion for human salvation. As such, it is a particularly appropriate choice for establishing the coherence of Romanos' soteriology and how the key themes of correction and perfection, new creation, and participation and anticipation fit together in one composition.

---

[1] Schork (1995), 115.

Dramatic Beginnings

On the Passion of Christ begins dramatically, setting the tone for the rest of the hymn. Romanos brings the events of the Passion into the present in the first proem with the word 'today' (Pr.1.1):

Today the foundations of the earth trembled ...[2]

Σήμερον ἐταράττετο   τῆς γῆς τὰ θεμέλια

Combined with imperatives in strophe 1 (e.g. 'stand back', 'do not dare'), the opening presents the events of the Passion as contemporary ones. This is a dramatizing device, which brings to life the church's liturgical calendar, and makes the events of Christ's crucifixion present. The congregation lives out this episode (and the whole Gospel week by week) through Romanos' hymns. The incarnation is made a present reality in much the same way in Romanos' famous Christmas hymn: 'Today a virgin gives birth to the one who is beyond being' (ἡ παρθένος σήμερον τὸν ὑπερούσιον τίκτει).[3] This dramatic device makes two connected theological points. Romanos believes that Christ's incarnation, death and resurrection dramatically changed the world; the incarnation was an eschatological event. Part of this was a change in the nature of time: time is not linear after the incarnation, but rather past, present and future events converge. This altered world is a new creation, in which Christians are called to participate. This period is one of confirmation of the eschaton before its final consummation. Romanos makes Gospel events present to encourage his congregation to participate in the life of Christ and thereby in God's life. By creating a vivid and contemporary narration of the crucifixion, Romanos enacts the change in time which he believes took place at the incarnation, and he calls his congregation to participate in the 'second' creation inaugurated at that point. These two ideas, new creation and participation, are important facets of Romanos' theology.

These changes in the nature of time are echoed by changes in the natural world, which increase the drama and emphasize the significance of the Passion (Pr. 1.1–2):

... the foundations of the earth trembled,
the sun hid, not able to endure seeing [what was happening].

... ἐταράττετο   τῆς γῆς τὰ θεμέλια,
ὁ ἥλιος ἠλλοιοῦτο   μὴ στέγων θεωρῆσαι·

---

[2] All references to Romanos' *kontakia* in this chapter are to Oxf. XX, *On the Passion of Christ*, unless otherwise stated.

[3] I.Pr.1. See also, for example, II.Pr.2; V.Pr.1.

Like the change in time, disruptions of nature demonstrate both how unnatural and how world-changing was Christ's crucifixion. The natural world cannot accept what humanity has done, so it rebels against it in earthquakes and eclipses. Romanos elides the events which Matthew's Gospel narrates at the death of Jesus (Matt. 27:45, 51):[4]

From noon on, darkness came over the whole land until three in the afternoon. … At that moment the curtain of the temple was torn in two, from top to bottom. The earth shook, and the rocks were split.

Romanos combines these Gospel verses and personifies the natural world, making its revulsion more personal and the events more dramatic. Such upheaval in the natural world was associated with divine displeasure in contemporary writings. The chronicler Malalas refers to earthquakes as 'the wrath of God' (e.g. 18.37, 18.40) and, according to the historian Procopius, the plague in Constantinople occasioned a change in behaviour for the unrighteous (*Wars* II.22–33), who felt that their sinfulness may have been to blame.[5] In the *Secret History* Procopius blames the plague (and many other disasters) on the impiety and immorality of the emperor Justinian (*SH.* 18.44–5).[6] If the emperor had behaved better, perhaps God would have spared the people. Overtones of this topos of divine displeasure manifesting itself in natural disasters would have resonated with Romanos' congregation. Thus the reaction of the natural world might suggest divine anger with those who crucified Jesus: the Jews.[7] Most fundamentally, these extraordinary events indicate the world-shattering significance of Christ's Passion. Like the conflation of time, Christ's entry into the world and the events of his life change the behaviour of the natural world. The incarnation transforms creation.

This theme continues in the first stanza after the two proems, in which Romanos calls (in a dramatic tricolon) on the natural world to respond to the crucifixion by being properly horrified (1.1–3):

Stand back, shuddering, O Heaven; plunge into chaos, O Earth;
do not dare, Sun, to look on your master
who hangs on the cross by his own will.

---

[4] Compare Mark 15:33 and Luke 23:44–5.
[5] For a list of the earthquakes in Malalas including those referred to as 'the wrath of God', see Jeffreys (1990), 155–9.
[6] Cf. Cameron (1985), 42. On the type of plague, where it came from, numbers of dead and aftermath, see Allen (1979). On Malalas' and Procopius' different interpretations of events, see Scott (1985).
[7] On the Jews in Romanos, see further below and in Chapter 3.

Ἔκστηθι φρίττων, ⟨ὦ⟩ οὐρανέ,   δῦνον εἰς χάος, ὦ γῆ,
     μὴ τολμήσῃς, ἥλιε,   σὸν δεσπότην
     κατιδεῖν ἐπὶ τοῦ ξύλου   βουλήσει κρεμάμενον·

These addresses and imperatives call for the correct (and expected) response from the natural world: one of horror. The most stable and most predictable elements in nature are repelled by the crucifixion of God's son to the point that they cannot bear to continue their normal behaviour. As we saw above, the Gospels emphasize the natural world's revulsion at this unnatural event. The direct addresses to heaven, earth and the sun, however, are Romanos' creation. The Gospel writers merely report the natural world's reaction, but Romanos enters the story and talks to the natural world in a dramatic use of apostrophe.[8] These imperatives personify and make characters out of the heaven, earth and sun. They have become players in the drama of the Passion, and Romanos (as director) calls on them to play their part.[9]

Romanos draws his tricolon to a dramatic close (the cross) and uses the rhetorical form to emphasize the significant theological point: the free will of Jesus Christ. Christ was not compelled to be crucified, but freely chose it. Here Romanos is influenced by the christological formulations of, among others, the Cappadocians. The freedom of Christ, according to Gregory of Nyssa, is evidence of his true humanity.[10] Freedom, or choice, is something which humans are granted by God, it is part of what it means to be human.[11] So Christ's willingness to go to the cross is evidence of his humanity but also of his divinity, since his actions are the perfection of humanity; he exercises perfect virtue and demonstrates the type of human God calls everyone to be.[12]

For those who supported the Council of Chalcedon in 451, it became important to acknowledge the free will of Christ, as it provided evidence

---

[8] On narrative apostrophe in Romanos, see Barkhuizen (1986a).
[9] Although I use a dramatic metaphor, I do not suggest that Romanos' *kontakia* were literally part of a liturgical drama. There is no firm evidence of liturgical drama in the sixth century in the East. La Piana suggested that dramatic homilies were delivered by several presbyters who performed the dialogues, and argued for the existence of trilogies of liturgical drama. See La Piana (1936). See also Carpenter (1936). So far nothing conclusive has been proved. *Contra* La Piana on the existence of Byzantine theatre before the iconoclast period, see Schork (1966). On liturgical dramas in the West, see Muir (1995). There were certainly dramatic homilies, by which Romanos was probably influenced. See, for example, Cunningham (2008), 875. On the influence of Greek drama on Romanos, see Tomadakis (1974), 401–9.
[10] *Antirrheticus adversus Apollinarium* in *Gregorius Nyssena Opera* (hereafter *GNO*) 3.1:181.14–22. For the edition, see Mueller (1958), 127–233.
[11] Harrison (1988), 40–1. See also Harrison (1992).
[12] *GNO* 3.1:198.1–7; 199.6–11. See also Daley (2002b), 482.

of his true humanity.[13] Their opponents, they believed, placed either too much emphasis on the divinity of Christ and so risked diminishing the importance of his humanity for the salvation of the world,[14] or emphasized the union of the two natures to the extent that the human nature was obscured by the divine.[15] So, in the passage above, Romanos emphasizes that Christ is divine (using the term 'master', line 2), while simultaneously drawing attention to that faculty of will which marks him as human.

One of Romanos' near contemporaries, Leontius of Constantinople, similarly mentions Christ's *willing* suffering at various points in his homilies.[16] In his fourteenth homily, entitled *A Homily on the Transfiguration of our Lord Jesus Christ*, Leontius says

… here Christ our rational sheep, even if
he was sacrificed,
was sacrificed nevertheless of his own will,
was buried of his own will,
rose of his own will,
ascending into heaven of his own will,
will come again of his own will in glory of his Father …[17]

ἐνταῦθα τὸ λογικὸν ἡμῶν πρόβατον Χριστός, εἰ
καὶ ἐσφάγη, ἀλλ᾽ ὅμως
βουλήσει ἐσφάγη,
βουλήσει ἐτάφη,
βουλήσει ἀνέστη,
βουλήσει εἰς οὐρανοὺς ἀνῆλθεν,
βουλήσει ἐλεύσεται ἐν τῇ δόξῃ τοῦ πατρὸς αὐτοῦ …[18]

Leontius' emphatic rhetorical repetition strongly underlines that Jesus, although incarnate, was not bound by human desires, but exercised his perfect human will freely to choose the path he did. In such insistence in Romanos and Leontius on Christ's voluntary suffering we see something of the christological concerns of the sixth century, informed both

---

[13] McLeod (2012), 382.

[14] Küng (1987), 515, McLeod (2012), 382. In the seventh century, concerns about the two natures of Christ translated into a debate about whether Christ had one or two wills. On which, see Hovorun (2008).

[15] Cyril of Alexandria was emphatic that Christ was fully human but that this did not diminish his divinity. See Young (2013), 217–18. On the importance of the human nature of Christ in Cyril's understanding of soteriology, see Anderson (2014), chapter 1.

[16] See the introduction in Allen and Datema (1991), 9–10.

[17] Translation taken from Allen and Datema (1991), 184.

[18] Homily XIV, lines 59–65: Allen and Datema (1987).

by the Council of Chalcedon and by earlier theologians such as Gregory of Nyssa.

The dramatic opening of the Passion *kontakion* continues with another ascending tricolon (1.4–7):

Let rocks shatter, for the rock of life is now wounded by nails.
Let the curtain of the temple be split,
since the master's body is being pierced with a lance by the lawless.
Let all creation together shudder and groan at the suffering of the creator.

ῥαγήτωσαν πέτραι,   ἡ γὰρ πέτρα τῆς ζωῆς
                              νῦν τοῖς ἥλοις τιτρώσκεται·
σχισθήτω τοῦ ναοῦ   τὸ καταπέτασμα,
σώματος δεσποτικοῦ   λόγχῃ νυσσομένου ὑπὸ ἀνόμων·
ἁπλῶς πᾶσα ἡ κτίσις   τοῦ κτίστου τὸ πάθος   φρίξῃ, στενάξῃ·

Once again Romanos calls for the Gospel events to take place, both exhibiting an authoritative relationship with scripture and playing the role of director or storyteller in bringing the events before his audience/congregation. The tension builds up through the reactions from the natural world (rocks) and an inanimate, man-made object (the temple curtain), leading up to Romanos' call for the whole creation to groan. Each reaction is a response to a particular part of Christ's suffering (the *arma Christi* in later tradition):[19] the whole creation mirrors the suffering of Christ. The repetition of 'rock' in line 4 creates a pun on Christ as the rock (1 Cor. 10:4) and the stones on the ground which react to the crucifixion (Matt. 27:51).[20] The temple curtain is another reference to this passage of Matthew and to the similar accounts of Mark 15:38 and Luke 23:45. Romanos also makes a word play on creation and creator in line 7, emphasizing it by juxtaposing the two words. This tricolon (and the word plays in it) highlights the paradoxical nature of Christ's crucifixion and the incomprehensibility of the salvific suffering of the creator.

Paradox is part of the new reality, in which the incomprehensible can and does happen. From the Gospels and the first Christian theologians, paradox had been at the heart of Christian doctrine.[21] The virgin birth, for instance, or the death of the immortal God on the cross, are events which require a different sort of discourse than that needed to talk about 'ordinary' events

---

[19] This tradition is mainly western and many centuries after Romanos, but is likely to have been influenced by Byzantine traditions. See Hirsh (1996), 127–9. On the *arma Christi* tradition more broadly, see Cooper and Denny-Brown (2014).

[20] On the witness of rocks, see also Luke 19:40.

[21] Cameron (1991a), 156, 158.

like human death or birth.[22] The apostle Paul famously used paradoxical language to talk about the crucifixion in 1 Corinthians 1:22–5:

For Jews demand signs and Greeks desire wisdom, but we proclaim Christ crucified, a stumbling block to Jews and foolishness to Gentiles, but to those who are the called, both Jews and Greeks, Christ the power of God and the wisdom of God. For God's foolishness is wiser than human wisdom, and God's weakness is stronger than human strength.

For Paul the Christian life is also one of paradox: 'For while we live, we are always being given up to death for Jesus' sake, so that the life of Jesus may be made visible in our mortal flesh.' (2 Cor. 4:11). Paul believed that living the life of an apostle necessarily meant participating in Christ's suffering,[23] and he endured many hardships as a result of his ministry. We will look further at paradox later in this chapter and in Chapter 3.

Direct Address and the Self

But before Romanos moves on to his imaginative narration and exploration of the biblical story, he addresses Jesus directly: the second strophe of the *kontakion* is a prayerful apostrophe which highlights in a personal way the significance of Christ's sacrifice on the cross (2):

My saviour, you took my [nature] so that I might take yours.
You accepted the suffering,[24] so that I now
might look down on sufferings. By your death I live again.
You were placed in a tomb and gave heaven to me as my home.
[By] going down into the depths, you raised me up.
[By] destroying the gates of Hades you opened the heavenly gates for me.
You withstood everything clearly because of the fallen one and endured everything,[25]
so that Adam might dance.

Εἵλου, σωτήρ μου, τὰ ἐμά,   ἵν᾽ ἐγὼ λάβω τὰ σά·
    κατεδέξω τὸ παθεῖν,   ἵν᾽ ἐγὼ νῦν

---

[22] I am indebted to Averil Cameron for her work on Christian discourse. See Cameron (1991a), especially chapter 5. Paradox was also used to talk about the nature of God, e.g. Ephrem *Nis* 3.2, in which he uses kataphatic and apophatic language to talk about God, setting the two up against each other in a paradoxical way. On this aspect of paradox in religious language, see Young (1979). We will deal here with paradoxes relating to the new creation, which are usually those relating to the incarnation or the crucifixion and resurrection.

[23] Savage (1996), 173–4.

[24] On the word play and the link between passions and suffering, see further below.

[25] The 'fallen one' is singular and could refer either to 'me' or to 'Adam', but the point is the same.

τῶν παθῶν καταφρονήσω· σῷ θανάτῳ ἀνέζησα·
ἐτέθης ἐν τάφῳ καὶ εἰς οἴκησιν ἐμοὶ ἐδωρήσω παράδεισον·
εἰς βάθος κατελθὼν ἐμὲ ἀνύψωσας·
πύλας Ἅιδου καθελὼν πύλας οὐρανίους ἠνέῳξάς μοι·
σαφῶς πάντα ὑπέστης διὰ τὸν πεσόντα· πάντα ἠνέσχου,
ἵνα χορεύῃ ὁ Ἀδάμ.

Through this direct address Romanos characterizes Jesus, but more importantly creates a persona for himself with which he expects the congregation to identify. He makes a statement about his salvation which nevertheless refers to human salvation in general: Romanos represents his congregation's experiences and hopes for salvation. Since Romanos recognizes the difficulties involved in imitating Christ without some assistance or mediation, he creates a persona for himself in which he represents both humanity in all its brokenness, and also an appropriately penitent Christian.[26] The congregation can thus identify with him but also seek to imitate him. So in this passage he relates Christ's actions directly to himself. The personal nature of this view of salvation is also intended to appeal to listeners, who can place themselves in the first-person pronouns: Christ's actions save humanity in general but also every person individually. This device, narrative apostrophe, works to connect Romanos (and thereby his congregation) closely with the events described.[27] Romanos becomes a player in the Passion drama and, through him, so does the whole congregation, living the life of Christ through this performance. Thus Romanos draws his congregation into a closer relationship with Christ.

Inserting himself as an example of redeemed humanity is not meant to elevate Romanos above his congregation. The purpose, rather, is to demonstrate that redemption is available to all. In other hymns, Romanos portrays himself with carefully constructed humility in a penitential persona. Perhaps the best example is from *On the Sinful Woman*, in which Romanos not only likens himself to the prostitute, but even says he is not as worthy as she (X.1.9–11):

... terrified, the prostitute no longer remained a prostitute.
But I, although terrified, persist
in the mire of my deeds.

... πτοηθεῖσα ἡ πόρνη οὐκέτι ἔμεινε πόρνη·
ἐγὼ δὲ καὶ πτοούμενος ἐπιμένω
τῷ βορβόρῳ τῶν ἔργων μου.

---

[26] Krueger (2006a), 256, 259. See also Krueger (2013), 290–302. On the influence of Romanos on later homilists including in relation to the penitential persona, see Cunningham (2010). See also Chapter 4 below.

[27] Barkhuizen (1986a), 19, 26.

Throughout this hymn Romanos plays the penitent, begging not only for forgiveness but for the ability to repent completely. As in the hymn on the crucifixion, the congregation is thus meant to identify with his sinfulness, just as he identifies with the prostitute's, and, like both characters, to repent of their sins. The prostitute is held up as the prime example of repentance,[28] but Romanos' calls for God's assistance indicate that all is not lost for listeners who find themselves unable to repent as completely as the sinful woman of the Gospels.[29] His portrayal of the possibility of redemption is consistently and characteristically optimistic.

The basis for this optimism is Romanos' insistence on the great exchange whereby sinful humanity is able to participate in the life of God. In this hymn on the crucifixion (stanza 2, above), metrical units emphasize the opposition of characters and roles being made in this passage and highlight the great exchange which takes place in the crucifixion. Romanos' references to Christ are always in the first metrical unit and the following units in each line are related to Romanos himself. This structural device and the paradoxical statements it houses emphasize the lengths to which God went to save humanity from death: he became human that humans might become divine (i.e. 'you took my [nature] so that I might take yours'). This exchange formula is central to the concepts of correction and perfection which will be important for Romanos (as we will see in Chapter 2): God became human in the person of Jesus to correct human sin and perfect human life.

The paradoxes in this paragraph reflect the counter-intuitive reality of the incarnation, crucifixion and resurrection. God's descent to earth dramatically altered norms and shattered expectations. Christ's descent means human ascent, his passion means an end to passions (and suffering – see further below); death now means life.

Narrative

Romanos follows the dramatic opening and direct address to Jesus with a creative narration of the story of the Passion.[30] *On the Passion of Christ* is based on the Gospel accounts of the events leading up to Christ's crucifixion (the Passion narratives), but rather than following a particular Gospel,

---

[28] Krueger (2013), 294.
[29] On Romanos' self-portrayal as a penitent Christian, see further in Chapter 4 below and Krueger (2006a), 255–74.
[30] On narrative and drama in the *kontakia*, see Eriksen (2013).

Romanos' hymn is a combination of the different accounts. For instance, Caiaphas' statement that it is better for one man to die (4.2–3) appears only in John's Gospel (John 18:14) and only in Matthew and Mark does Jesus make no reply to Pilate's charges (7.1–6; Matt. 27:14; Mark 15:5). This blend of stories reflects Romanos' conception of scripture as a unity, but also his emphasis on creating the fullest possible context for the reading of the day. While we know that Romanos used a (Syriac) harmonized Gospel (*diatessaron*) – another reflection of his belief in the unity of scripture – as well as the four individual Gospels, it is not clear that he does so here.[31] Rather, we can see in Romanos a concern to contextualize the daily lection, drawing on other scriptural passages where necessary to create the richest reading of the Passion possible.

Romanos is also concerned with crafting a good story and with teaching. So he chooses from the different accounts the details of the story which are relevant to his purpose.[32] Caiaphas' statement 'Did I not say rightly before: "It is fitting | that this man alone die and not the whole nation?"' (Οὐ καλῶς εἶπον τὸ πρίν· 'συμφέρει | ἀπολέσθαι τοῦτον μόνον καὶ μὴ ὅλον τὸ ἔθνος;') (4.2–3), for instance, allows Romanos to digress (in a highly rhetorical strophe) on the miracle that makes an enemy of God foretell the truth (4.4–7):

Who [ever] saw the snake bringing forth sweet honey instead of its own venom?
Who [ever] beheld a flame sprinkling dew?
Who ever heard a liar speaking the truth like Caiaphas?
Without meaning to, he prophesied that you would die for the sake of all …

τίς εἶδεν ἀσπίδα   ἀντὶ τοῦ ἰοῦ αὐτῆς   γλυκὺ μέλι προφέρουσαν;
    τίς ἐθεάσατο   φλόγα δροσίζουσαν;
    τίς ἀκήκοε ποτὲ   ψεῦδος ἀληθεῦον ὡς Καϊάφαν;
μὴ θέλων προφητεύει   ὅτι ὑπὲρ πάντων   θνῄσκεις …

The three rhetorical questions of lines 4 to 6 form a tricolon, ending in the true-speaking liar, Caiaphas.[33] The first two lines of the tricolon help to

[31] A *diatessaron* is a unification of the four Gospels. Petersen has made a detailed study of phrases in Romanos which seem to have been borrowed from a Syriac *Diatessaron*. See Petersen (1985b), especially 52–168. Petersen does not argue that Romanos only used a *diatessaron*, but that he made use of one in addition to the four individual Gospels. See Petersen (1983), 491.

[32] Constructing a narrative always involves choosing to include some elements and leave out others. See Nilsson (2006), 28, White (1980), 14.

[33] Schork's argument that Caiaphas comes to recognize the truth of his statement seems unlikely: Schork (1957), 311. Romanos is concerned rather to show that nothing is impossible for God. He can enable even liars to speak the truth.

make the third more dramatic and contradictory. The anaphora (repetition of 'who' at the beginning of each line) emphasizes the tricolon. The paradoxes employed in this passage emphasize the miracle: the power of God to prophesy through an enemy.

Paradoxes also signify that nature has been changed because of Christ. Snakes now spit out honey instead of venom, liars now speak the truth, and so on. Honey and venom, and fire and water go together in the new creation just as life and death go together in Christ's crucifixion. He died, but by his death he saved all humankind from sin and death. Rhetorical questions highlight how impossible these paradoxes are. Jesus' silence before Pilate similarly allows Romanos to employ clever paradoxes, emphasizing the significance of the crucifixion for humanity. Paradoxes change reality and thus perform and are symbols of the post-incarnation reality.

Romanos also uses Caiaphas' statement to dwell on the faults of the Jews, who not only refuse to recognize the Messiah but actually put him to death. The first paradox in the passage above is a reference to Psalm 140: 'They make their tongue sharp as a snake's, and under their lips is the venom of vipers' (Ps. 140:3). It is a call for deliverance from enemies.[34] Through this biblical allusion Romanos places Caiaphas (and thus the Jewish crowd) in the place of the enemies who plot Christ's downfall (Ps. 140:4). Romanos excludes the Jews from the new creation, blaming them collectively for the death of Jesus and claiming that their rejection of him as their Messiah excludes them from participation in the new reality which he instituted.[35]

Romanos' freedom with the text allows him to combine different Gospel accounts into one narrative about Caiaphas. It also enables him to change and augment the story. The *kontakion* focuses on a dialogue between Jesus and the crowd (strophes 8 to 12) which is not part of the Gospel Passion narratives but draws on an earlier event in the Gospels (Mark 2:23–3:1–5; Luke 6:1–10, John 5:9b–18) in which Jesus heals on the Sabbath and the Pharisees are angered. In this story Jesus says, 'The Son of Man is lord of the Sabbath' (Luke 6:5), just as he does in Romanos' dialogue (10.2–3). But Romanos' dialogue moves well beyond this Gospel story. Romanos gives Jesus a lengthy speech and allows the Jews only

---

[34] Psalm 140 is part of a group of lament psalms. See Wallace (2009), 188.

[35] Romanos' theological understanding of the Jewish place in salvation history will be explored further below and in Chapter 3. For a theological reading of references to Jews in contemporary Orthodox liturgy, see Theokritoff (2003a), (2003b).

short responses. Jesus rebukes the crowd with the imagined retorts of the Gentiles (11.1–2):

You have heard the blame from the many [nations] dwelling around you,
that you observe the Sabbath and [yet] are sick

Ψόγον ἠκούσατε ἐκ πολλῶν   τῶν παροικούντων κύκλῳ,
ὡς τηροῦντες σάββατα   καὶ νοσοῦντες·

Through this creative extension of the biblical narrative, Romanos argues that the Jews, along with their laws and the Sabbath, represent the old order, which no longer defines reality. It no longer suffices to observe the Sabbath; now humanity must live Christ-like lives in preparation for the final judgement and consummation of the eschaton. Romanos' imaginative recreation and extension of the Gospel story is one way in which he expounds scripture and teaches his congregation about the new reality and how they should live in it.

This freedom with the text places Romanos firmly within the homiletic tradition. The preacher is vested with authority to interpret and teach the scriptures and this enables him to play around with the story for interpretive and teaching purposes. One Syriac writer used the story of the 'Good Thief' who was crucified with Jesus (Luke 23:40–3) to develop a long dialogue between the Thief and the Angel who guards the entrance to paradise.[36] This dialogue enabled the author to explore various themes around the crucifixion, resurrection and salvation of humanity. Leontius, presbyter of Constantinople, expands the dialogue of the story of the raising of Lazarus (John 11:1–44) to allow Jesus to counter Arianism.[37] Leontius' Jesus interprets Martha's statement ('if you had been here, my brother would not have died') as a foreshadowing of Arianism and corrects her. In Romanos' creative reinvention of the Passion narrative, he focuses on Jesus' miracles (8.4–8) to emphasize his divinity. This reminder of the miracles and the debate over the Sabbath together point out the Jews' lack of understanding and faith. Jesus' remarks about the Sabbath also allow Romanos to explore God's reasons for becoming human: to save humanity from sin and death.

For Romanos, constructing a good story involves imaginative creation.[38] The freedom to bend the Gospel narratives a little, combined with

---

[36] Brock (2002).

[37] Homily II, lines 291–312. See also Allen and Datema (1991), 48.

[38] We know from numerous other Byzantine authors that storytelling was an important element of Byzantine culture. Roger Scott has demonstrated that the one story may be adapted by different authors for quite different purposes, so that a story which was once propaganda for Emperor Michael III becomes anti-propaganda in the hands of Pseudo-Symeon. See Scott (2009), 41–2, (2010), 115–31.

the sorts of rhetorical devices available for a poet, enables Romanos to construct a coherent narrative and persuasive theology. By appealing to his congregation's desire for a good story Romanos makes the Gospel account more vivid and thus draws the congregation into participation in the life of Christ.

Dialogue

Romanos constructs a vivid narrative primarily through dialogue and related techniques.[39] He makes extensive use of biblical and non-biblical dialogues and monologues in his hymns, using both biblical and invented characters. They add drama to his homilies, as he creatively invents speeches and situations which help to draw the congregation into participation in the performed life of Christ. In *On the Passion of Christ*, Romanos has Jesus refute the arguments of the crowd in a fairly one-sided dialogue which asserts Jesus' superiority over his opponents. It is a highly rhetorical speech, full of repetition, antistrophe, alliteration, and assonance, clearly designed to persuade. The speech lasts for over five strophes, but here is one extract (9.3–6):

[Crowd:]: 'You are not crucified for the sake of these things,
                    but for breaking the Sabbath.'
[Jesus:]: 'And what is better, to have mercy on the sick
                    or to honour the Sabbath?
You have broken Sabbaths many times,
and I did not come from my Father's bosom for the sake of Sabbaths ...'

'Χάριν τούτων οὐ σταυροῦσαι,   ἀλλ' ὡς λύων τὸ σάββατον'.
'Καὶ τί καλὸν ἄρα,   ἐλεῆσαι ἀσθενεῖς   ἢ τιμῆσαι τὸ σάββατον;[40]
    ἐλύσατε ὑμεῖς   πολλάκις σάββατα,
    καὶ ἐκ κόλπων πατρικῶν   οὐ παρεγενόμην χάριν σαββάτων ...'

Repetition of 'Sabbath' in the antistrophe here and throughout the speech (e.g. 10.3–5) emphasizes the main point of contention. Romanos repeats

---

[39] On the importance of dialogue in homiletics and poetics before Romanos, see Cameron (1991b), 92, 95, Cunningham (1995), 71, (2003), 101, Kecskeméti (1989), (1993). On dialogue as a dramatizing device, see also La Piana (1936), 176. On Syriac dialogue hymns, see Brock (1983), (1987), (1991), Upson-Saia (2006). On their naissance, see Brock (2001). See further in Chapter 4 below.

[40] I have followed the SC edition in the accentuation of καὶ τί. See Grosdidier de Matons (1967), 214.

'for the sake of', 'honour' and 'to crucify' throughout, focusing on the coming crucifixion and its effects, as opposed to the effects of honouring the Sabbath. We will look at this section of the speech again shortly. Yet it is not the crowd who is to be persuaded by all this rhetoric, but rather Romanos' congregation. He does this through the technique of characterization.

Characterization (*Ethopoeia*)

Characterization (*ethopoeia*) is defined in rhetorical handbooks as the 'imitation of the character of a person supposed to be speaking'.[41] In *On the Passion of Christ,* Romanos works hardest to develop the character of Jesus. Christ is characterized as a clever speaker as an excess of rhetorical figures are put into his mouth. He employs numerous devices including repetition, anaphora, antistrophe, rhetorical questions, assonance and synecdoche. Christ is also a vivid and engaging character: his argumentative speech is lively and heartfelt and makes him seem present to the listeners.

Most importantly, however, Romanos sets Jesus up as a formidable opponent and an authoritative interpreter of scripture. Jesus reverses the arguments of the Jews, turning their own words against them; his opponents are silenced by his arguments; his interpretation of God's words confounds them. Christ's apparent disrespect for the Sabbath is not disrespect at all, but rather by healing on the Sabbath he has glorified it. In the Gospel stories (Matt. 12:9–14; Mark 3:1–6; Luke 6:6–11) Jesus confounds the Pharisees by responding to their query about whether it is lawful to heal on the Sabbath with 'Is it lawful to do good or to do harm on the Sabbath, to save life or to kill?' (Mark 3:4). Naturally the Pharisees cannot respond that it is lawful to do harm on the Sabbath, and since their only possible response is to admit that healing on the Sabbath is lawful, they remain silent. In these accounts, Jesus does not need to berate his opponents further, since their silence is proof of his victory. In contrast, Romanos' Jesus does not hold back. He argues that the Jews have made many other transgressions and that his purpose in coming was not to uphold a small facet of the Law, but rather to restore health to all creation. Romanos' Jesus says that the Jewish observance of the Sabbath has done them little good (11.1–2, 7):

You have heard blame from the many who dwell around you,
that 'they observe the Sabbath and [yet] are sick' ...

---

[41] Hermogenes, *Progymnasmata*. See Kennedy (2003), 84. See also Patricia Matsen's Appendix II in Rollinson (1981), 160ff.

but I, by saving all on the Sabbath, have brought much glory

[to the Sabbath] …

Ψόγον ἠκούσατε ἐκ πολλῶν   τῶν παροικούντων κύκλῳ,
    ὡς τηροῦντες σάββατα   καὶ νοσοῦντες·…
ἐγὼ δὲ πάντας σώσας   τ[ῷ σαβ]βάτῳ πλέον

κλέος παρέσχον …

Jesus gives voice to the Gentile critics of the Jews, sympathizing with their rebuke of the law-abiding Jewish community. Their observance of the Law has gone too far; it has caused them to be blind to their own Messiah and to the plights of their fellow human beings, like those Jesus healed. Romanos asserts that, although the Jews do not realize it, Jesus' acts of healing are part of the new reality which he has instituted. In this *kontakion* and throughout the corpus, Romanos reminds his readers of the Jews' incomprehension and blind rejection of Jesus. This resonates with contemporary violence against Jews and other non-Christian groups, and encourages listeners to maintain this stance against Judaism. Romanos' general treatment of Jews in the *kontakia*, including such damaging rhetoric, will be explored further in Chapter 3, and at the conclusion of this chapter.

Refrain

The debate between Jesus and the Jews is another way in which Romanos weaves his congregation into the events of the Passion story, making them play first the crowd and then Jesus through the refrain. This refrain, 'so that Adam might dance' (ἵνα χορεύῃ ὁ Ἀδάμ), which concludes each stanza and which the congregation (or perhaps a choir representing them) sang, is the most obvious way in which listeners participate.[42] Romanos puts this line into the mouths of the various characters in the hymn, thereby making the congregation enact different roles within one *kontakion*. In strophe 7 (lines 7–8), the crowd says to Pilate:

'He is liable for death for what we claim he did. For this reason he is silent, so that Adam might dance.'

… Ἔνοχος ἔστιν   ὧν ἡμεῖς αἰτοῦμεν·   ὅθεν κωφεύει,
ἵνα χορεύῃ ὁ Ἀδάμ.

---

[42]   Grosdidier de Matons (1980–1), 40, Maas (1910a), 289. On the role of the congregation, see further in Chapter 4 below.

The congregation sings the refrain, playing the part of the crowd. Then (at 8.7–8) the same words are spoken by Jesus:

'Perhaps it is not because of these things, rather in pay for them,
                                                            that I suffer and die
so that Adam might dance.'

μὴ τάχα διὰ ταῦτα,   μᾶλλον δ᾽ ἀντὶ τούτων   πάσχω καὶ θνήσκω,
ἵνα χορεύῃ ὁ Ἀδάμ

Now the congregation plays Jesus. By performing parts of the narrative they perform the life of Christ. They thus participate in the new reality inaugurated by the incarnation. But they also perform the exclusion of the Jews. The congregation plays both saviour and sinner, concluding the debate between Jesus and the crowd in the role of the former. The congregation is to imitate Christ, and this means living in the new reality, not being bound into the old pre-incarnation reality (exemplified by the Jews).

There is also a theological irony in placing the same words in the mouths of both Jesus and his attackers: the crowd speaks the truth without realizing it. Christ does indeed keep silent for Adam's sake (7.7–8). The end of this strophe mirrors the close of the previous one, which ends with Romanos' explanation of Jesus' silence (6.7–8): 'But he, so that he might suffer, endures in silence for a while, standing wordless, so that Adam might dance' (αὐτὸς δὲ ἵνα πάθῃ, σιγῶν τέως στέγει, ἄλαλος στήκων, | ἵνα χορεύῃ ὁ Ἀδάμ.).[43] Christ's silence is calculated to bring about the restoration of humanity: Jesus could have prevented his death, but he chose silence so that he might die for the sake of his creation. The Melodist's explanation is thus echoed by the unwitting crowd. This irony would not have been lost on the congregation, which played all three roles in the refrain: narrator (Romanos), crowd and Jesus.

Irrespective of which character says the refrain, its theological significance in this *kontakion*, as well as helping to enact the congregation's participation in the new reality, is that it points to the ideas of correction and perfection. Christ, the second Adam, came into the world to correct the first Adam's sins, perfect human existence and overturn human death. Thus, all Christ's actions bring redemption and life to the first Adam: the bound Adam will be free and dance for joy as a result of God's descent to earth in Jesus Christ. In moving the congregation through different roles, from the blind, sinful crowd to the persona of Jesus, the *kontakion* performs the redemptive correction and perfection of the Passion.

---

[43] Ignatius, among others, recognized the importance of silence in confessing God as well as speaking. See *Letter to the Ephesians* 15.

Although for most of Romanos' hymns the refrain remains the same throughout the hymn, in *On the Passion of Christ* it changes. Initially it is 'only Adam dances' (μόνος χορεύει ὁ Ἀδάμ), but in the second strophe it changes to 'so that Adam might dance' and continues as such for the rest of the hymn. This change might suggest that a select group sang the refrain, perhaps a trained choir. But I see no reason why the cantor could not have explained the change before beginning. The change makes more grammatical and semantic sense and so would not have been difficult for the whole congregation to pick up.[44]

Paradox

The long speech Romanos gives Jesus, and in which the congregation takes part, infuriates the crowd (whom Romanos describes as bloodthirsty and like lions) and Pilate sends him to be whipped. The following strophe is an extended paradox (14.1–8):

The Redeemer endures scourgings, the Releaser was bound,
stripped and stretched out on the cross.
He who in a pillar of cloud once was speaking with Moses and Aaron,
he who made firm the pillars of the earth, as David said, is bound to a pillar;
he who showed to the people a path in the desert –
for the fiery pillar appeared before them – is held fast to a pillar.
The Rock is on the pillar, and the church is hewn for me
so that Adam might dance.

Μάστιγας φέρει ὁ λυτρωτής,   δέσμιος ἦν ὁ λύτης,
　　γυμνωθεὶς καὶ ἐκταθεὶς   ἐπὶ στύλου
　ὁ ἐν στύλῳ πρὶν νεφέλης   Μωσῇ καὶ Ἀαρὼν συλλαλῶν·
　ὁ τῆς γῆς τοὺς στύλους   στερεώσας, ὡς Δαβὶδ
　　　　　　　　　　　　ἔφη, στύλῳ προσδέδεται·
　　ὁ δείξας τῷ λαῷ   ὁδὸν εἰς ἔρημον –
　πύρινος γὰρ πρὸ αὐτῶν   ἔφαινεν ὁ στῦλος – στύλῳ προσήχθη·
ἡ πέτρα ἐπὶ στύλου,   καὶ λαξεύεταί μοι   ἡ ἐκκλησία,
ἵνα χορεύῃ ὁ Ἀδάμ.

---

[44] The changes in the pronunciation of Greek from the classical period to the sixth century mean that there would have been little if any difference between the vowels ει and η, so that χορεύῃ would sound just like χορεύει, but the replacement of μόνος with ἵνα remains a problem. See Moleas (2004), Palmer (1996), 176. Grosdidier de Matons, while agreeing that a changing refrain makes it unclear, nevertheless argues for the participation of the whole congregation in the refrain on the basis of Romanos' invitations to take part in some of the hymns. See Grosdidier de Matons (1977), 46. Cf. *On Judas* XVII.23.7–9 where Romanos calls for listeners to cry out directly before the refrain.

As we have noted, the central mysteries of the Christian faith are paradoxes (e.g. the virgin birth, the incarnation, the crucifixion, the resurrection). Like other early Christian writers, Romanos employs paradox repeatedly; paradoxes and oxymorons are recurrent devices in this and almost every *kontakion*. In this passage, Romanos develops an elaborate layered paradox involving 'pillar' or 'cross' (*stulos*). The word is repeated again and again in different contexts, linking the Redeemer on the cross with the God of the Old Testament, and finally concluding the paragraph by making a connection with the Christian church. This strophe illustrates the contradictions inherent in the crucifixion. Verbal and structural repetition, alliteration and allusions to well-known biblical stories make this layered paradox particularly effective. Line 1 emphasizes Christ's role as the saviour of humanity by naming him 'Redeemer' and 'Releaser', two words cognate with the verb for loosing or releasing, while simultaneously connecting the Redeemer with words of scourging and bondage (*mastigas, desmios*). These contrasts emphasize, as does the whole stanza, the miraculous nature of the crucifixion, the extent of God's sacrifice. Christ, who by definition is associated with release and redemption, is bound and whipped. Wonder at God's miracles and full realization of his sacrifice on the cross are two important themes which run throughout the corpus of Romanos' hymns. Lines 3 to 5 in this paradoxical stanza all define God by referring to different events in the Old Testament, as we will see shortly. The pillars of the Old Testament which associated God with strength and power are contrasted with the pillar (i.e. the cross) which makes God in Christ suffer.

The pillar, and in particular the 'fiery pillar [which] appeared before them', recalls the Exodus. Romanos uses the same word (*stulos*) as that used in the Septuagint for the pillars of cloud and fire: 'The Lord went in front of them in a pillar (*stulō*) of cloud by day, to lead them along the way, and in a pillar (*stulō*) of fire by night, to give them light, so that they might travel by day and by night' (Exodus 13:21). In the Exodus story, God leads and protects his vulnerable people. Romanos compares this narrative with the behaviour of the Jews towards God when he is vulnerable: they crucify him; whereas before God became a pillar for their salvation, now they have made a pillar for his destruction. Line 4 recalls Psalm 75:3: 'When the earth totters, with all its inhabitants, it is I who keep its pillars (*stulous*) steady.' God is the one who protects the foundations of the earth, who can keep the earth from being destroyed by its inhabitants. God, who has been a pillar for the Jews in numerous ways, protecting and guiding them, is rewarded by being bound to a pillar until he dies.

An interesting allusion to a biblical pun finishes this extended paradox in the reference to the rock as the foundation of the church. This simultaneously refers to Jesus and to his disciple Peter. In 1 Corinthians, Paul says: 'For they [i.e. the Israelites in the desert] drank from the spiritual rock that followed them, and the rock was Christ' (1 Cor. 10:4). Paul's imagery is cleverly mixed, connecting the rock from which the Israelites drank not only with Christ but also with God in the pillars of fire which followed them at night as they journeyed through the desert (Exodus 13:21). In Matthew's Gospel Jesus says to Peter: 'And I tell you, you are Peter (*petros*), and on this rock (*petra*) I will build my church, and the gates of Hades will not prevail against it' (Matt. 16:18). Both passages spring to mind here. Romanos' substantial point is the strength of the church and its foundation in Christ, which is the cause of its strength. Just as death (Hades) did not prevail against Christ who was crucified on the cross, death will not prevail against the church which is founded on Christ, the Rock, through his disciple, Peter (rock).

This is the most elaborate paradox in *On the Passion of Christ*, but Romanos uses other paradoxical imagery and oxymorons elsewhere in the *kontakion* to re-enact in language the incongruity of the crucifixion. Standing before Pilate, Jesus refuses to speak (7.1):

The Thunderer stands silent, the Word is without a word.

Ἄφωνος ἵστατο ὁ βροντῶν,   λόγου ἐκτὸς ὁ Λόγος·

How can the thundering one not thunder? God is all powerful and controls the heavens and all the dramatic weather which emanates from them. Yet here God stands without making a sound. It is equally incomprehensible that Jesus, who is called the Word (e.g. John 1:1), and who is defined in terms of his role as the Word of God, should say nothing. Romanos explains why (7.2–3): 'for if he had broken into speech, he would not have been beaten; and if he had won he would not have been crucified nor saved Adam' (εἰ γὰρ ἔρρηξε φωνήν, οὐχ ἡττᾶτο | καὶ νικῶν οὐκ ἐσταυροῦτο καὶ Ἀδὰμ οὐκ ἐσῴζετο·). What seems most natural is changed in the crucifixion. Death means life: Christ's death on the cross means life for all humanity. We have seen this sort of natural change expressed already in the opening of the hymn. Human categories break down in the face of this miraculous deed of God, and language is left with paradox, which performs the new creation.[45]

---

[45] See further in Chapter 3 below.

Another paradox in this *kontakion* reverses the roles of Jesus and Pilate (6.5):

A condemned man judges the righteous judge …

τὸν δίκαιον κριτὴν   [κρίνει κ]ατάκριτος,

Jesus is the condemned man in the Gospel story, since he is the one brought before Pilate for judgement and condemned to death. But Romanos makes Pilate the condemned man, doomed to die like all humanity, and particularly damned for his role in Christ's crucifixion. By contrast, Jesus, whom Romanos places at the beginning of the line to emphasize his importance, is the 'righteous judge'.

Later Romanos emphasizes that Pilate made the wrong choice, through a paradoxical rhetorical question (16.4–6):

For hearing that he would be Caesar's enemy, the coward was scared.
Did he wish to be an enemy of the almighty or of Caesar,
by honouring life now rather than the Life?

ἀκούσας γὰρ ὅτι   ἔσται Καίσαρος ἐχθρός,   ἐπτοήθη ὁ δείλαιος·
   τοῦ παντοκράτορος   ἢ γὰρ τοῦ Καίσαρος
   θέλει εἶναι δυσμενής,   τῆς Ζωῆς τὴν ζωὴν νῦν προτιμήσας;

Pilate's decision to honour Caesar above God is laughable when put in these terms. Who would willingly choose to be an enemy of God rather than an enemy of a mortal ruler? Pilate's choice is a short-sighted one, focusing on his earthly life 'now' rather than on eternal life. Romanos encourages his listeners to avoid Pilate's mistake and orient their lives towards eternal life.

Another brief oxymoron once again emphasizes the reversal of all norms in the crucifixion, this time using the imagery of taste (22.1):[46]

They gave the Fount of Sweet Streams vinegar to drink

Ὄξος ἐπότισαν τὴν πηγὴν   τῶν γλυκερῶν ναμάτων

By drawing on the sense of taste (and perhaps smell), Romanos makes the contrast more bodily and vivid, and therefore more immediate to his audience.

Vivid Description (*Ekphrasis*)

The vivification achieved through taste imagery in this paradox (and in dialogic and narrative techniques) is extended to events and objects through *ekphrasis*. *Ekphrasis* or 'vivid description' was a way to bring an

---

[46] On Romanos' use of the senses, see chapter 2 below.

object or scene before the eyes of the listener.[47] The fourth-century rhetorician Aphthonius defines *ekphrasis* as 'a speech which leads one around, bringing the subject matter vividly before the eyes' (Ἔκφρασίς ἐστι λόγος περιηγηματικὸς ὑπ' ὄψιν ἄγων ἐναργῶς τὸ δηλούμενον).[48] 'Leads one around' is an appropriate translation for περιηγηματικὸς since the speech should take the listener around the object being described. If it is an *ekphrasis* of a church (for example, Procopius of Caesarea's *ekphrasis* on Hagia Sophia),[49] then the *ekphrasis* should describe the church in such a way that the listener feels as if they are being led around the church itself. It was supposed to do this so vividly that the person listening to the *ekphrasis* would actually see the thing being described in their mind's eye. Nicolaus the Sophist says: 'the former [i.e. *ekphrasis*] tries to make listeners into spectators' (ἢ δὲ πειρᾶται θεατὰς τοὺς κούοντας ἐργάζεσθαι) (68).[50]

Byzantines did not see *ekphrasis* simply as a description of a work of art (as it is still often conceptualized today despite the definitive studies of scholars such as Ruth Webb), but rather an advanced narrative exercise, used to describe people, places, times, events, nature and so on.[51] So narrative and *ekphrasis* are closely connected in Byzantine rhetoric.[52] Vivid description is certainly part of the way in which Romanos constructs a coherent and dramatic narrative. These *ekphraseis* are not simply digressions from the narrative, unrelated to the meaning or flow of the story. They are carefully integrated into the narrative and although they may at first seem to create a gap, closer inspection proves they often assist the temporal movement of that narrative.[53] In strophe 18, Romanos describes human thirst and Christ's quenching of it in an *ekphrasis* followed by a short speech by Jesus:

The earthly race was destroyed by thirst, consumed by burning heat
as they wandered in the desert, and in waterless land
the wretched [race] has not found a cure for its thirst.
For this reason my Saviour, the fount of good things, gushed forth a stream of life,

---

[47] James and Webb (1991), 4, Macrides and Magdalino (1988), 49.

[48] Rabe (1926), 36, line 22. The translation is Ruth Webb's: Webb (1999b), 11.

[49] Procopius, *Buildings* I.i.23–65.

[50] Nicolaus *Progymnasmata* section 68: Kennedy (2003), 166.

[51] Webb (1999b), 11. See also Webb (2009), 61–86. Webb includes a useful table (p. 64) on the subjects of *ekphraseis* in the different *progymnasmata*, and art works appear in only one of these. Even in cases where the subject matter could be broadly defined as art, as in the Shield of Achilles, the first-century (AD) rhetorician Theon sees the *ekphrasis* as a description of the process of manufacture rather than a description of a work of art. See Theon *Progymnasmata* section 119 and Webb (1999b), 11.

[52] James and Webb (1991), 6, Webb (1999a), 64.

[53] On the relationship between narrative and *ekphrasis* and how the latter can involve temporal as well as spatial movement, see Nilsson (2005), 127–8.

saying, 'You were thirsty because of your side.
Drink from my side and do not ever thirst.
This is a twofold stream. It washes those who are dirty and quenches thirst,
so that Adam might dance.'

Ὤλετο δίψῃ ὁ γηγενής,   καύσωνι κατεφλέχθη
    ἐν ἐρήμῳ πλανηθείς,   ἐν ἀνύδρῳ
    καὶ ἰάσασθαι τὴν δίψαν   οὐχ εὗρεν ὁ δύστηνος·
διὸ ὁ σωτήρ μου,   ἡ πηγὴ τῶν ἀγαθῶν,   ζωῆς νάματα ἔβλυσε
    βοῶν· ʽΔιὰ τῆς σῆς   πλευρᾶς ἐδίψησας,
    πίε τῆς ἐμῆς πλευρᾶς   καὶ οὐ μὴ διψήσεις εἰς τὸν αἰῶνα·
διπλοῦν ταύτης τὸ ῥεῖθρον·   λούει καὶ ποτίζει   τοὺς ῥυπωθέντας,
    ἵνα χορεύῃ ὁ Ἀδάμ.'

The thirst of those in the desert is emphasized by repetition of 'thirst' and words related to water ('fount', 'stream'), and by the juxtaposition of 'in the desert' and 'in waterless land'. Adam's side is a metaphor for Eve, who caused human thirst, and the image of drinking from Christ's side recalls the eucharist. Romanos creates a picture of a spiritually and physically thirsty humanity, which is redeemed and whose thirst is quenched by Christ's crucifixion. This is an image of correction (Christ corrects the sins of Eve) and perfection (he stops humanity thirsting).

The motif of thirsting in the desert also calls to mind the water which burst from a rock to quench the thirst of the Israelites in their journey through the desert (Exodus 17:1–6): 'The Lord said to Moses, "… strike the rock, and water will come out of it, so that the people may drink."' (17:6). Yet this water did not quench human thirst forever, nor did it restore humanity to everlasting life. It is in the eucharist, which is both a symbol of and a participation in Christ's sacrifice on the cross, that human thirst is quenched.

This reference to the eucharist, which links Romanos' preaching with other rites of the church or parts of the liturgy, reminds the congregation of the most obvious way in which they participate in the life of Christ: by receiving the sacrament of his body and blood. This reminder is central to Romanos' endeavour to make his congregation participate in the new creation which he believes is present after the incarnation. Participation does not only take place in the eucharist, but these references may keep the idea of participation in the minds of listeners. They are also appeals to the senses, encouraging the congregation to remember the taste of the bread and wine;[54] the *ekphrasis* thus appeals not only to sight, but also

---

[54] On the senses, see further in Chapter 2 below and Frank (2005), 163–79, Harvey (2006).

to the feeling of thirst, both physical and spiritual. The congregation is made to picture the Israelites in the desert and not only to imagine but also to identify with, even feel, their thirst. This Good Friday *kontakion* looks forward to Easter Day, the day in which Christ is resurrected anew in the liturgical year and the eucharistic feast is celebrated. Lay eucharistic communion was infrequent, but Easter was one major feast at which lay Christians usually received the eucharist.[55] Romanos prepares his congregation to receive the sacraments, making them thirst for the 'stream of life'.

Romanos also invokes memory of baptism and perhaps foreshadows approaching Easter baptismal rites. Biblical allusions to water often carry connotations of baptism, at least as far as many patristic exegetes were concerned, and Romanos' allusion is no exception.[56] The waters of baptism save in a way that the water which burst from the rock did not. Romanos elsewhere makes the comparison between the parting of the Red Sea and baptism (Exodus 14:26–9; XXXVI.8): baptism saves eternally, whereas the parting of the Red Sea only saved those particular Israelites from being killed (or returned to slavery) by the Egyptians.[57] Baptism is another rite which, although it only takes place once in a person's life, is an important participatory moment. Through baptism Christians participate in the baptism of Christ and, as we will see later (Chapter 3), Romanos sees this as the point in which humans are re-clothed in the divine garment which they lost at the Fall and restored to paradise.[58] In Jesus' speech following the *ekphrasis*, he connects his crucifixion and death both with the eucharist and with baptism: it is a twofold stream (18.7). It is perhaps a reference to the blood and water which came forth from Jesus' side: the blood is the thirst-quenching eucharistic wine and the water the restorative waters of baptism.

Ekphrasis is itself a way in which Romanos makes his congregation perform and participate in the story, irrespective of whether eucharistic imagery is involved. Its vividness is designed to make the listener visualize the situation and react in a particular way.[59] As discussed above, many rhetoricians and commentators have explained these techniques as ways

---

[55] Krueger (2006b), 13.

[56] See, for example, Ambrose *On the Mysteries* 3.1.3 in which he sees the waters in Genesis as a type for baptismal waters. On Old Testament types for baptism, see Daniélou (1956), 70–113. On fish and water images and their relation to baptism, see Drewer (1981).

[57] See Chapter 3. On this type for baptism more generally, see Daniélou (1956), 86–98.

[58] On this type of clothing metaphor in Syriac homiletics and poetry, which probably influenced Romanos, see Brock (1982a).

[59] Webb (1997), 112 and passim.

of making eyewitnesses out of listeners.[60] By employing these devices Romanos changes the congregation from passive listeners into active participants in the events he vividly describes. They are no longer simply listening to him tell them about the thirsting Israelites, but they see the Israelites before them and experience their thirst. Romanos thus encourages his listeners to recognize their thirst, their sinfulness and therefore their need for God. He makes them thirst for God. But it also enables him to emphasize that Christ quenches thirst. Unlike the Israelites who will go on thirsting, his congregation's thirst will be eternally sated by Christ.

Structure

This *ekphrasis* also helps to cover a temporal gap in the story, between Pilate's decision to crucify Jesus (stanza 17) and the carrying of the cross and the crucifixion (stanza 21). Far from the *ekphrasis* causing a halt in time and thereby making the narrative disjointed, we are carried through a change of scene and time in the narrative proper by this vivid description of human thirst.[61] The *ekphrasis* holds the attention of the audience, elaborating on an important point through vibrant imagery and at the same time helping to move the narrative from one scene to the next. This type of structural device adds to the drama of the musical homily.

The Passion story is interspersed with such stanzas of analysis, *ekphrasis* or Old Testament references, which help to set up the story as a drama by assisting the temporal and spatial movement of the narrative. Between the stanzas on Caiaphas (3–4) and Pilate (6ff.), Romanos analyses Caiaphas' statement and links the events to the Old Testament story of Cain and Abel (4–5). Like the *ekphrasis* above, this analysis covers a gap in time and a change of scene. The drama moves from the courtyard of Caiaphas to Pilate's headquarters in the time it takes for Romanos to examine Caiaphas and his actions.

Dramatic comparisons or oppositions of two characters are also supported by structural techniques (2.1–3):

My saviour, you took what was mine, so that I might receive what is yours.
You accepted the suffering, so that I now
might look down on passions.

---

[60] See, for example, Nicolaus the Sophist, section 11, quoted above, and Dionysius of Halicarnassus *De Lysia* 7. See also, for example, James and Webb (1991), 4, Webb (1997), (1999b), esp. 13, Zanker (1981), 297.

[61] On *ekphrasis* as a narrative technique in Konstantinos Manasses, see Nilsson (2005), (2006). On temporal movement as an element of *ekphrasis*, see Nilsson (2005), 128.

Εἵλου, σωτήρ μου, τὰ ἐμά,   ἵν’ ἐγὼ λάβω τὰ σά.

κατεδέξω τὸ παθεῖν,   ἵν’ ἐγὼ νῦν

τῶν παθῶν καταφρονήσω·

The first half of each line (and first metrical unit) refers to what Christ has done, the second to the reason and effect on Romanos (and therefore on all humanity). The word play, which strengthens the comparison, is difficult to render in English, but the word for suffering and the word for passions come from the same root in Greek so that a paradox is created: Christ accepted suffering to get rid of human passions. This word play is repeated in several places in this *kontakion*, including in the acrostic.

Romanos also highlights the comparison through repetition of the following construction: a) a clause in which Christ is the subject, describing his actions; b) caesura; c) a clause expressing Christ's purpose in so acting. This sort of structural repetition, using the metrical caesura to separate the two phrases, is not uncommon for Romanos.[62] Here it accentuates the significance of the incarnation and crucifixion for human salvation: that Christ perfects our human life. The metre is similarly used in *On the Annunciation II* (XXXVII.8.1–3). Metre and structure combine to play the role of much of Romanos' rhetoric in his hymns: emphasizing theological points.

Similar structural repetition occurs at 8.1, 4–6:

'Do I now owe you my death,' my Saviour said …

'because I once "demanded back" Jairus' daughter with a single word,

because I "gathered in" the only son of the widow

and with my voice showed to all lifeless Lazarus hastening [from the tomb]'

'Θάνατον ὤφειλον νῦν ἐγώ,'   ἔφησεν ὁ σωτήρ μου …

'ἀνθ’ ὧν Ἰαείρου   τὸ θυγάτριον ποτὲ   λόγῳ μόνῳ ἀνέπραξα,

ἀνθ’ ὧν μονογενῆ   τῆς χήρας ἤγειρα[63]

καὶ τὸν Λάζαρον φωνῇ   τρέχοντα τὸν ἄπνουν ἔδειξα πᾶσι'

The repetition of lines 4–5 accentuates the miracles Jesus performed, and suggests a plethora of others unmentioned. The placement of the repeated 'because' at the beginning of these lines matches the placement of 'death' in the first line, emphasizing the paradox that such miraculous reversals of death should necessitate Jesus' death.

---

[62]   On the metre of Romanos' *kontakia*, see Maas and Trypanis' metrical appendix: Maas and Trypanis (1963), 511–38. The metrical scheme for this *kontakion* is xix, Maas and Trypanis (1963), 526.

[63]   This word is ambiguous. It could come from ἐγείρω or ἀγείρω. I have chosen the latter, because I think Romanos is using debt imagery, following ὤφειλον, but 'raised' would certainly be an appropriate translation in this context, so I do not argue that my reading is the only possible one. On this use of imagery, see below.

Word Play

Contrasts and comparisons of characters are also made through etymological word plays. In strophe 8 Romanos makes a play on 'word' (*logos*) (8.2–3):

for he did not judge Pilate worthy of a word,
since he considered him irrational.

τὸν Πιλᾶτον
οὐδὲ λόγου γὰρ ἠξίου   λογισάμενος ἄλογον-

Romanos contrasts Jesus with Pilate. Jesus is silent in response to Pilate's questioning. In the story Pilate speaks, but Jesus considers him 'wordless' or 'reasonless' (*alogos*). By contrast, Jesus is the one who 'reasons'. *Alogos* has also come to mean 'horse' or 'animal' by this period, further strengthening the notion of Pilate's irrationality.[64]

This strophe also plays on images of debt, money and exacting payment. Jesus asks whether he 'owes' death (1), because he 'demanded back' or 'exacted' Jairus' daughter (4) and 'gathered in' the widow's son (5). These miracles are put in terms of debt recoupment and money collection. In line 7 he says that 'in pay for these things' he must suffer and die. To suggest that raising someone from the dead is equivalent to collecting a debt makes a mockery of the Jewish claim. Romanos' use of money imagery thus demonstrates how ridiculous the suggestion is that Jesus 'owes' the Jews anything. But it also uses everyday language, monetary terminology which would have been familiar to all, to appeal to (or even amuse) his audience, giving them a more accessible route to an understanding of the text.

In strophe 21, Romanos makes plays on the word 'cross' to reverse roles in the crucifixion: it is Christ who is crucifying Satan/Death by his death (21.1–3):

Providing victory to the humble, bearing, in the manner of triumph,
the cross on his shoulders, he went out
to be crucified and to crucify the one who severely wounded us.

Νίκην παρέχων τοῖς ταπεινοῖς,   δίκην τροπαίου φέρων
    ἐπὶ ὤμων τὸν σταυρὸν   ἐξῆλθε
    σταυρωθῆναι καὶ σταυρῶσαι   τὸν ἡμᾶς κατατρώσαντα·

Death's apparent victory over Jesus is actually defeat. By this word play Romanos enacts the paradox of the crucifixion. Jesus turns death on its head and by his crucifixion crucifies death for all humanity.

---

[64] Lampe (1961), 78, A.1.a.

These sorts of close connections between words and ideas are made using alliteration and assonance as well. These devices enable a type of word play where there is no etymological link between the two words. For instance (5.1–4):

Thus the priest spoke, but he did not understand it.
For envy did not allow him,
but roused him to murder. For murder follows envy.
And the martyr Abel was envied by Cain, and afterwards murdered.

οὕτω μὲν ἔφη ὁ ἱερεύς,   τοῦτο δὲ οὐ συνῆκεν·
    οὐ γὰρ εἴασεν αὐτὸν   ὁ φθόνος,
    ἀλλ᾽ ἠρέθισε πρὸς φόνον·   φθόνῳ φόνος γὰρ ἔπεται·
καὶ μάρτυς ὁ Ἄβελ   ὑπὸ Κάϊν φθονηθείς,   φονευθεὶς δὲ μετέπειτα·

In this passage Romanos asserts that murder (*phonos*) and envy (*phthonos*) are closely associated: murder follows envy. He makes this association all the more prominent by alliteration, assonance and repetition, and the juxtaposition of these similar-sounding words in lines 3 and 4. The reference to the story of Cain and Abel (Genesis 4), a story in which one brother murders another out of envy, hammers home the connection (on the typology of which, see further below). Here is a moral lesson in word play. Romanos provides a negative moral example in Caiaphas; he speaks the truth but is unable to comprehend it because of his envy of Jesus. Again, Romanos uses the biblical stories to educate his listeners about true Christian behaviour: avoid envy as it leads to murder. As we will see shortly, this could also be read as instructing listeners to avoid 'Jewish' behaviour.

Typology and Prophecy

Towards the end of this *kontakion*, Romanos presents Old Testament people as types for Jesus and Old Testament events prefigure events in the life of Christ.[65] Following earlier theologians, Romanos sees Isaac as a type for Christ and his resurrection (19.6–7):[66]

Of whom [i.e. Christ] the patriarch Isaac on the mountain was a type.
He was slaughtered in the ram and brought down living like my saviour.

---

[65] We will look further at typology and prophecy in Chapters 2 and 3. For discussions of typology in Romanos, see also Reichmuth (1975), Schork (1962).
[66] For example, *Epistle of Barnabas* 7:3.

οὗ καὶ τύπος ὁ πατὴρ   Ἰσαὰκ ἐγένετο ἐν τῷ ὄρει·
ἐσφάγη ἐν ἀρνίῳ   καὶ ζῶν κατηνέχθη   ὡς ὁ σωτήρ μου

Romanos explicitly marks this comparison as a type (*tupos*): Isaac fore-shadows Christ's resurrection, since he was taken to be sacrificed and only replaced by the ram at the last minute (Genesis 22:9–13). He was therefore sacrificed (in the ram, which is his substitute) and yet returned alive with his father Abraham; Christ is sacrificed on the cross and then resurrected. Antitype surpasses type: the ram is substituted for Isaac and so Isaac returns alive, whereas Christ truly undergoes suffering and death and returns to life. It was important in Christian tradition, which Romanos certainly follows here, that Isaac did not suffer, but that he prefigured the one who would suffer for the sake of all.[67] This was in contrast to rabbinic interpretations of Isaac as the suffering one, whose blood was truly shed and who thereby demonstrated his willingness to obey God and his father.[68]

Jonah is also a type for Christ and the resurrection (20.1–6; Jonah 1:17, 2:10):

Another type for Jesus was the prophet
Jonah in the belly of the whale.
He was swallowed but not digested, like the Lord in the tomb.
This man came out from the whale after three [days],
                                        like Christ from the tomb.
This man, having preached to Nineveh, saved it,
but Christ redeemed every land and the inhabited world.

Ἄλλος δὲ τύπος τοῦ Ἰησοῦ   γέγονεν ὁ προφήτης
   Ἰωνᾶς ἐν κοιλιᾷ   τοῦ κήτους·
   κατεπόθη, οὐκ ἐπέφθη   ὡς ἐν τάφῳ ὁ κύριος·
ἐκεῖνος ἐξῆλθεν   ἐκ τοῦ κήτους μετὰ τρεῖς,
                              ὡς Χριστὸς ἐκ τοῦ μνήματος·
   ἐκεῖνος Νινευὶ   κηρύξας ἔσωσε,
   πᾶσαν δὲ τὴν γῆν Χριστὸς   ἐλυτρώσατο καὶ τὴν οἰκουμένην·

Jonah's descent into the belly of the whale foreshadows Christ's descent into the tomb and into hell, and the 'resurrection' of Jonah from the belly of the whale foreshadows the resurrection of Christ. Having been spat out by the whale, Jonah went on to save the people of Nineveh from destruction. From the New Testament (Matt. 12:38–41), Jonah had been seen as a type for Christ.[69] Romanos uses this incident as a type for Christ's salvation of the

---

[67] Kessler (2004), 131–7.
[68] Kessler (2004), 136.
[69] On patristic interpretations of Jonah, see Duval (1973).

whole world, clearly stating that the latter surpasses the former: Jonah only saved one city (and not eternally) whereas Jesus saves all humanity and restores them to everlasting life through his death and resurrection.

A less marked example of typology in this hymn is the reference to the murder of Abel by Cain (5.4–6; Genesis 4:1–8):

And the martyr Abel was envied by Cain, and afterwards was murdered.
Christ also submitted to this.
Being fond of the envious people, he drove them to hatred by showing them love.

καὶ μάρτυς ὁ Ἄβελ   ὑπὸ Κάϊν φθονηθείς,
                                    φονευθεὶς δὲ μετέπειτα·
ὃ δὴ καὶ Χριστὸς ὑπομεμένηκε·
βάσκανον λαὸν ποθῶν εἰς ὀργὴν ἐκίνει στοργὴν δεικνύων …

In the Genesis story, Cain kills Abel after God accepts Abel's sacrifice but not Cain's. Cain was envious of Abel's acceptance by God, and this led him to kill his brother.[70] In keeping with contemporary Christian interpretations of the story, Romanos sets up this first murder as a type of the most significant murder: that of Jesus Christ.[71] The envy of Cain is a type for the sin of the Jews who are going to murder Jesus.[72] God's love for the Jews, demonstrated in his sacrifice on the cross, led them to hate him rather than love him.

Abel is also described as a martyr, placing this Old Testament Jewish figure in a Christian role.[73] The 'martyr' Abel, whose sacrifice and death (the ultimate sacrifice) are acceptable to God, becomes an important type for Christ's sacrifice (or 'martyrdom') in late antique Christianity.[74] In Romanos, the 'martyrdom' of Abel foreshadows the ultimate martyrdom, the one which established the concept of martyrdom: the crucifixion of Jesus. Such moves point to the strongly typological mode of thinking that supports much of Romanos' imagery and argument.

Likewise, specific Old Testament prophecies are fulfilled in Christ. Such prophecies do not appear in this hymn, but occur frequently in others. For instance, in *On the Entry into Jerusalem* (XVI.10.1–2) Romanos refers to the

---

[70] We have seen the link made between murder and envy through assonance.
[71] See Grypeou and Spurling (2013), 118–19.
[72] On Abel as a type for Christians and Cain as a type for the Jews, see Byron (2011), 202–4.
[73] This image emerged in the New Testament (Matthew 23:35; Hebrews 11:4, 12:24) and was developed by patristic writers. See Byron (2011), 191–5, Hayward (2009), 110.
[74] Byron (2011), 196–8. Irenaeus of Lyon was the first to present Abel's sacrifice as a eucharistic type (*Adv. Haer.* IV.17.5–18.4): Hayward (2009), 114–15. The image of Abel takes on the same significance in the mosaics of San Vitale, Ravenna: Jensen (2000), 85. On the tradition which makes Abel a symbol of all the righteous who unfairly suffer, and even presents him as a vengeful judge, see Byron (2011), 181–90.

prophecy by Zechariah that the king would enter Jerusalem triumphantly, riding a donkey (Zech. 9:9); Christ fulfilled this prophecy, just as he does all other Old Testament prophecies. Fulfilment of prophecies is part of Christ's recapitulation of human life, but also a symbol of the new creation.

Old Testament types and prophecies are fulfilled in Christ. In this hymn and throughout the extant corpus of *kontakia* Romanos uses the fulfilment of prophecy to argue for a changed reality as a result of the incarnation. This new reality brings with it a radical change in the nature of time.[75] Before the incarnation, history was governed by prophecy; all events looked forward to the coming of the Messiah. Now that the Messiah has come, in Christ, there is no longer any need for prophecy. All prophecies are fulfilled and therefore the time of prophecies has ended. No longer are there types for the coming Messiah, his incarnation, death and resurrection. Instead of waiting for the coming Messiah and looking for signs which signal his advent, now Romanos believes humans are called to participate in the new creation and to recognize that all prophecies are fulfilled.

Anti-Judaism

And yet, as we saw above, 'humans' for Romanos does not include the Jews. Throughout his *kontakia*, Romanos characterizes the Jews as subhuman; he presents them as murderers and liars and paints them with images of bitterness and poison. In Chapter 3 we will look at Romanos' anti-Judaism in more detail and contextualize it in more depth; here it suffices to glimpse the anti-Judaism of *On the Passion of Christ*.

References to biblical imagery contrast the behaviour of the Jews and Jesus (13.1–3):

When Jesus spoke they heard these things, bloodthirsty,
the savage people, and like lions
they roared over the seizing of the life of Christ the lamb.

Λέγοντος ταῦτα τοῦ Ἰησοῦ   ἤκουσεν αἱμοβόρως,
    ὁ ἀνήμερος λαός,   καὶ ὡς λέων
    ὠρυᾶτο τοῦ ἁρπάσαι   τὴν ψυχὴν τοῦ ἀμνοῦ Χριστοῦ·

The image of the lamb carries with it connotations of helplessness, especially in comparison with lions. Romanos turns the Jewish crowd into a group of bloodthirsty, roaring lions, who rejoice in killing a helpless lamb. The characterization of Jews as murderers was a common one in Christian

---

[75] See MacCormack (1982), 287–309.

polemics against the Jews from the Gospels onwards and Romanos taps into this tradition. Ephrem the Syrian, for example, creates an image of the Jews from all time up to the present as killers, using the death of Jesus as the ultimate evidence of their murderous nature.[76]

Romanos' use of animal imagery reveals Christ as God, while demonstrating that the Jews do not recognize him. The depiction of Christ as the slaughtered lamb recalls John 1:29, and the lamb in Revelation (5:6), which is also identified with Christ's sacrifice on the cross: 'Then I saw between the throne and the four living creatures and among the elders a Lamb standing as if it had been slaughtered …'. The Jews are ignorant of the truth and sub-human in their actions.

Romanos figures Jewish rejection of Jesus through the image of taste (9.1–2):

And when the crowd heard the honey-flowing words,
as though filled with bitterness they replied

Ὅτε δὲ ἤκουσεν ὁ λαὸς   τῶν μελιρρύτων λόγων,
        ὡς πικρίας ἐμπλησθεὶς   ἀπεκρίθη·

Romanos often makes such appeals to the senses, sometimes creating an *ekphrastic* passage for different senses than sight. Here it is as though the sweetness of Jesus has caused the Jews to be filled with bitterness (just as his love for them only engendered hatred); it is evidence that they have turned away from God and refuse to be drawn into his recreation of the world. We can see similar uses of the senses in earlier anti-Judaic literature and notably in Ephrem, who contrasts the foul stench of the Jews with the sweet scent of Christ.[77] Romanos uses simple physical contrasts like bitter and sweet to perpetuate the split between Judaism and Christianity, making them into direct opposites: bitter Judaism becomes completely incompatible with Christ's sweet paradise.

As suggested above, this depiction of the Jews illustrates Romanos' belief that they are excluded from the new creation. They turned their back on the Messiah who came to restore them to proper communion with God; they crucified him. In stanza 17 Romanos compares the Jews with his congregation:

Hurling the blame at them, [Pilate] killed Christ through them,
because he found them conducive, the ones who said,
that 'His blood will be on them and their children.'

---

[76] See Shepardson (2008), 56. See further in Chapter 3 below.

[77] See Harvey (1998), 109–28, Shepardson (2008), 49, 53. On the use of scent more broadly in late antiquity, see Harvey (2006). For a specific discussion of the use of scent in Syriac homilies on the repentant harlot, including Romanos' *kontakion On the Sinful Woman*, see Harvey (2002), 69–89. Also see further below (Chapter 2).

On the sons not [yet] begotten,[78] the fathers have prepared a cloak of curse,[79]
they added blow to blow against their offspring,
amassing liability for wrongs for their race forever.
But we, receiving the blood of our Saviour, have found redemption,
so that Adam might dance.

Ῥίψας τὸ ἔγκλημα ἐπ᾽ αὐτοὺς   κτείνει Χριστὸν δι᾽ αὐτῶν,

ὑπουργοὺς αὐτοὺς εὑρὼν   τοὺς εἰπόντας·

<ὡς> ῾τὸ αἷμα αὐτοῦ ἔσται   ἐπ᾽ αὐτοὺς σὺν τοῖς τέκνοισιν᾽.[80]

υἱοῖς μὴ τεχθεῖσιν   οἱ πατέρες τῆς ἀρᾶς

τὸν χιτῶνα ηὐτρέπισαν·

τοῖς γόνοις τῇ πληγῇ   πληγὴν προσέθηκαν,

δίκην ἕλκοντες κακῶν   εἰς τὰς γενεὰς αὐτῶν εἰς αἰῶνας·

ἡμεῖς δὲ τοῦ σωτῆρος   τὸ αἷμα λαβόντες   εὕρομεν λύτρον,

ἵνα χορεύῃ ὁ Ἀδάμ.

Romanos contrasts the blood that curses and the blood that redeems.[81] The Jews have Jesus' blood on their hands, and have allowed this blood curse to pass on to their children as well (*eis tas geneas*), whereas Christians ('we'), or particularly Romanos' congregation, find redemption by receiving Christ's blood at the eucharist. The Jews forced Jesus to die, whereas Christians are the recipients of Christ's outpouring of his own life on the cross.

Through the imagery of eternity and generation, Romanos argues that the Jews have rejected their own inheritance, which is now received by Christians.[82] He describes the sin or 'curse' of the Jews as 'on their race' or 'on their generations' 'forever'. This recalls the passage in Luke 1:50 and 55: 'his mercy is on those who fear him for generations and generations (*eis geneas kai geneas*) … as he said to our forefathers, Abraham and his seed for ever'. This song of Mary specifically mentions Abraham and the Jewish heritage of Christianity. By alluding to this biblical passage, Romanos argues that the Jews have stopped fearing God and have been denied their inheritance: God's mercy. In fact, they seem to have openly rejected it, and have thereby brought upon themselves and their offspring an everlasting curse.

---

[78] The negative particle (μή) seems to imply that they may not be able to have sons. I have followed Grosdidier de Matons's 'encore à naître' here. See Grosdidier de Matons (1967), 225.

[79] On the curse, cf. Matthew 27:25, Psalm 109:17–18.

[80] I have followed the SC edition in the insertion of <ὡς>.

[81] Again, Ephrem does similarly, see Shepardson (2008), 34–5.

[82] This is called 'supersessionism' and was the common belief amongst early Christian theologians. Athanasius, for example, argued that the Christian 'passover' (Easter) should have supplanted the Jewish one. See Brakke (2001), 454.

There is no room in Romanos for continued Jewish identity in paradise: God's promises to the Jews are instead confirmed in the Christian community alone. While Romanos' hymns nowhere advocate violence towards the Jews, and his emphasis is on the new creation which is in principle available to all humanity, his theological scheme and imagery sit all too easily with contemporary violence towards Jews. Contemporary chroniclers speak in similar terms of the unhuman nature of the Jews and their blind rejection of Jesus, and record contemporary efforts to convert Jews and constrain their worship. Such actions fit with a theological view that sees no continuing role for the Jews in the history of salvation after the coming of Christ.[83]

Final Strophe

Many of Romanos' hymns end with a prayer and others with an exhortation to the congregation.[84] Both have the effect of relating the events described in the hymn strongly to the members of the congregation (and to readers). They either ask God for forgiveness or assistance, or call on the congregation to behave in a particular way. In *On the Passion of Christ,* it is the latter (23):

Hymn him, O earthly race. Praise the one who suffered
and died for your sake. Receive him whom a short time ago
you saw living, into your soul.
For Christ is about to rise up from the tombs
                                    and make you new, humanity.
So make ready a pure soul,
in order that, by dwelling in it, your King might make it his Heaven.
In a short time he will come and will fill with joy those in pain,
so that Adam may dance.

Ὕμνησον τοῦτον, ὦ γηγενῆ,   αἴνεσον τὸν παθόντα
    καὶ θανόντα διὰ σέ,   ὃν καὶ ζῶντα
    μετ᾽ ὀλίγον θεωρήσας   τῆς ψυχῆς ἔνδον εἴσδεξαι·
τῶν τάφων γὰρ μέλλει   ἐξανίστασθαι Χριστὸς
                                    καὶ καινίζειν σε, ἄνθρωπε·
    ψυχὴν οὖν καθαρὰν   αὐτῷ εὐτρέπισον,
    ἵνα ταύτην οὐρανὸν   κατοικῶν ποιήσῃ ὁ βασιλεύς σου·
μικρὸν ὅσον καὶ ἥξει   καὶ χαρᾶς ἐμπλήσει   τοὺς λυπηθέντας,
    ἵνα χορεύῃ ὁ Ἀδάμ.

---

[83] The anti-Judaic rhetoric of Romanos' *kontakia* is treated in more detail in Chapter 3 below.
[84] On final prayers in Romanos, see Barkhuizen (1989), (1991a).

Romanos concludes his hymn on Christ's Passion in praise and exhortation. He calls on the world to praise God for the miracle of the crucifixion and exhorts his congregation to be ready for the coming of Christ: to purify themselves and prepare for Christ to dwell within them. This eschatological language is a reflection of Romanos' temporal and liturgical theology: Romanos' congregation relives the life of Christ in the liturgical cycle, made all the more vivid and real by the *kontakia*. This *kontakion* was sung on Good Friday, the day when Christ died. In this final strophe Romanos reminds listeners that they have witnessed this death. Only a day or so earlier they were witnesses of the living Christ ('whom a short time ago you saw living', lines 2–3), when they attended holy week services and perhaps heard another of Romanos' *kontakia* – *On Judas* perhaps, or *On Peter's Denial*.[85] And, as Easter fast approaches, Romanos tells his listeners that they will soon see him resurrected ('Christ is about to rise', line 4; 'in a short time he will come', line 7).

This final strophe is also somewhat self-referential. Romanos calls for a hymn to be sung to the crucified one having just finished singing such a hymn. The reason for this is that praise of God and participation in his new creation is not something which finishes with Romanos' *kontakion*, nor is it something which applies only to his congregation. Since the Byzantines believed that their liturgy was an imitation of that taking place in heaven and was partaking in worship in all time and space,[86] Romanos' call for a hymn to be sung by all the earthly race applies to all Christian worship, not just Good Friday in a particular year in sixth-century Constantinople. The change in the nature of time is evident in this final stanza as well. In lines 2–3, the congregation (and all humanity) is associated with the disciples who saw Christ alive after his crucifixion and resurrection. The events of Christ's life are not distant and removed, but ever-present; the disciples of the sixth century are not completely distinct from the disciples of the first century. Romanos' congregation is part of the Gospel account and the first disciples are part of sixth-century Constantinople.

The contrast between the opening strophe and the final one could not be greater. Romanos opened his hymn with the dramatic revulsion of the natural world at the crucifixion and ends with a joyous hope for the

---

[85] Maisano proposes that both these *kontakia* were written for Maundy Thursday: Maisano (2002), 100. There are several other *kontakia* likely composed for holy week. For example, *On the Sinful Woman*, and perhaps *On the Ten Virgins I* and *II*. See Maisano (2002), 100.

[86] See, for example, Pseudo-Dionysius *The Ecclesiastical Hierarchy* II.ii.4. See also the discussion in Chapter 4 below.

eschaton, looking forward to the resurrection of Christ, which is relived in the liturgy about to take place on Easter Day, and ultimately to the general resurrection.

Conclusions

The foregoing analysis has served as an introduction to Romanos' poetry. He adeptly employed a wide range of rhetorical figures and his *kontakia* are indebted for their imagery and rhetoric especially to biblical narratives and contemporary homiletics and liturgical poetry. The *kontakion* is carefully constructed, using a variety of devices, such as dialogue and characterization, *ekphrasis*, paradox, and various narrative and structural techniques. These literary devices are designed to attract the audience's attention and to make the poetry vivid and engaging.

Throughout the investigation of Romanos' use of rhetoric in his *kontakia*, we have seen that his literary devices are intimately connected with his theology. Poetic devices support, communicate and embody Romanos' theology. Many, particularly metaphor, typology, structural devices and narrative apostrophe, help to emphasize Christ's correction of Adam's sin (see Chapter 2). Others, including paradox, typology and prophecy, and characterization, make Romanos' congregation aware of a fundamental newness in the world around them. This is the subject of Chapter 3: new creation. Other devices, such as *ekphrasis*, characterization, use of the refrain and dialogue, are designed to make the congregation participate in this new creation and anticipate the eschaton. This is the subject of Chapter 4. All these themes are to a greater or lesser degree evident in the *kontakion* analysed in this chapter. In the following chapters we will investigate these theological ideas in detail, examining how Romanos uses the rhetorical devices we have seen in this chapter to argue for his theological agenda.

2 | The Second Adam: A Typology of Salvation

> For since death came through a human being,
> the resurrection of the dead has also come through a human being;
> for as all die in Adam, so all will be made alive in Christ.
>
> 1 Cor. 15:21–2

The restoration of Adam's fallen race by Christ's incarnation, death and resurrection is central to the theology expressed in Romanos' *kontakia*. First present in the writings of the apostle Paul,[1] famously expounded by Irenaeus of Lyons, and foundational for thinkers such as Athanasius, Ephrem the Syrian and the Cappadocians, this is the concept of *recapitulation*: that God became human to perfect human existence, to right the wrongs Adam and his race had committed and to restore humanity to its rightful and eternal relationship with God.[2] Romanos likewise believes that by his life on earth, and particularly by his sacrifice on the cross, Jesus corrected the sins of humanity and restored humans to their proper relationship with God.

This chapter focuses on the correction of sins and the perfection of humanity which God achieves by becoming, in Jesus Christ, the second Adam. Romanos uses three main rhetorical techniques to explore these ideas of correcting human wrongs and perfecting the human race: typology, comparison and metaphor. Types for Christ, Mary and the cross show Christ as the second Adam, Mary as the second Eve and the cross as the second Tree (of Life or Knowledge), all demonstrating that by the life and death of Jesus Christ God restores humans to life. Comparisons show the counter-action which takes place in God's assumption of human form: the wrong actions of Adam are countered by the right actions of Christ. The rhetorical form of metaphor embodies the form of this exchange and its miraculous results; different metaphors explore various aspects of the correction of sin and renewal of humanity.

---

[1] On which, see Hooker (1990).

[2] Adam represents all fallen humanity, so his redemption means the redemption of all humanity: Brümmer (2005), 67.

Correction and Perfection in Earlier Theology

The apostle Paul sets up a comparison between Adam and Christ: Adam brought about death for humanity, whereas Christ provided eternal life (1 Cor. 15:22). This comparison continues throughout 1 Corinthians 15: the first Adam became a living spirit, but the second became a *life-giving* spirit (1 Cor. 15:45); the first man was from earth and made of dust, whereas the second man was from heaven (1 Cor. 15:47).[3] Likewise, in Romans (5:12–21), Paul compares and contrasts Adam and Christ.[4] The contrast is between sin and grace: sin (brought into the world by Adam) brings death, whereas grace (brought into the world by Christ) brings eternal life (5:21).[5] The wrongful actions of Adam are corrected by the right actions of Christ; the gift which Christ brings – divine grace – undoes Adam's sin (5:15). The righteousness of Christ makes up for Adam's trespass, which condemned all humanity (5:18). The result is that death has been put to death: by uniting himself to humanity, Christ brings immortality for humankind (Romans 6:5, 9–11). This is the perfection of humanity and its restoration to immortality. We will see that Romanos sets up similar contrasts between Adam and Christ, and between mortality and immortality, to emphasize and explain what God has done for humanity.

Irenaeus of Lyons employs and expands this Pauline idea in his *Against Heresies*.[6] He argues that human death and sinfulness were brought about by the initial sin of Adam and Eve, who disobeyed the commands of God. Human disobedience is corrected by Christ's obedience (5.21.2).[7] This concept of correction will be particularly important for Romanos. Christ is the second Adam who corrects the disobedience of the first Adam (5.16.2; 3.9.1).[8] Just as Christ's obedience counters the disobedience of Adam, the tree in Eden which caused the downfall of humanity is redeemed by the tree of the cross, which restores humanity to paradise.[9] In a similar way, Irenaeus argues that Mary redeems Eve, that Mary's obedience to the commands of God corrects the disobedience of Eve in the garden (5.19.1; 3.22.4).[10] This correction enables Christ to impart perfection to humanity (4.20.4):[11] God became human that humans might become God.

---

[3] See also Heil (2005), 240.
[4] Byrne (1996), 173.
[5] Fantino (1998), 419.
[6] The text used is Roberts (1979).
[7] Steenberg (2008), 160.
[8] Steenberg (2009), 46.
[9] We will see this image in Romanos too.
[10] Harrison (2008), 79.
[11] Fantino (1998), 418.

These concepts became pervasive in orthodox theology and important for closer contemporaries to Romanos such as Athanasius, Ephrem the Syrian, Gregory of Nyssa and Gregory Nazianzus. Key ideas from thinkers like these were also significant for Romanos, demonstrating his connection to the theological traditions of the church. The Pauline–Irenaean tradition is clear in Athanasius:

For since Adam, the first man, turned away, and through sin death came into the world, because of this it was fitting for the second Adam not to turn away.

Ἐπειδὴ γὰρ ὁ πρῶτος ἄνθρωπος Ἀδὰμ ἐτράπη, καὶ διὰ τῆς ἁμαρτίας ὁ θάνατος εἰσῆλθεν εἰς τὸν κόσμον, διὰ τοῦτο τὸν δεύτερον Ἀδὰμ ἔπρεπεν ἄτρεπτον εἶναι.[12]

Athanasius focuses on human mutability and divine steadfastness: Christ's unchanging obedience corrects Adam's changeable disobedience. While Adam turned away from God and disobeyed his command, Christ was obedient to God's will when he entered the world as a human to eradicate sin and death and thus he corrected the original flaw.[13] Correction, then, for Athanasius, is part of a wider argument about Christ's change-lessness and immortality over and against general human mortality. In his *On the Incarnation of the Word*, Athanasius emphasizes that humans were intended by God to remain uncorrupted, but that Adam's sin led the race into corruption and death (4).[14] In spite of this transgression against God's commands, God could not allow humanity, which was made in his image, to remain in a fallen state (13–14). To counter this fall, and because of his love for his creation, God made the great exchange: he became truly human in the person of Jesus Christ in order to destroy death and restore humanity to eternal life (8–10). The incarnation was needed because death was woven into the very fabric of human existence (44); Christ had to become properly human, assuming a body which was woven with life rather than death, in order to restore humanity to incorruption (44).[15] Unlike the first Adam, the second Adam had complete control over his body's passions and thereby divinized humanity.[16] Thus, Athanasius argues, in his incarnation, death and resurrection, Christ not only participated in our humanity, but

---

[12] *Three Orations against the Arians*, PG 26.117.

[13] The description of Christ as the second Adam is also found in Cyril of Alexandria, among many others. On Adam–Christ typology in Cyril of Alexandria, see Wilken (1966).

[14] Athanasius argued that corruption was always possible, but that by contemplating God and God alone, like a true ascetic, Adam and Eve could remain in their perfect state. It was when they turned away from God and towards contemplation of the flesh that they fell into sin. See Brakke (1995), 146–8.

[15] See Brakke (1995), 149–54.

[16] Brakke (1995), 150.

united all humanity in himself, perfecting it and making it what God had intended. The restoration of humanity in Christ means that Christ became human so that humans might become God (54).

Articulating this 'christology of transformation' became vital for both Gregory of Nyssa and Gregory Nazianzus in the late fourth century, as they argued against the christological formulations of Apollinarius.[17] For Gregory of Nyssa, Apollinarius' Christ was too unlike humanity to have any impact on human salvation.[18] Gregory argued that it was Christ's true humanity, complete with human will and participating in human suffering, that enabled human divinization.[19] Once again, obedience is the key: the obedience of the second Adam even to death heals the wound of the first Adam's disobedience and destroys death forever.[20] And it is through participating in Christ, in his perfect human virtue, that all humanity is transformed from corruption to incorruption.[21]

Likewise, in his *Theological Orations*, Gregory Nazianzus argues that the union of divine and human natures in Christ at the incarnation enables human divination (*Theol. Or. 3.* xix). Christ is the second Adam who takes on human sin and disobedience for the sake of their salvation (*Theol. Or. 4.* i, v–vi). For Gregory, the great contrasts inherent in Jesus' divine mortality emphasize the miraculous nature of God's actions: Jesus is sold cheaply but redeems the whole world at great price to himself; Jesus weeps but by his death causes human tears to cease, and so on (*Theol. Or. 3.* xx).

Christ's actions divinize Adam, restoring him to his former state. In the Syriac tradition particularly, this is figured by clothing: the second Adam re-clothes the first in the 'robe of glory' which he lost when he sinned.[22] This metaphor also became important for Romanos, as we will see. For Ephrem the Syrian, this re-clothing comes through Mary: 'Through Mary Adam had another robe' (*HPar* IV.5).[23] Just as we saw in Irenaeus, Mary becomes the second Eve; she is the perfection and therefore the redemption of womankind.[24] Ephrem contrasts the first and second Eve, characterizing Mary

---

[17] For this terminology, see Daley (2002b), 479. See also Daley (2002a), 501–3.

[18] Daley (2002b), 478.

[19] In his *Antirrheticus*: *GNO* 3.1:151.14–20. On the Logos taking on human will, see *GNO* 3.1:181.14–22.

[20] *GNO* 3.1:160.27–9; 161.1–5. See also Daley (2002b), 482.

[21] *GNO* 3.1:223.2–10. On Gregory of Nyssa's understanding of this participation, see Harrison (1992), 88–131.

[22] Murray (1971), 376. See also Brock (1982a), 11–38. And see further below.

[23] Translation taken from Brock (1990), 99.

[24] Harrison (2008), 79–81.

as light and sight and Eve as darkness and blindness (*HEccl* 37), and associating shame with Eve and glory with Mary (*HNat* 17.4). The redemption
of humanity comes through Mary, whereas death came through Eve (*HVirg*
23.9).[25] Childbirth is redeemed: Eve gave birth in pain, whereas for Mary
it was painless (*HVirg* XXIV.11).[26] The recapitulation of human life thus
began *in utero* (*HNat* 4.160–1):[27]

> While His body in the womb was being formed,
> His power was constructing all the members.
> While the fetus of the Son was being formed in the womb,
> He Himself was forming babes in the womb.[28]

In these thinkers before Romanos, who all helped to construct the theological *koinê* of the sixth century, often in the context of theological and
political controversy, we see the common themes of correction through
obedience, and perfection of humanity. Christ corrects Adam's wrong-
doing by being obedient to God; Christ is human in the way in which
God intended. This analogy between Christ and Adam also extends to an
Eve–Mary relationship.

Correction and Perfection in Romanos

These themes are also evident in the *kontakia* of Romanos. In the *kontakion
On Jacob and Esau*, Romanos contrasts the obedience of Christ with Adam's
faithlessness and disobedience (XLII.1.1–10):

> The one who through obedience saved the human race,
> having trampled on the serpent and illumined the cosmos,
> and who was born from the virgin without seed,
> the one who delivered the whole creation from its curse,
> who destroyed the transgressing angels
> and who raised up the fallen Adam by the hand,
>   let us hymn him, let us praise him.
> Let us know what the Fall did to us
> in the disobedience of transgression,
> as the book of creation tells
> of the faithlessness of the first-formed man.

---

[25] For Mary as the new Eve and contrasts between the two women, see, for example, *HNat* 17 and *HEccl* 37.
[26] Murray (1971), 378–9.
[27] Murray (1971), 375.
[28] Translation taken from McVey (1989), 101.

Τὸν διὰ τῆς ὑπακοῆς   σώσαντα γένος ἀνθρώπων,
    πατήσαντα τὸν ὄφιν   καὶ φωτίσαντα τὸν κόσμον
    καὶ ἐκ τῆς παρθένου   τεχθέντα ἀγεωργήτως,
τὸν τῆς κατάρας   ἀπαλλάξαντα κτίσιν ἅπασαν,
    τὸν τοὺς παραβάντας   ῥήξαντα ἀγγέλους
    καὶ παραπεσόντα   χειρὶ ἐγείραντα Ἀδὰμ
                                                 ὑμνήσωμεν, δοξάσωμεν·
γνῶμεν τί   ἔδρασεν   ἡμῖν τὸ πτῶμα
    τῆς παραβάσεως   ἐν τῇ παρακοῇ,
καθὼς καὶ ἡ βίβλος[29]   τῆς κτίσεως λέγει
    τοῦ πρωτοπλάστου τὴν ἀθεσίαν·

Just as we saw in earlier theologians, Romanos sets up a comparison
between Christ and Adam. This strophe is a particularly nicely balanced
comparison.[30] The first five lines of the strophe are about Christ, his
obedience and what it achieved. The last four lines are about Adam's disobedience. In between these two sections is a direct reference to Adam
and the result of Christ's obedience for Adam: it allows Christ 'to raise
up the fallen Adam'. Romanos finishes off this middle line with a performative call for the congregation (and humans generally) to praise
God who made this happen. Romanos is enacting this hymning as he
sings. This contrast between the obedience of Christ, through which
humanity is saved, and the disobedience of Adam, through which death
was brought upon humanity, emphasizes Christ's correction of Adam's
sin. We will see later that Romanos also uses Mary as a second Eve in a
similar way.

The central image for Christ's obedience is his suffering on the cross
(e.g. *On the Resurrection V* (XXVIII.1.7–8)):

You are, one and the same, the one who received suffering according to [God's]
    salvation plan
in order that you might grant freedom from suffering to all.

εἷς ὁ αὐτὸς κατεδέξω   τὸ πάθος οἰκονομίᾳ,
ἵνα τῶν παθῶν δώσῃς   ⟨ἅπασιν⟩ ἐλευθερίαν

But the divine obedience which corrects human sin is also figured through
a complex of other images. In *On the Entry into Jerusalem*, Jesus voluntarily
becomes poor because of his love for humans (XVI.12); in another hymn,
Romanos talks about Jesus fasting to give humans eternal life (LI.1). As well

---

[29] Romanos uses *biblos* as the word for 'book' to make a play on 'Bible'.
[30] See below for more structural comparisons.

as being examples of how to live, such passages highlight how far Christ went to correct the misdeeds of humankind.[31]

This correction removes the bondage under which humanity suffered until the advent of Christ. In *On the Entry into Jerusalem,* Romanos refers to the freedom which Christ brings (XVI.11.6–7):

I am being sold on your behalf, and [thereby] I will free you.
I am being crucified because of you, and [therefore] you will not die.

πωλοῦμαι ὑπὲρ σοῦ   καὶ ἐλευθερῶ σε·
    σταυροῦμαι διὰ σέ,   καὶ σὺ οὐ νεκροῦσαι·

Like earlier theologians, Romanos emphasizes that humanity was made captive by sin and death. Christ became human to suffer this captivity (Romanos depicts him being sold like a slave). The paradox is that Christ's bondage releases humankind from slavery. The liberty of Christ unties Adam's chains.

The freedom which Christ brings is specifically freedom from corruption. In *On the Resurrection III,* Adam says to Hades (XXVI.10.3–4):

For I have now been bought by his precious blood.
The one who is without corruption has set me free from corruption.

αἵματι γὰρ τιμίῳ   νῦν ἐγὼ ἠγοράσθην·
    φθορᾶς ἀπήλλαξέ με   ὁ ἄνευ φθορᾶς.

In fact, this is a return to the proper state. In *On the Adoration of the Cross,* the angel who guards the gate of Eden speaks of the 'restoration of Adam' (τὴν ἀνάκλησιν τὴν τοῦ Ἀδάμ) (XXIII.13.9). Romanos reworks a traditional theme to explore this concept of restoration, through a dialogue at the gates of paradise.[32] The good thief arrives at the gates and asks to be admitted, explaining to the guarding angel the world-changing event which makes this possible: the crucifixion. The angel recognizes that this means Adam has been restored to eternal life in paradise.

This means Adam's restoration to immortality, to perfection (VI.3.3–7):

This one, whom you feared when you were deceived,
                                became like you for your sake.
He came down to the earth in order that he might take you up.
He became mortal in order that you might be divine

---

[31] For how exemplars like this relate to participation, see Chapter 4 below.
[32] There is a Syriac tradition of this debate between the angel at the gate of Eden and the thief which Romanos may be drawing on. Cf. Brock (2002). On debate literature in the Syriac tradition and its naissance, see Brock (1991), (2001).

and might put on the foremost dignity.
Wishing to open Eden again he lived in Nazareth.

οὗτος ὃν ἐφοβήθης,　ὅτε ἐξηπατήθης,　διὰ σὲ ὡμοιώθη σοι·
　　κατέβη ἐπὶ γῆς,　ἵνα λάβη σε ἄνω·
　　ἐγένετο θνητός,　ἵνα σὺ θεὸς γένη
　　καὶ ἐνδύση　τὴν πρώτην εὐπρέπειαν·
θέλων ἀνοῖξαι πάλιν τὴν Ἐδὲμ　ᾤκησε τὴν Ναζαρέτ·

This, we can see straight away, is the exchange formula employed by Irenaeus, Athanasius and Gregory (and many other theologians). God's incarnation enables human divinization.[33] As a result of Adam's sin humans experienced death, but because of God's descent to earth in Jesus Christ, Romanos argues that humans are brought into the life of God.

In order to do this Christ takes on human lowliness and suffers, like humanity has since the Fall. In *On the Baptism of Christ*, God says to Adam (V.2.4–7):

Where are you, Adam? Do not hide from me. I wish to see you.
Even if you are naked, even if you are a beggar, do not be ashamed,
　　　　　　　　　　　for I have become like you.
Although you wished it, you did not become god,
but now I have of my own will become flesh.

Ποῦ εἶ, Ἀδάμ; ἀπάρτι　μὴ κρύπτου με·　θέλω θεωρεῖν σε·
　　κἂν γυμνὸς εἶ,　κἂν πτωχὸς εἶ,　μὴ αἰσχυνθῆς·
　　　　　　　　　　σοὶ γὰρ ὡμοιώθην·
αὐτὸς ἐπιθυμῶν　θεὸς οὐκ ἐγένου·
ἀλλ᾽ ἐγὼ νῦν βουληθεὶς　σὰρξ ἐγενόμην·

Adam was not able to make himself into God, although he tried (by taking the knowledge-giving fruit). This sin took him away from God and away from the immortality intended for him. Nothing Adam could do would restore him to his perfect state. But God cared for his creation and wished to redeem it; and so God became human. The unification of mortal and immortal in the person of Christ unites humans with immortality.

This passage also draws attention to the goodness and love of God and his desire to bring humans back into relationship with him. Romanos joins together the stories of the garden of Eden and the incarnation in this one passage in a summation of all human history. The incarnation thus brings about a return to the garden, to paradise, and therefore a restoration of the proper relationship between humans and God.

---

[33] Cf. also, for example, XX.2.

In his concept of God's correction and perfection of humanity through the second Adam, Romanos draws on existing theological and homiletic traditions as he seeks to preach faithfully to his congregation in matters which pertain to their salvation. I now investigate three different rhetorical devices – typology, comparison and metaphor – which Romanos uses to talk about this restoration of humanity. These are by no means the only devices Romanos uses, but I believe they are the most significant. In their different ways, they each mirror the idea of correction and perfection closely, making them appropriate vehicles for Romanos' theological teachings.

Typology

Before we investigate Romanos' use of typology in detail, I present a short overview of the use of typology in the Greek and Syriac homiletic and poetic traditions to situate Romanos' distinctive poetry within a tradition. Ephrem the Syrian used typology in a similar way to Romanos.[34] According to Ephrem, typology is one of the central ways in which God is made known to humanity.[35] God reveals himself through biblical types and in symbols in the natural world (*Faith* 32:9):

Lord, You bent down and put on humanity's types
so that humanity might grow through your self-abasement.[36]

Ephrem makes typology part of the correction of humanity. By lowering himself to assume an understandable form, both in the incarnation and in types and symbols, God enables humanity to 'grow' back into their pre-Fall state. Events from the Old Testament foreshadow events in the life of Christ and are surpassed by them, showing the fulfilment of time and history in Jesus Christ, particularly at the point of the incarnation.[37] Ephrem's hymns on the Nativity are full of Old Testament types for the incarnation and virgin birth. In the first hymn of this group the types greatly outnumber the antitype. There is no simple one-to-one correlation between an Old Testament event and a New Testament event. Within a few lines, in the first strophe, numerous prophecies and statements are said to be fulfilled in

---

[34] On Ephrem's use of typology and symbolism, see Brock (1992), Murray (2006).

[35] Brock identifies three main ways in which God reveals himself to humans according to Ephrem, one of which is in types and symbols. The others are through metaphors, and in the incarnation: Brock (1992), 40–3.

[36] Translation taken from Brock (1992), 54. On the 'recapitulative force' of typology, with reference to Ephrem, see Young (1994), 42–5.

[37] Brock (1992), 57. See also Buchan (2007), 151.

Christ: prophecies of David, Micah, Balaam and Zachary (*Nat.* 1). Jacob's blessing and Ruth's vow are fulfilled, Solomon's proverb finally makes sense, and Eve (and all womankind) is saved. The story of the flowering rod of Aaron is fulfilled in the virgin who gives birth. This hymn overflows with types, pointing to the inability of one single Old Testament event to fore-shadow the incarnation. The whole of time has been leading up to this point. And, in fact, everything converges at this point, the point at which it is fulfilled. We could go further and suggest that the whole of history converges in this hymn which makes the incarnation present.

One Greek homilist whose use of typology parallels that of Ephrem is Proclus of Constantinople. Typologies for the incarnation abound in Proclus' homilies 1–5. The first of these homilies is full of types for the virgin birth.[38] The Virgin is a second burning bush ('the living bush of human nature, which the fire of a divine birth-pang did not consume') (lines 16–17),[39] and even a second paradise ('the spiritual paradise of the second Adam') (14),[40] but Proclus also describes her using an allegorical metaphor: 'the awesome loom of the divine economy upon which the robe of union was ineffably woven' (21–2).[41] All of these images and many more appear within a few lines in Proclus' homily. As in Ephrem's hymn, the pro-liferation of images here serves to illustrate at once how many past events the incarnation fulfils and also to express the miraculous nature of God becoming human through a virgin.[42]

In Proclus' second homily he explains Adam–Christ typology (section VII, lines 74ff.). Each aspect of Adam's life and fall is paralleled by an action of Christ:

That one stretched forth his hand to the tree and plucked forth death, but this one stretched out his hands on the cross and embraced the world, and in the Gospels he cries out: 'When I am raised up I will draw all men to myself.' That one had a woman as his accomplice, but this one had a virgin as his bridal chamber.[43]

ἐκεῖνος τὴν χεῖρα εἰς δένδρον ἐξέτεινεν καὶ θάνατον ἐτρύγησεν, οὗτος τὰς χεῖρας ἥπλωσεν ἐν τῷ σταυρῷ καὶ τὸν κόσμον ἐνηγκαλίσατο, καὶ βοᾷ ἐν εὐαγγελίοις· 'ὅταν ὑψωθῶ πάντας ἑλκύσω πρὸς ἐμαυτόν.' ἐκεῖνος γυναῖκα ἔσχεν ἐπίβουλον, οὗτος παρθένον ἔσχεν θάλαμον.

---

[38] Edition used is Constas (2003), 136ff. See also the section on imagery in Constas' introduction to the hymn: Constas (2003), 131–5.

[39] ἡ ἔμψυχος τῆς φύσεως βάτος, ἣν τὸ τῆς θείας ὠδῖνος πῦρ οὐ κατέκαυσεν. Constas's translation: Constas (2003), 137.

[40] ὁ λογικὸς τοῦ δευτέρου Ἀδὰμ παράδεισος. Constas's translation: Constas (2003), 137.

[41] ὁ φρικτὸς τῆς οἰκονομίας ἱστὸς ἐν ᾧ ἀρρήτως ὑφάνθη ὁ τῆς ἑνώσεως χιτών. Constas's translation: Constas (2003), 137. On Proclus' use of the image of the loom, see Constas (1995).

[42] Cunningham (1988), 54–5.

[43] Constas's translation: Constas (2003), 169.

Adam's life is paralleled, but more importantly surpassed by Christ's. Each of Adam's early misdeeds is matched and outdone by a perfect, selfless and miraculous deed of Christ.

I have presented these homilists as precursors for Romanos in their use of typology to explain doctrine and to praise God's marvellous works, but it is important to realize that they are themselves part of an extensive patristic tradition.[44] What these two great exponents of typology in homiletics reveal is the rich array of images available to Romanos as he composed his *kontakia*.

Typology and Correction

Romanos uses typology to explore the themes of correction and perfection. He joins Adam and Christ and links the first sin with the crucifixion, but the two are not joined as equals.[45] Typological connections like this convey the idea that the antitype is the fulfilment of the type, so Romanos can use them to argue that Christ is the fulfilment of Adam, the correction of Adam's sin and the perfection of his humanity. Romanos draws on well-known typologies used by some of the theologians discussed above, principally Christ as the second Adam. Mary is sometimes a second Eve. The cross as a type for the tree in Eden is another important typology we will look at in this section, before investigating other types for the cross.

Christ–Adam

Romanos draws the link between Adam as the first human in the first creation and Christ as the first human of the new creation. In *On the Victory of the Cross,* Romanos has the devil say to Hades (XXII.2.7–8):

For it is a cross, to which I fastened Christ,
wishing by a tree to destroy the second Adam.

ἐστὶ γὰρ σταυρός,   ᾧ προσήλωσα Χριστὸν
ξύλῳ θέλων ἀνελεῖν   τὸν Ἀδὰμ τὸν δεύτερον·

The devil destroyed the first Adam by means of a tree: he tempted Eve to taste the forbidden fruit of the tree in the garden of Eden, which she then

---

[44] Constas (2003), 131.
[45] Schork (1975), 135.

gave to Adam. This sin caused them to be thrown out of paradise and into a life of hardship and, finally, death. Here the devil attempts the same strategy against the second Adam. This connection between Adam and Christ emphasizes Christ's true humanity: he must be sufficiently like Adam for the devil to try equivalent tactics. Word placement heightens the connection: 'Christ' and 'second' are placed in the same position, at the end of the line.

In *On the Resurrection V,* Christ tells the devil that he is 'earthy Adam' (Ἀδὰμ ὁ γεώδης) (XXVIII.28.7). The devil says to Hades that (XXVIII.31.2–3):

for the sake of humans he was seen as a man
                                        and willingly took on flesh,
in order that, as God, he might give life to Adam as well as Eve.

δι᾽ ἀνθρώπους ὡράθη ὡς [ἄνθρωπος]
                                        καὶ ἀνέλαβε σάρκα βουλόμενος,
ἵνα τὸν Ἀδὰμ   σὺ[ν] τῇ Εὔᾳ ζωώσῃ [[ὡς]] θεός.

Christ is both the 'earthy Adam' and God. Adam's earthiness is redeemed by Christ's godliness, but Christ had to become earthy to do it. Here, again, is the central idea of exchange: God took on flesh (and therefore death) to bring life to Adam and Eve. The divine–human exchange emphasizes Christ's humanity (Romanos draws attention to God's willingness to take on *flesh*), as well as Christ's divinity (as *God*, he gives life), and thus sits well within post-Chalcedon orthodoxy. The expansion of the biblical story here as elsewhere functions to accentuate orthodox doctrinal positions, and shows that Romanos was aware of and connected to live theological debates. In focusing on the exchange, Romanos frames debates about the nature of Christ in terms of salvation. He argues that redemption comes about through the Adam–Christ exchange, through Christ's assumption of human flesh.

Clever word placement highlights this in the second annunciation hymn (XXXVII.8.1-2):

Adam was thrust out. Therefore God, devising resurrection for Adam,
assumed Adam from your [i.e. Mary's] womb.

Ὥσθη Ἀδάμ·   διὸ θεὸς Ἀδὰμ   τῷ Ἀδὰμ μηχανώμενος ἔγερσιν
       τῆς σῆς κοιλίας τοῦτον ἀνέλαβεν·

The threefold repetition of 'Adam' in the first line and the juxtaposition of 'God' and 'Adam' draw attention to both the reasons for the incarnation and the enormity of the exchange itself. In order to construct a resurrection or 'awakening' for Adam, God became human.

And as a human, Christ fulfils and surpasses Adam's life. When the devil and Hades realize what the effect of the crucifixion has been, the devil cries out (XXII.11.9–12):

> For it is not the first,
> but the second Adam who carried Eve,
> the mother of the living,
> again to paradise.

οὐχ ὁ πρῶτος γάρ,
ἀλλ' ὁ δεύτερος Ἀδὰμ   Εὔαν ἐβάστασε,
τὴν μητέρα τῶν ζώντων,
πάλιν εἰς τὸν παράδεισον.

Christ's assumption of humanity enables him to restore 'the mother of the living' to paradise. Ordinary humanity could not achieve such a thing: the first Adam could not carry Eve back into paradise. Christ, as the second Adam, corrects the fault of Adam, he fulfils Adam's life, but also surpasses it. By the cross he restores the first Adam, and Eve, to paradise (XXIII.3.7–8):

> For I am the true second Adam
> and I have come willingly to save my Adam.

ἐγὼ γάρ εἰμὶ   δεύτερος Ἀδὰμ ἀληθὴς
    καὶ ἦλθον ἑκὼν   σῶσαι τὸν Ἀδὰμ τὸν ἐμόν·

Romanos draws on Exodus 3:14 and the sayings of Jesus in the Gospel of John to emphasize Christ's divinity: he is the 'I am'.[46] God has willingly become part of his own creation to restore that creation to proper life with him. Truth and goodness play a part in this passage too. As the 'true second Adam' Christ is the perfect Adam, the fulfilment of what Adam should have been. The words are in the mouth of Adam in *On the Resurrection III* (XXVI.5.1–4):

> Just as for my sake he would not beg off from blows,
>   for my sake he will become a second Adam, my saviour.
> for my sake he will endure my punishment,
>   since he bears my flesh, even as I do.

Ὥστε καὶ πληγὰς δι' ἐμὲ   οὐκ ἂν παραιτήσηται,
    δεύτερος Ἀδὰμ δι' ἐμὲ   γενήσεταί μου ὁ σωτήρ·
τὴν ἐμὴν τιμωρίαν   δι' ἐμὲ ὑπενέγκη
    τὴν σάρκα μου φορέσας   καθάπερ κἀγώ.

Salvation is personal and particular: Adam repeatedly uses 'my' and 'for my sake'. Christ, the second Adam, acts on behalf of the first. But since Adam

---

[46]   The Gospel 'I am' statements are at John 6:35, 8:12, 10:9, 10:11, 11:25, 14:6, 15:1.

also represents all humanity, Romanos means his listeners to feel personally implicated in God's salvific actions; it is their flesh, as well as that of Adam, which God takes on: 'he bears my flesh, even as I do.' Romanos reinforces that Christ was truly human; his flesh was the same as Adam's, the same as that of all humans. To highlight this, Romanos links flesh with blows and punishment, which Christ, in his obedience, does not avoid; Christ's flesh combined with his divinity make him the antitype, the fulfilment of Adam.

Christ as the second Adam thus communicates a complex, interwoven set of claims about who Christ is and human salvation. As immortal God, Jesus took on flesh in order to bring humans immortality. This exchange of opposites is the basis of human redemption; it reunites humanity with God. Christ's human life is the fulfilment of Adam's life: he makes it what it was supposed to be. As both human and divine, however, Christ also surpasses Adam, and it is his two natures which enable him to correct Adam's wrongs, obediently submitting to suffer and die for Adam's sake. Thus Christ recapitulates Adam's life. Through Adam–Christ typology Romanos argues that Christ corrects and perfects human existence.

Mary–Eve

Although Romanos mostly focuses on the second Adam as the antitype of the first, he also presents Mary as the second Eve and the corrector of Eve's sins. In *On the Nativity I*, Mary is the intercessor and defender of humanity, and the means by which humans return to paradise. Mary speaks to the Christ-child (I.23):

For I am not simply your mother, compassionate saviour,
not by chance do I suckle the one who supplies my milk,
but on behalf of all I entreat you.
You made me both mouth and boast of my whole race,
for your inhabited world has me
as a mighty shelter, wall and support.
Those cast out from the luxuries of paradise
look to me, because I bring them back
to understanding all things, through me who bore you,
just now a child, God before all ages.

Οὐχ ἁπλῶς γάρ εἰμί   μήτηρ σου, σῶτερ εὔσπλαγχνε·
    οὐκ εἰκῇ γαλουχῶ   τὸν χορηγὸν τοῦ γάλακτος·
    ἀλλὰ ὑπὲρ πάντων   ἐγὼ δυσωπῶ σε·
ἐποίησάς με   ὅλου τοῦ γένους μου   καὶ στόμα καὶ καύχημα·
    ἐμὲ γὰρ ἔχει   ἡ οἰκουμένη σου
        σκέπην κραταιάν,   τεῖχος καὶ στήριγμα·

ἐμὲ ὁρῶσιν   οἱ ἐκβληθέντες

τοῦ παραδείσου τῆς τρυφῆς,   ὅτι ἐπιστρέφω αὐτοὺς

λαβεῖν αἴσθησιν πάντων   δι' ἐμοῦ τῆς σε τεκούσης

παιδίον νέον,   τὸν πρὸ αἰώνων θεόν.

Mary has a God-given role as intercessor for humanity, and as a fortress, a strong defender of the race. She explains her different roles: for her baby, she is a gentle, caring mother, nursing her son at the breast; for humanity she becomes intercessor and model and a military bulwark, protecting humanity from the invasion of sin and death.[47] Mary is the one who returns humanity to paradise (8–9). The verb 'to bring back' (*epistrephō*) also has connotations of correction so that we could translate lines 8–9 as 'because I correct them to the point that they can understand all things'. Through the son she bore, Mary is the corrector of human sin. Mary is an important part of the redemption of Adam in *On the Nativity I*, in which she is seen as the quencher of Adam's (and David's) thirst (I.1.7–8). We will look at this passage in more detail in the section on metaphor below.

In *On the Annunciation II,* Mary is specifically the antitype of Eve (XXXVII.8.3–5):

Before, a woman brought [Adam] down, and now a woman raises him up,
>   a virgin, from a virgin.
Adam did not know Eve then,
>   and Joseph does not know the God-bearer now.

γυνὴ τὸ πρὶν κατέβαλε,   καὶ γυνὴ νῦν ἀνιστᾷ,
>   ἐκ παρθένου παρθένος·
τὴν Εὔαν ὁ Ἀδὰμ   οὐκ ἔγνω τότε,
>   οὐδὲ τὴν θεοτόκον   ὁ Ἰωσὴφ νῦν·

Whereas Eve brought sin and death upon humanity by eating the forbidden fruit and giving it to Adam, Mary brings redemption and life by giving birth to Jesus Christ, that is, by being the *Theotokos* or 'God-bearer'.[48] We will investigate this term in more detail shortly.

The disobedience of the first woman must be undone by a woman. This sort of typology works on symmetry, which is always so important for Romanos' word plays. Romanos also focuses on the actions of the two women. Through Christ-like obedience, Mary redeems Eve's disobedience; Mary corrects the wrongs of Eve. Romanos sets up a structural comparison between the two women, further emphasizing their differences. Eve is on one side of the caesura and Mary on the other. This physical boundary

---

[47] On Mary's different roles in the *kontakia*, see Arentzen (2014), Gador-Whyte (2013a), 77–92.
[48] On the translation of this term, see Wright (2004), 22.

(a 'weak sense pause' in the poetry) makes the contrast the greater.[49] Through the phrase 'a virgin from a virgin', and the following lines (4–5), Romanos also draws attention to Eve's virginity, which was another way in which Mary was seen as an antitype for Eve.[50] Eve was a virgin before she tasted the fruit and her descendent Mary was also a virgin. The first virgin, Eve, foreshadows this significant virgin, Mary.

But, unlike the first virgin, Mary remains a virgin. In this sense she is also the perfection of Eve. The refrain of this *kontakion* (XXXVII) is

A virgin gives birth and after the birth still remains a virgin.

παρθένος τίκτει   καὶ μετὰ τόκον   πάλιν μένει παρθένος.

Likewise, in *On the Nativity I*, Mary says (I.2.7–10):[51]

And I look at you among your swaddling clothes,
but I observe my virginal bloom sealed
for you guard it, you approved of it, you were born
just now a child, God before all ages.

καὶ σὲ μὲν βλέπω   μετὰ σπαργάνων,
    τὴν παρθενίαν δὲ ἀκμὴν   ἐσφραγισμένην θεωρῶ·
σὺ γὰρ ταύτην φυλάξας   ἐγεννήθης εὐδοκήσας
    παιδίον νέον,   ὁ πρὸ αἰώνων θεός.

Both the conception and birth of Mary's child are divine and so keep her virginity intact. By contrast, Eve's experiences of childbirth are normal human ones. She is 'the one who brought forth children in pain' (ἡ ἐν ὀδύναις τεκοῦσα τέκνα, II.3.3–4). The second Eve surpasses the first, and shows what perfect womanhood means.

Romanos draws attention to this perfection by describing Mary using adjectives like 'blameless' or 'unblemished' (I.22.1). Her womb is also blameless (XXXVI.15.5), and she is 'all-holy' (IV.10.1). Descriptors like 'radiant' (XXXVI.15.3), which is used of the stars or the dawn (e.g. Paul Sil. *AP* 5.227), give Mary a divine status.

One of the most significant epithets Romanos uses for Mary is *Theotokos* (God-bearer). According to Gregory of Nazianzus, this title reveals the two natures of Christ: divine, since Mary conceived divinely, and human, since

---

[49]   On this terminology, see the metrical appendix in Maas and Trypanis (1963), 511.

[50]   It perhaps also suggests that virginity alone is not enough to guarantee salvation or to be classed as godly and virtuous. See, for example, Romanos' hymns on the story of the ten virgins. Five of the virgins are excluded from the kingdom because they did not lead virtuous lives in spite of their virginity. Cf. XLVII.13–26.

[51]   See also stanza 20.

Christ was born of a human woman.[52] In the fifth-century christological disputes the term came under scrutiny by the bishop of Constantinople, Nestorius, who argued that Mary could only give birth to the human nature of Christ (i.e. she was the *anthropotokos*, 'bearer of the man') but that since the two natures were united in the person of Christ it would be best to call Mary *Christotokos* (Christ-bearer).[53] Like Gregory, Cyril of Alexandria saw the title *Theotokos* as safeguarding the two natures of Christ and their union; he thought Nestorius' arguments placed too great a separation between the two natures and therefore moved close to suggesting that there were two Sons.[54] Polemically, Cyril linked Nestorius with the Jews and others who rejected the divinity of Christ.[55] Cyril saw Mary's role as *Theotokos* as ensuring the redemption of humanity, the lifting of the curse which humanity brought upon itself.[56]

We have seen that Romanos' conception of Mary's role in salvation is in keeping with that of Cyril (and Gregory, and others), and his use of the title *Theotokos* is similarly in line with these theologians' concerns about the two natures of Christ and the salvific nature of the incarnation. At times Romanos calls Mary *Theotokos* when he particularly wants to stress the miracle of the incarnation. So, in a *kontakion* which foregrounds Mary's virginity *post partum*, Romanos likens Mary to the rain on the fleece, the burning bush and the rod of Aaron and addresses her as *Theotokos* (XXXVII.Pr).[57] The miracle of Mary the God-bearer both fulfils and surpasses all these Old Testament miracles.

At the opening of *On the Presentation in the Temple* (IV.1.1), Romanos calls for his congregation to rush to the *Theotokos*, creating an image of Mary as

---

[52] *Ep.* 101, section 16. See also Cameron (2004), 7, Price (2007), 56.

[53] On Nestorius' views, see *III Epistula Nestorium ad Celestinem*: Loofs (1905), 181–2 and Socrates Scholasticus *Eccl. Hist.* VII.32. See also Price (2007), 57, (2008), 89–90, Young and Teal (2010), 293. Price makes it clear that the disputes of the fifth century were over christology and not mariology and that the term *Theotokos* was not the main issue of the debates: Price (2004), 31–8. It is only in the fifth century that this term was disputed. Earlier theologians of various christological persuasions used the term without concern. See Starowieyski (1989), 239, Wright (2004), 22–3. On the use of *Theotokos* before the fourth century, see McGuckin (2001), 10–13, Starowieyski (1989), 236–42.

[54] Perry and Kendall (2013), 30.

[55] Price (2007), 60, Wessel (1999), 2. On Cyril of Alexandria's incarnational theology, see Weinandy (2003), 23–54, Young (2003), 55–74. See also McGuckin (1994). Cyril's position was vindicated at the Council of Ephesus (431), although there was no decree officially supporting the term *Theotokos*, and at the Council of Chalcedon in 451 Mary was named the *Theotokos* in the definition of the faith (section 4): Stevenson (1966), 337.

[56] *Third Letter to Nestorius (Letter 17)*. Translated in McGuckin (2009), 130.

[57] The refrain of this *kontakion* is 'A virgin gives birth and after the birth still remains a virgin' (Παρθένος τίκτει καὶ μετὰ τόκον πάλιν μένει παρθένος). For the rain on the fleece, see Judges 6:3; for the burning bush see Exodus 3:2–4; for Aaron's rod see Numbers 17:23.

an ordinary and contemporary mother living amongst them. And yet the use of the title reinforces that she is far from ordinary; rather, she was chosen by God and her son is God. Again it is the miracle of the incarnation and Mary's perpetual virginity which Romanos has his characters emphasize. Later in that same *kontakion* Simeon addresses Mary as *Theotokos*, proclaiming that the prophets marvelled at her (IV.9.5):

because you are the closed gate, *Theotokos.*

ὅτι ἡ πύλη   ἡ κεκλεισμένη   ὑπάρχεις, θεοτόκε.

Romanos combines the title *Theotokos* with an image of Mary's perpetual virginity, which guarantees both her role as God-bearer and Christ's divine nature.

Most often, however, Romanos uses the term *Theotokos* in phrases which either call for or assume the intercession of the Virgin (VII.21.7–10):[58]

But save us, blameless one,
from the lamentation of your judgement, since you are the merciful God,
by the prayers of the holy *Theotokos* and virgin,
[you] who made all things in wisdom.

ἀλλὰ ῥῦσαι   ἡμᾶς, ἀναμάρτητε,
τοῦ ὀδυρμοῦ τῆς κρίσεως τῆς σῆς   ὡς ἐλεήμων Θεός
   ταῖς εὐχαῖς τῆς ἁγίας   Θεοτόκου καὶ παρθένου,
   ὁ τὰ πάντα   ἐν σοφίᾳ ποιήσας.

These phrases often appear at the end of the *kontakion* as part of the final prayer, joining the prayers of Romanos and his congregation with those of Mary.[59] Their formulaic nature may imply a growing appreciation of Mary's role as intercessor in popular piety and reflect the developing Marian cult.[60]

For Romanos, Mary is a redeemer through her role as the *Theotokos*. She brought Christ into the world and thereby plays an essential role in salvation; she intercedes with Christ on behalf of humanity. As in the Christ–Adam parallel, salvation, framed in terms of correction by obedience and

---

[58] See also IV.18.7; VII.Pr.3; VIII.Pr.3; VIII.18.7; XI.25.7; XVII.Pr.2.5; XXIII.Pr.4; XXXIV.24.8; XXXIX.24.3; XLIV.22.15; XLIX.22.11; LI.24.8; LII.Pr.6. Romanos also calls for Mary's intercession without using the term *Theotokos*, e.g. III.18.

[59] On final prayers in Romanos, see Barkhuizen (1989), (1991a).

[60] See Gador-Whyte (2013a), 83–7, Shoemaker (2007), 135. On the development of the cult of Mary in late antiquity, see Cameron (2004), Cunningham (1988), Shoemaker (2008). Mary's role as intercessor became increasingly important from this period on. Theoteknos, for example, emphasized the ambassador role in the early seventh century. See Cunningham (1988), 58, Daley (1998), 75.

the restoration of true humanity, is the central purpose of the comparison. Romanos presents Mary as the perfect woman, who by her purity and her obedience redeems the impurity and disobedience of Eve, who was tempted and sinned and brought death upon humanity. Through Mary's mothering of Jesus, humans are restored to life.

Cross–Tree

The second Adam restores the first to paradise through the crucifixion. Romanos explores this through the image of the tree and plays on the word 'wood' (ξύλον). Paradise is symbolized by the tree of life, to which the cross restores Adam; the tree of knowledge, which led to Adam's fall, is redeemed by the cross. Romanos underlines the typological nature of certain Old Testament stories and images of redemption through word play.

The image of fruit-bearing connects the tree in Eden and the cross in *On the Victory of the Cross* (XXII.5.6–8):

For behold, this tree, which you say is dry and barren,
brings forth fruit, after tasting which the robber
became the heir of the good things of Eden.

Ἰδοὺ γὰρ τὸ ξύλον ἐκεῖνο, ὃ λέγεις   ξηρὸν καὶ ἄκαρπον,
    βλαστάνει καρπόν,   οὗ γευσάμενος λῃστὴς
    τῶν ἀγαθῶν τῆς Ἐδὲμ   κληρονόμος γέγονεν·

Death speaks here and, unlike Satan, he recognizes the significance of the crucifixion: Adam is restored to the tree of life. Death chides Satan, rebuking him for being caught in his own snare (lines 1–5). The supposedly barren tree is the cross on which Christ is crucified. Rather than a fruitless plank of wood, it is the life-giving tree in Eden. It gives life to the robber who was crucified with Christ (and to all humanity). The robber now inherits paradise, with its life-giving fruit (8). The return to paradise, as well as signifying the inauguration of the new creation, suggests a new relationship with God. The cross reunites humanity with God.

The cross both is and reveals the tree of life in *On the Resurrection V* (XXVIII.22.1–5):

Death cried these things, dismissing the lifetime accomplishments
of the Wanderer.[61]

---

[61] Eusebius seems to use 'wanderer' for Satan in his *Demonstratio Evangelica* PG 22, 118B. The term is also used of heretics, those who 'wander' from the truth. Romanos makes a word play on 'wandering' and Plato in XXXIII.17.4: τί πλανῶνται πρὸς Πλάτωνα.

For both of them the much-revered cross fixed in the earth
                              had wrought defeat.
[But] to humans it had revealed the tree of life,
on which the fruit of good things was nailed,
in order that, by dying, he might bring to bloom the resurrection
                              for mortals in the meadows below.[62]

Ὁ μὲν Θάνατος ταῦτα ἐφθέγξατο   διελέγχων τὸν π[λά]νον
                              ὅσα ἐν βίῳ   ἀπετέλεσεν·
    ἀμφοτέροις μὲν ἧτταν [εἰρ]γάσατο
                              ὁ παγεὶς ἐπὶ γῆς πολύτιμος σταυρός·
    ξύλον τῆς ζωῆς   τοῖς ἀνθρώποις δεδήλωται,
ὅπου ὁ καρπὸς   τῶν ἀγαθῶν πρ[οσ]ηλώθη,
    ἵνα θνῇσκων ἀνθήσῃ βροτοῖς
                              ἐκ τῶν κάτ[ω λειμ]ώνων ἀνάστασιν

Whereas in the passage from *On the Victory of the Cross* Romanos associated the cross with the tree of life, in this passage the cross reveals the tree which had been hidden because of human sin. But it also *is* the tree 'on which the fruit of good things was nailed' (line 4). Christ is this fruit and by his crucifixion he brings about the general resurrection. Images of fruit and blossoming emphasize that Christ inaugurates a new existence, bringing new life through his death and resurrection. The juxtaposition of 'dying' and 'bring to bloom' also helps to highlight the connection between the death of Christ and the new life he offers.

In *On the Adoration of the Cross*, Romanos refers to both trees (XXIII.4.5–7):

Because of a tree sin was entered by the forefather [i.e. Adam]
because of which, as it was unlawful, he was thrown out of paradise,
but he enters again through the tree of life …

διὰ ξύλου δὲ ἡ παράβασις   εἰσήχθη τῷ προπάτορι,
    δι' οὗ ὥσπερ ἄνομος   παραδείσου ἐκβέβληται·
εἰσέρχεται δὲ   πάλιν διὰ ξύλου ζωῆς·

Adam was thrown out of paradise because of the tree of the knowledge of good and evil; he re-enters through the tree of the cross, the tree of life which redeems the knowledge tree.[63] We might see this redemption also as a renewal of human intellect. Previously the tree of knowledge was forbidden to Adam, and when he ate of it he disobeyed God's command; after

---

[62] John Chrysostom refers to the 'meadows below' in his *Ad populum Antiochenum* to refer simply to 'earth' as opposed to heaven: PG 49, 114.

[63] Barkhuizen (1992), 161.

the crucifixion Adam is restored to the tree, because he has matured, and is now allowed to eat of it. Through the goodness and truth of God, human intellect is perfected and renewed. Romanos stresses this redemption by the repetition of 'because of the tree'.

Romanos uses the word 'wood' to show how Old Testament redemption narratives foreshadow the ultimate redemption of humanity: the wood which makes the water sweet at Marah (Exodus 15:23–5), the thicket which traps the ram to be sacrificed in place of Isaac (Genesis 22:13) and the staff which Elisha uses to raise a sunken axe-head to the water's surface (2 Kings 6:5–7). There is an extended contrast between bitter and sweet in *On the Victory of the Cross*, which presents the sweetening of the water at Marah as an image of the recapitulation of human life which takes place in the crucifixion.[64] Death says (XXII.15.1–8):

By the wood which he showed to Moses,
which once sweetened the water at Marah,
didn't the Master teach what it was and from what root?
Then he did not say, for he did not want to,
but now he has revealed it to all.
For look, everything has been sweetened, but we are embittered.
From our root, a cross has sprung up,
which was planted in the earth and became sweet.

Ἄρα ὅπερ ἔδειξε   τῷ Μωϋσῇ ὁ δεσπότης
ξύλον ὃ ἐγλύκανε   ποτὲ τὸ ὕδωρ εἰς Μέρραν,
ἐδίδαξε τί ἦν   καὶ τίνος ἡ ῥίζα;
τότε οὐκ εἶπεν·   οὐ γὰρ ἤθελε·
νῦν δὲ τοῖς πᾶσι   τοῦτο ἐφανέρωσεν·
ἰδοὺ γὰρ τὰ πάντα ἡδύνθη, ἡμεῖς δὲ   παρεπικράνθημεν·
ἐκ ῥίζης ἡμῶν   ἀνεβλάστησε σταυρός,
ὃς ἐνεβλήθη τῇ γῇ   καὶ γλυκεῖα γέγονεν·

In the Exodus narrative (15:22–5), the Israelites spent three days in the wilderness without water and when they arrived at Marah they found the water bitter and undrinkable. God rescued them from death through a piece of wood: Moses threw the wood into the water and the water became drinkable. Not surprisingly, theologians often linked this story with baptism and the crucifixion, the redemption through water that comes about through the cross.[65] In Romanos' *kontakion*, Death recognizes that this Old Testament episode foreshadowed the crucifixion. The wood of the cross and

---

[64] See also XXVIII.30, although ξύλον is reconstructed here.
[65] See, for example, Tertullian *On Baptism* 9.2 and Ambrose *On the Mysteries* 3.14.

Moses' wood are of the same ilk. Antitype again surpasses type: the cross sweetens everything (and embitters Death and Satan), whereas the wood at Marah only sweetened the water; the cross saves eternally, whereas the wood at Marah only rescued the Israelites temporarily.

In *On Abraham and Isaac*, Isaac's salvation from sacrifice at his father's hand prefigures the cross (XLI.23.1–5):[66]

Just as this man, your own Isaac, carried the wood on his shoulders,
on his shoulders my son will carry the cross.
Your great love has also shown you the things to come.
And now see where the ram is caught in the thicket.
Seeing, understand the mystery.

Οὗτος δ' ὡς ἐβάσταζε   ξύλα τοῖς ὤμοις   ὁ σὸς Ἰσαάκ,
    ἐπ' ὤμων φέρει   ὁ ἐμὸς υἱὸς [[τὸν]] σταυρόν·
ὁ πόθος ὁ πολύς σοι ἔδειξε   καὶ τὰ μέλλοντα·
βλέψον ἄρτι   καὶ κριὸν τὸν ἐν τῷ ξύλῳ
    πόθεν κρατεῖται·   βλέπων καταμάνθανε τὸ μυστήριον·

Romanos sees a double typology in this Old Testament story. Isaac carries the wood (*xula*) for his own sacrifice, just as Christ carried the cross for his own crucifixion ('wood' and 'cross' are equated here), but the ram is also a type for Christ, and the thicket (*xulō*) a type for the wood of the cross.[67] The 'ram in the thicket' is placed in the same position in the line as 'my son [will carry] the cross'. Ephrem the Syrian likewise makes this second-level typology, depicting the ram hanging in the tree just as Christ hangs on the cross.[68]

Once again the image of wood is central to the typology in the narrative of Elisha rescuing a sunken axe-head (2 Kings 6:5–7).[69] Romanos presents this event as a type for the crucifixion and harrowing of hell in *On the Victory of the Cross* (XXII.3):

'Go, Beliar, come to your senses,' cried Death,
'Run, uncover your eyes and see
the root of the wood within my soul.[70]

---

[66] Brock identifies similarities between this *kontakion* and two anonymous Syriac *memre*, and argues that they (or the Syriac tradition of which they are part) influenced Romanos in his composition of the Isaac *kontakion*. See Brock (1986), 91–6.

[67] Athanasius makes the same link between the ram and Christ, claiming that Abraham recognized Christ in the ram: *Epistle 6*. See Kessler (2004), 133.

[68] *Commentary on Genesis* 20.3.

[69] This story was often seen as a type for Christ's baptism as well as his crucifixion. Cf. Jensen (2010), 119.

[70] The image of Hades pierced by the cross of Christ becomes an important one in the visual arts as well. See Frazer (1974).

It has gone down to my depths,
so that it might draw up Adam like iron.
Elisha once painted an image of this,
raising the axe-head from the river.
With a light thing, the prophet drew up the heavy,
foreshadowing it for you and teaching you
that by wood Adam would be led up
from wretchedness
again to paradise.'

Ὕπαγε, ἀνάνηψον,   Βελίαρ, κράζει ὁ Ἅιδης,

    δράμε, ἀποκάλυψον   τοὺς ὀφθαλμούς σου καὶ ἴδε

    τοῦ ξύλου τὴν ῥίζαν   ἐντὸς τῆς ψυχῆς μου·

κάτω κατῆλθεν   εἰς τὰ βάθη μου,

    ἵν' ἀνασπάσῃ   τὸν Ἀδὰμ ὡς σίδηρον·

τὴν τούτου εἰκόνα ποτὲ Ἐλισσαῖος   προεζωγράφησεν

    ἐκ τοῦ ποταμοῦ   τὴν ἀξίνην ἀνελών·

        τῷ ἐλαφρῷ τὸ βαρὺ   ὁ προφήτης εἵλκυσε

προοιμιάζων σοι   καὶ διδάσκων σε

    ὅτι ξύλῳ ὁ Ἀδὰμ   μέλλει ἀνάγεσθαι

    ἀπὸ ταλαιπωρίας

πάλιν εἰς τὸν παράδεισον.

With urgency, signalled by the imperatives placed emphatically at the beginning of the first two lines and by their rhyming endings, Death encourages Satan to see the significance of the crucifixion. He likens it to Elisha's miraculous restoration of the sunken axe-head, asserting that Elisha himself taught Satan the truth if only Satan could recognize it. And so Death opens his address with the command: 'uncover your eyes and see': a light bit of wood restores something heavy. 'Light thing' and 'wood' in lines 8 and 10 respectively are equated, as are 'heavy' and 'Adam', which are also in the same position in their lines. The weak sense pauses which come after 'heavy' and 'Adam' perhaps also help to emphasize the heaviness of each. Romanos also likens Adam to iron: a heavy rock which is drawn up to the surface. Adam is redeemed from the depths just as the borrowed axe-head was from the deep water.

Redemption and punishment go together in God's correction of humanity through the cross and this is reflected in the typologies Romanos uses: the just are redeemed and the unjust punished. Once again, it is Death who points out the significance of past events (XXII.13):

O how did we not remember the types of this tree?
For they have been shown for a long time in many and diverse ways

in the saved and in the lost.
Noah was saved by a tree,
but the whole world, having been disobedient, was destroyed.
Moses was glorified by one, when he took a rod as a staff,
but Egypt drowned with the many plagues that came from it,
as though she had fallen into deep waters.
For what it has done now, the cross showed long ago
in an image. So why are we not lamenting?
For Adam is brought in
again to paradise.

Ὦ πῶς οὐκ ἐμνήσθημεν   τῶν τύπων τούτου τοῦ ξύλου·
    πάλαι γὰρ ἐδείχθησαν   πολυμερῶς, πολυτρόπως
    ἐν τοῖς σῳζομένοις   καὶ ἀπολλυμένοις·
ξύλῳ ὁ Νῶε   διεσῴζετο,
    κόσμος δὲ ὅλος   ἀπειθήσας ὤλλυτο·
Μωσῆς δι᾽ αὐτοῦ ἐδοξάσθη,   τὴν ῥάβδον
                                                        καθάπερ σκῆπτρον λαβών,
    ἡ Αἴγυπτος δὲ   ταῖς πληγαῖς ταῖς ἐξ αὐτοῦ
    ὥσπερ βαθείαις πηγαῖς   ἐμπεσοῦσα πνίγεται·
ἃ νῦν γὰρ ἔπραξε,   πάλαι ἔδειξεν
    ἐν εἰκόνι ὁ σταυρός·   τί οὖν οὐ κλαίομεν;
    ὁ Ἀδὰμ γὰρ ὑπάγει
πάλιν εἰς τὸν παράδεισον.

Death's lament encourages listeners to make the connections he made all too late. Romanos emphasizes that all history has foreshadowed the life of Christ through the words 'long time', 'many' and 'diverse'. The wood of Noah's ark (Genesis 6:11–8:19) is a type for the wood of the cross: it was the salvation of the righteous in the flood, but the unrighteous were destroyed. Likewise, Moses' staff saved the Israelites from slavery, but destroyed the enslaving Egyptians. The image of water here draws together the plagues of Egypt, which decimated the population, with the parting of the Red Sea (Exodus 14:16), which literally drowned the Egyptians. One group is saved, but the other destroyed. So the redemption of humanity means destruction for Satan and Death.

Such images, of redemption and punishment, abound in *On the Adoration of the Cross* (XXIII). Images of the cultivation of nature highlight that the cross restores humans to paradise and demonstrate the growth, health and beauty of God's redeeming actions. In strophe 6, the robber describes the cross as a graft for sterile souls (line 5), a plough (5), a thought-cleansing cultivation (6), the root of resurrection life (7). Healing images are teamed with those of punishment: the cross is a rod which beats down Adam's enemies (8).

The other image which recurs in *On the Adoration of the Cross* is a royal one. The cross becomes an inscription, sealed with Christ's royal, purple blood, or a royal signature (XXIII.11.1–2; 5–6):[71]

'Receive the certain seal and divine inscription,
the signature of the king, God, the all-merciful.'

'Σφραγῖδα δέχου βεβαίαν   καὶ θεῖα ἐγχαράγματα,
   ὑπογραφὴν βασιλέως   θεοῦ τοῦ πανοικτίρμονος.'

And, having received them, the cherubim recognized the writing
shining forth with the grace of the purple blood.

Χερουβὶμ δὲ ὑποδεξάμενα   ἐγνώριζε τὰ γράμματα
   ἐκλάμποντα χάριτι   πορφυρίδος τοῦ αἵματος.

In this *kontakion*, the good thief takes the cross to the gates of Eden as proof that he may re-enter paradise. The cross becomes a royal pass-key or signet ring by which the cherubim can recognize the true 'heir'. By means of the cross, Christ has corrected the wrongs Adam did which caused him to be expelled from paradise. Humanity has now been perfected and may reclaim its inheritance: Eden.

For Romanos, typology models the restoration of humanity: the antitype fulfils and surpasses the type. Adam is a type for Christ in this way, as is Eve for Mary. Christ takes on Adam's humanity – and this means the depth of his 'humanness' – even to the point of death. Christ corrects the wrongs of Adam and, by being the fulfilment of Adam, brings him to perfection. He inaugurates the new creation, just as Adam was the beginning of the first creation. Christ saves Adam (and all humanity) and brings him into the new reality. Romanos suggests that Mary is similarly redemptive for Eve; by her obedience to God's call, Mary corrects the disobedience of Eve. She brings life into the world by giving birth to Jesus, whereas Eve brought death into the world by her sin. As we have seen, Romanos uses a number of different permutations of cross typologies, whereby the cross displays Christ as the fulfilment of Old Testament prophecies, forgiving redeemer and royal saviour. The cross redeems the sin of Eden (which is symbolized by the tree of the knowledge of good and evil) and restores humanity to the tree of life. Romanos plays on the word 'wood' to strengthen typological links between Old Testament redemption narratives and that of the crucifixion

---

[71] On writing imagery, see Krueger (2003), (2004), 165. Also see further below.

and resurrection and thus brings to the fore the redemption which Christ achieves through the restoration of humanity.

Comparisons

We have already seen some comparisons between Adam and Christ set up by the structure of the stanza or the hymn, or through repetitions of words or structure. Romanos uses structural techniques to create a sort of *syncrisis* between Adam and Christ.[72] Structural comparisons set up Adam's actions against Christ's.[73] Each act of disobedience on Adam's part is counteracted by an obedient action of Christ; each of Christ's actions has a salvific effect for Adam.

In *On the Epiphany*, as we have seen above, Romanos says to Adam (VI.3.4–5):

[Christ] came down to earth,   so that he might take you up,
He became human,   so that you might become God.

κατέβη ἐπὶ γῆς,   ἵνα λάβῃ σε ἄνω·
ἐγένετο θνητός,   ἵνα σὺ θεὸς γένῃ

Romanos uses the sense pause (shown here by a larger space, following the convention of the Maas–Trypanis edition) in each line to create a comparison.[74] Before the pause, he refers to Christ, after it, to Adam. The repetition of 'so that' in each line after the pause adds to the structural contrast. Christ's descent to earth enables Adam's restoration to paradise. Christ's humanity enables human divinity.

Caesurae and 'so that' are again used for this purpose in *On the Nativity II*. Christ says to his mother (about Adam and Eve) (II.14.8):

I came down to earth,   so that they might have eternal life.

κατέβην εἰς γῆν,   ἵνα σχῶσιν ἄφθαρτον ζωήν·

The pattern is the same as that above. There is space to marvel at Christ's action and anticipate the 'so that' clause which brings about a new existence for humanity, just as the proper response of humans to the new creation is

---

[72] For a definition of syncrisis, see Kennedy (2003), 113.

[73] Visually, we can see something similar in the eighteenth-century redemption rose window in the cathedral of Saint Jean, Lyon, in which the stages of Adam's creation, sin and expulsion from the garden, which are illustrated on the right, are balanced by the actions of Christ, from incarnation to resurrection, on the left.

[74] See the metrical appendix in Maas and Trypanis (1963), 511.

wonder, praise and living in anticipation of heaven. Christ's descent to earth enables human ascent to heaven.[75]

Romanos also sets up comparisons between Adam and Christ through the use of cognates or repetition of a word in different forms. Adam has suffered, so Christ takes on this suffering in order to relieve Adam's (XXIII.4.3–4):

And I became a curse,
so that I might release Adam and his own from the curse.

καὶ κατάρα ἐγενόμην,
    ἵνὰ κατάρας   ἐλευθερώσω τὸν Ἀδὰμ   καὶ τοὺς αὐτοῦ

Romanos' use of 'curse' (*katara*) recalls Paul's letter to the Galatians, in which he says: 'Christ redeemed us from the curse (*kataras*) of the law by becoming a curse (*katara*) himself – for it is written, "Cursed is anyone who hangs on a tree"' (Gal. 3:13). Paul was referring to Deuteronomy 21:23, which states that anyone who hangs on a pole is cursed. The form of Jesus' death made him a curse in Jewish (and Greco-Roman) eyes. Jesus took this curse upon himself, by being crucified, in order to remove the curse of the Law from Adam (and all his people). The placement of 'curse' in the same position in each line heightens the comparison.

In *On the Annunciation II*, Romanos repeats the word 'to wound' to emphasize the close connection between what has happened to Adam and what God does in the person of Christ (XXXVII.2.3):

for this reason God, seeking to wound the one who wounded Adam,
                                                    became flesh from a virgin.

διὸ θεὸς τὸν τρώσαντα   τὸν Ἀδὰμ τρῶσαι ζητῶν
                                ἐκ παρθένου σαρκοῦται

Adam has been 'wounded' and so Christ seeks to 'wound' the perpetrator: Satan. Romanos highlights the correction of the wrongs done by or to Adam and shows that Christ is the fulfilment of the perfection to which Adam was called.

All these comparisons set up Christ as Adam's counterbalance. Each action of Christ is a response to one of Adam's. In fact, it is *the* response, the perfect human action which redeems fallen humanity. Comparison and typology are thus useful tools for Romanos to examine how Christ is the second Adam, that is, how he corrects the sins of Adam and perfects the human race. Perhaps the most significant rhetorical device Romanos uses in his exposition of this theme, however, is metaphor.

---

[75] See also XX.2.1–3.

Metaphor

Metaphor takes words and ideas which relate to one thing and connects them with another, putting together two disparate things to say something which cannot be captured in straightforward language.[76] In a formal sense, this models God's restoration of humanity, in which God connected two disparate things (human and divine) in the person of Christ in order to do something which could not be done elsewise: to restore humanity to God. There are several images and associated metaphors which Romanos uses to explore the correction and perfection of humanity through the second Adam: opening of closed paradise, clothing and nakedness, blindness and sight (and the senses more generally), thirst and hunger, writing, and healing. Many of these metaphors draw on existing scriptural metaphors, which carry with them certain fertile connotations. Romanos draws on the tradition as well as creating new metaphors, using the rhetorical form to illustrate the sort of process which takes place in Christ's correction and perfection of humanity.

If I am right about metaphor, then explaining it will always fail to capture the newness of its meaning. What I can hope to do in the following is show how different images and metaphors cohere, and identify particular ways in which metaphor embodies or seeks to explain the theological idea of the second Adam.

Reopening Paradise

In *On the Nativity I*, both Mary and Christ are described as a door or gate (I.9.4–10):

She opens the door and receives the company of the Magi.
She opens the door, she the unopened gate,
whom Christ alone broke through.
She opens the door, she who had been opened
and yet never cheated of the treasure of her purity.
She opened the door, from whom was born the door,
a child now, God before all ages.

ἡ δὲ ἀνοίγει   θύραν καὶ δέχεται   τῶν μάγων τὸ σύστημα·
    ἀνοίγει θύραν   ἡ ἀπαράνοικτος

---

[76] Soskice (1985), 15, 44, 49 and passim. This view of metaphor is not unlike that of Aristotle, who argued that metaphor enables a superior mode of knowledge than a mere gloss. On which, see Dalimier (2004), 127–41. See also Cohen (1978), 3–12. Against this view of metaphor, Davidson, Rorty and others claim metaphors have no meaning other than the literal interpretation of their constituent words: Davidson (1978), 31–47, Haack (1987–8), 293–301.

πύλη, ἣν Χριστὸς   μόνος διώδευσεν·
ἀνοίγει θύραν   ἡ ἀνοιχθεῖσα
    καὶ μὴ κλαπεῖσα μηδαμῶς   τὸν τῆς ἁγνείας θησαυρόν·
αὐτὴ ἤνοιξε θύραν,   ἀφ᾽ ἧς ἐγεννήθη θύρα,
    παιδίον νέον,   ὁ πρὸ αἰώνων θεός.

Metaphor, imagery and typology are mixed in this passage. Romanos combines the image of Mary opening the door to the Magi with the metaphor of Christ as the door to heaven (cf. John 10:8–10). Insistent repetition creates an image of opening that which was firmly closed before. Romanos argues that Christ has opened the door to heaven. At the start of the hymn, the door to heaven is the gate to Eden (I.1.1): 'Bethlehem has opened Eden, come, let us see!' (τὴν Ἐδὲμ Βηθλεὲμ ἤνοιξε, δεῦτε ἴδωμεν). 'Bethlehem' becomes a metaphor for the birth of the incarnate God. Jesus opens Eden, which was closed by Adam's sin. By correcting this sin, Christ is the way humans return to paradise. The final line (the refrain) emphasizes the union of human and divine in the person of Jesus Christ. By joining these together, Christ restores humanity to relationship with God, acting as the door to heaven, and initiating the new creation. We will explore this in more detail in the following chapter. The door that was closed from the Fall has been reopened as a result of Christ's descent to earth as a human being. Mary is the vessel which allowed Christ to do this. Romanos draws attention to the fact that it is through the motherhood of Mary, who is herself described as a gate, perhaps conjuring up images of a *hortus conclusus* (and yet it is the image of opening that is the more dominant), that the door to heaven is opened.[77]

By referring to the biblical type of the closed gate (Ezekiel 44:1–3), Romanos also stresses Mary's perpetual virginity, which, as we saw above, is an important aspect of her role as the second Eve. Likewise, in line 8 Romanos uses a biblical reference to focus on the significance of Mary's continuing virginity. The imagery of Mary's purity as a treasure (*thesauron*) which is never stolen (*klapeisa*) refers to Matthew 6:19–20, in which Jesus instructs people not to store up treasures (*thesaurous*) on earth, which thieves can steal (*kleptai*), but treasures in heaven. In this sense, Romanos argues that virginity is a heavenly treasure rather than an earthly one.[78] One effect is to place the human Mary on the heavenly side of the equation, allowing her to function as the second Eve to Christ's second Adam.

[77] Arentzen (2014), 139.
[78] On the debate about virginity and marriage in Byzantium, see Cameron (1989), Hunter (1987), (1989), Meyendorff (1990).

These metaphors are, of course, firmly grounded in the biblical tradition. Jesus calls himself a gate in John's Gospel (10: 8–10):

'... I am the gate for the sheep. All who came before me are thieves and bandits; but the sheep did not listen to them. I am the gate. Whoever enters by me will be saved, and will come in and go out and find pasture. The thief comes only to steal and kill and destroy. I came that they may have life, and have it abundantly.'

Christ is the door to salvation, the pathway on which those who wish to be saved should travel. He opens up new life to all who would enter it through him. Romanos responds to the language of the Gospel in *On the Nativity I*, highlighting that redemption of humanity and their restoration to paradise comes through Christ, who came to give humans eternal life. He associates Mary with this imagery, picking up on patristic theology about the *Theotokos*, and augments New Testament imagery with images and metaphors from the Old Testament to demonstrate the consistency of God's saving promises.

Old Testament resonances also abound in passages where the cross is the central door to salvation. In this passage from *On the Adoration of the Cross* the good thief crucified with Christ addresses the cross (XXIII.6.7–11):

You beautiful root of my resurrection life,
You rod of the blow which strikes the enemy of Adam,
You have opened the doors of delight, which sin once closed,
[the sin which] Adam then committed[79]
in paradise.

σὺ ῥίζα καλὴ   τῆς ἀναστάσης μου ζωῆς·
    σὺ ῥάβδος πληγῆς   τύπτουσα ἐχθρὸν τοῦ Ἀδάμ·
σὺ τὰς θύρας ἤνοιξας   τὰς τῆς τρυφῆς,   ἃς ἀπέκλεισε ποτὲ
    ἡ ἁμαρτία,   ἥνπερ τότε   ⟨ὁ⟩ Ἀδὰμ ἐπλημμέλησεν
ἐν τῷ παραδείσῳ.

The cross has opened the door to paradise, which was closed by the sin of Adam. The cross does not simply represent Christ here. Romanos draws attention to the fact that it is through the crucifixion of Christ that humans are restored to paradise. The crucifixion is part of Christ's correction of Adam's sin. The cross as a 'beautiful root' links it to the tree of life of Genesis. In this passage there is an explicit reference to sin closing the door to paradise. Sin closed the door and the cross opened it; Adam closed the

---

[79] Baud-Bovy would no doubt be disappointed that I have been unable to think of a musical translation for ἐπλημμέλησεν. He is determined that we should not lose sight of the fact that the *kontakia* were sung: Baud-Bovy (1938b), 217.

door and Christ opened it. Once again, Christ is doing the addition and getting the sums right, where Adam went wrong.[80]

Romanos' images of opening have quite direct, literal force: paradise was closed to humans because of Adam's sin and Christ has opened it again by correction of Adam's sin, by being incarnated, living, suffering, dying and being resurrected. By these actions, Christ summed up human life, correcting the mistakes which had accrued from the Fall, and perfected human nature to fit it for paradise.

Clothing and Nakedness

Romanos also explores these concepts of correction and perfection through clothing and nakedness metaphors in *On the Baptism of Christ* and *On the Epiphany*, drawing particularly on the Syriac tradition. Sebastian Brock has explored this metaphor in Syriac texts and sets out four stages of salvation history in which clothing plays a part:[81] a) Adam and Eve are clothed in a 'robe of light' in the garden;[82] b) they are stripped of their clothing at the Fall;[83] c) God 'puts on Adam' in the incarnation;[84] and d) at the baptism of Christ, Christ takes the garment of light and places it in the river Jordan. This part of the scheme seems to be predominantly Syriac.[85] The initiate then retrieves the robe at their own baptism, so that baptism is the moment at which Christians are reclothed in the robe of light (or 'glory').[86] This fits with Paul's statement that baptism is when Christians are clothed with Christ, although probably Paul never envisaged quite such an elaborate interpretation of his words. Similarly, Proclus of Constantinople refers to Adam's robe of glory of which he was stripped at the Fall.[87]

---

[80] For this type of accounting imagery in Irenaeus of Lyons, see Osborn (2001), 97–110.

[81] Brock (1982a), 12, Brock (1990), 66–72.

[82] E.g. Ephrem *Vir.* 16.9; *Par.* 15.8–9. These examples refer to the robe of glory of which Adam was stripped at the Fall.

[83] See previous note. See also, for example, Ephrem *Nat.* 23.13 and his commentary on Genesis 11.14ff.

[84] E.g. Ephrem *Nis.* 35.8.

[85] Brock argues that this particular use of clothing metaphors is uniquely Syriac, since the Greek theologians focus on the clothing of Adam and Eve in skins as they leave paradise. Nakedness then becomes a symbol of purity for the Greeks. See Brock (1982a), 12, 22. There are early uses of such phrases as 'robe of glory' in Assyrian and Akkadian literature. It is arguably present in the Epic of Gilgamesh: Freedman (1972), 92. On the use of clothing imagery to mean 'overwhelm' first in Sumerian and Akkadian literature and then influencing Hebrew and Syriac uses, see Waldman (1989).

[86] Brock (1982a), 12.

[87] PG 65.712D–713A. Cf. Constas (1995), 182–3 and passim.

In Romanos, as in Ephrem and other Syriac writers, nakedness refers to human brokenness and clothing usually to Christ and perfection. In *On the Epiphany*, Romanos combines images of blindness and nakedness (VI.2.1–3):

When Adam was willingly maimed, having tasted the blind-making fruit, straightaway he was unwillingly made naked. For, finding him, the
                              maiming one stripped him like a blind man.
So he was naked and maimed …

Ὅτε ἑκὼν ἐπηρώθη Ἀδὰμ   καρποῦ γευσάμενος τυφλοποιοῦ
  εὐθέως ἄκων ἐγυμνώθη·   ὡς τυφλὸν γὰρ εὑρὼν
                            ὁ πηρώσας ἀπέδυσεν·

ἦν οὖν γυμνὸς καὶ πῆρος …

Although in Genesis it says that Adam and Eve came to 'know' or 'realize' that they were naked as a result of eating the fruit (Genesis 3:8), Romanos refers to Adam being 'stripped naked' by the devil. The theme of 'maiming' likewise recurs in this passage. The devil is 'the maimer' who causes harm to Adam as well as stripping him naked. Like the nakedness, this harm may be physical but more importantly points to the harm done to mortals when removed from their life with God. Nakedness is a metaphor for the fallen state of humanity (V.2.1–2):

God did not overlook the one who was stripped by trickery
                             within paradise
and who lost the God-woven robe.

Οὐχ ὑπερεῖδεν ὁ θεὸς   τὸν δόλῳ συληθέντα
                       ἐντὸς τοῦ παραδείσου·
  καὶ ἀπολελωκότα τὴν θεοΰφαντον στολήν·

Adam was clothed in a 'God-woven robe' before he was tempted by the devil. The devil's deception and his sin left him naked when he left the garden. A precise explanation of the robe is not forthcoming, but the point is clearly made: Adam was clothed by God in the garden, but is unworthy of such clothing after his temptation and sin. The robe here is a metaphor for Adam's purity, and nakedness for his fallen and sinful state. Romanos reverses the Genesis story, in which Adam and Eve were 'naked, and were not ashamed' (2:25) in the garden and only when they sinned did they need clothing.[88] God then sends them out of the garden clothed in skins (Genesis 3:21).

---

[88]   In the Genesis account, it was the realization of nakedness, rather than the nakedness itself which caused Adam and Eve shame: Peterson (1993), 560.

For Romanos, nakedness, unlike the purity and innocence it symbolizes in Genesis, is a metaphor for human brokenness. When God becomes
human in Jesus Christ Romanos talks about him being stripped naked. In
On the Baptism of Christ, God tells Adam not to hide himself in the garden 'since because of you I am stripped naked and baptized' (διὰ σὲ γὰρ
τὸν γυμνὸν γυμνοῦμαι καὶ βαπτίζομαι) (V.3.3).[89] In the previous passage,
Romanos talks about Adam being stripped when he left the garden. In
order to recall him, Christ is stripped naked. He thus takes on humanity, in
all its brokenness, and corrects the brokenness. The metaphor of nakedness
is about correcting Adam's sin.

But it is also about restoring humans to perfection. Jesus is stripped
naked in order to perfect human existence and return humanity to its former, 'clothed' state. So, at the opening of *On the Baptism of Christ,* Romanos
speaks, in Pauline fashion, of 'putting on Christ' (V.1.6–8):

On account of which, come, all those who are naked from Adam,
let us put [Christ] on in order that we might be warmed.
For [he is] shelter for the naked and daylight for those in darkness.

διὸ οἱ ἐξ Ἀδάμ   γυμνοὶ δεῦτε πάντες,
    ὑποδύωμεν αὐτὸν   ἵνα θαλφθῶμεν·
σκέπη γὰρ γυμνοῖς   καὶ αἴγλη ἐσκοτισμένοις

And Romanos keeps emphasizing this through repetition of 'naked'. He
conjures up an amusing image of shivering naked people putting on the
nice warm woollens of Christ, keeping the imagery real and vivid: being
naked means being cold. Separation from God becomes an image not
unlike homelessness: cold, dark and alone. Humans are naked as a result
of Adam's sin (and continued human sin). Christ comes as a garment for
naked humanity, to clothe, warm and enlighten them in their dark and sinful state. Here Romanos refers to Paul's letter to the Galatians (3:27): 'As
many of you as were baptised into Christ have clothed yourselves in Christ.'
Baptism is the moment when Christians are 'clothed in Christ'.[90] As we have
seen, this passage greatly influenced Syriac theologians, and this in turn
suggests influence of Syriac theology on Romanos.[91]

---

[89] On the conflation of time that this passage suggests, see Chapter 4 below.

[90] This is thought, by Anson (among others), to be part of the motivation of cross-dressing
saints: Anson (1974), 7. On gender identity in such stories, see Davis (2002).

[91] Although the use of clothing imagery was, of course, not exclusive to Syriac writers. Justinian
himself used clothing imagery in his edict on the Three Chapters Controversy. Nakedness is a
negative image, likened to those who dishonour the council, and the veiling of nakedness is a
positive image. See Albertella et al. (1973), 100, Price (2009), 151.

In *On the Epiphany* Romanos changes the metaphor slightly, and suggests that Christ's incarnation (and revelation as God in his baptism) tears away the human mourning robe, with which humanity was clothed after the Fall. The idea of a mourning robe suggests that humans have been in a state of lament – often a sign of recognition of sinfulness and consequent repentance in early Christian literature – since leaving paradise and being removed from God.[92] Tearing away the mourning robe is a metaphor for the reunification of humans with God; Christ provides humans instead with a white robe (VI.12.1–2):

Now the mourning garment is torn, we have received the white robe
which the Spirit wove for us from the holy wool of the lamb and our God.

Ῥήγνυται νῦν ὁ πενθήρης χιτών·

        ἐλάβομεν τὴν στολὴν τὴν λευκήν,

ἣν ὕφανεν ἡμῖν τὸ πνεῦμα   ἀπὸ πόκων ἁγνῶν

        τοῦ ἀμνοῦ καὶ θεοῦ ἡμῶν.

Once again, humanity is restored to its 'God-woven robe' and to proper, consummated, communion with God. The image of the Lamb of God being shorn to provide garments for mortals is rather amusing, and is perhaps an example of humour helping to communicate ideas. But, most importantly, we see the involvement of the three persons of the Trinity in the reclothing of humanity. Father, Son and Spirit are all involved in reclothing humanity, in restoring humanity to relationship with God. This restoration and consummation of the relationship between God and humanity is achieved through correction of human sin.

The clothing and nakedness metaphors of these two hymns on divine revelation (*On the Baptism of Christ* and *On the Epiphany*) illustrate Romanos' concept of the process from the Fall to Christ's restoration of humanity to eternal life. Adam was clothed in a 'God-woven robe' in paradise, which he lost when he sinned. He was stripped and sent out of the garden into hardship and death. Nakedness evokes Adam's sinfulness and separation from God. Romanos then uses this image to depict Christ taking on human form and entering into the depths of human brokenness. Christ is likewise stripped, but this time willingly. He takes on human nakedness in order to correct the wrongs done by Adam. The restoration of mortals to their former clothed state is a metaphor for Christ's perfection of humanity.

---

[92] For a detailed study of repentance in late antiquity, see Torrance (2013).

For Romanos, drawing on Greek and Syriac traditions, nakedness is a metaphor for human sin and departure from God, whereas clothing signifies a return to proper relationship with God and perfect existence in paradise. Christ takes on nakedness, correcting human sin. He reclothes humanity, perfecting human life. The metaphor of nakedness embodies the incarnation in a way in which other descriptions or explanations could not. Romanos does not view the incarnation as a sanitary, neat transaction, but concludes rather that Christ enters into the dirt and depravity of humanity. The image of God being stripped naked conveys this and thus emphasizes the truly radical event which is taking place. The clothing metaphor also points to the inauguration of a new creation (reclothing of humanity) and final restoration of humanity to relationship with God (removing the mourning robe which represents the separation between humans and God). We will look further at these aspects of Romanos' theology in Chapters 3 and 4.

Blindness

Nakedness, as we saw above, is sometimes linked with blindness; both are metaphors for human sinfulness. Adam is described as blind and Romanos refers to his restoration to perfect humanity as a revelation of light and a restoration of sight (VI.1.1):

A Sun from Bethlehem shone on blinded Adam in Eden.

Τῷ τυφλωθέντι Ἀδὰμ ἐν Ἐδὲμ   ἐφάνη ἥλιος ἐκ Βηθλεέμ

Eden and Adam are in darkness, and the Sun (Christ), coming from Bethlehem, restores the light to them. Associations between blindness and sin abound in the *kontakia*. In *On Mary at the Cross,* Mary calls those who kill Jesus blind (XIX.15.5–6):

I will look on the daring of those who honour Moses.
For they say it is to avenge him that these blind men came to kill you.

κατίδω τὴν τόλμαν   τῶν τιμώντων τὸν Μωσῆν·
αὐτὸν γὰρ ὡς δῆθεν   ἐκδικοῦντες οἱ τυφλοὶ κτεῖναι σε ἦλθον.

Those 'who honour Moses' are the Jews, whom Romanos calls 'blind' because in their determination to protect their prophet they did not recognize their own Messiah. We will look further at Romanos' characterization of the Jews in Chapter 3.

So, ignorance or lack of recognition are figured as blindness. Death and the devil are so labelled in *On the Victory of the Cross* for their inability to recognize either Christ as God or the significance of Christ's crucifixion (XXII.7.1–3):

And suddenly Hades cried out to the devil,
Sight-maimed to one who does not see, blind to the blind, he said, 'Look.
You are walking in darkness. Grope about, lest you fall …'

Ἔκραζε δὲ ἄθροον   πρὸς τὸν διάβολον Ἅιδης·
πῆρος τῷ μὴ βλέποντι,   τυφλὸς τυφλῷ λέγει·   ʽΒλέψον·
ἐν σκότει πορεύει,   ψηλάφα μὴ πέσης…'

This seems to be a case of the blind leading the blind! Romanos creates this comical situation to demonstrate that both Hades and the devil missed the fact that Christ was the incarnate God. Darkness and blindness go together as metaphors for ignorance.

The guards at Christ's tomb in *On the Resurrection II* deliberately fashion themselves as blind (XXV.16.1–2):

What we know, this we also set forth,
                    for even if we kept these things silent now,
the stones will cry out and betray our hardness and blindness.

Ὅπερ] οἴδαμεν, τοῦτο καὶ δηλοῦμεν·
                    κἂν ἡμεῖς γὰρ αὐτὰ νῦν σιωπῶμεν,
[[οἱ]] λίθοι κράξουσι   καὶ ἐλέγξουσι τὴν πώρωσιν
                    ἡμῶν καὶ τὴν τύφλωσιν·

This *kontakion* was likely sung on Easter Sunday and Romanos draws on the Gospel account of that resurrection day in Matthew 28:11–15:

… some of the guard went into the city and told the chief priests everything that had happened. After the priests had assembled with the elders, they devised a plan to give a large sum of money to the soldiers, telling them, 'You must say, "His disciples came by night and stole him away while we were asleep." If this comes to the governor's ears, we will satisfy him and keep you out of trouble.' So they took the money and did as they were directed. And this story is still told among the Jews to this day.

Romanos takes this passage and creates an imaginative dialogue around it to explore the reality of the resurrection. Since the guards were not supposed to speak, he has them refer to the Gospel of Luke (19:40) in which Jesus says to the Pharisees who want him to stop the crowd from praising him that the stones would cry out if the people were silent. In this case, the stones would cry out about the resurrection if the guards did not speak. They tell the story despite being determined to remain blind – they have been paid for this purpose by the Jews (XXV.20). Unlike Adam (and even Hades and the devil), the guards remain blind of their own free will.

Vision was considered to be both a tactile sense and a true one – a sense which did not corrupt the essence of the thing observed. No doubt this high evaluation of sight was partly a function of the overlap in Greek between words for knowing and seeing. This connection was bolstered by physical theories of how people see. Extramission was a prominent conceptualization of sight in late antique thought. According to this theory, optical rays come out from the eyes, touch the object being looked at, and take back the essence of the object to the eyes.[93] The Pythagoreans and Euclid were among the proponents of this conceptualization of vision.[94] Even for someone like Lucretius, who did not believe in extramission, sight and touch were connected.[95] He argues that an object handled in the dark will be recognized as the same object when seen in the light (*De rer. nat.* 4.230). This close connection between sight and touch continued in Christian late antiquity. A suppliant to the monk Paphnutius says: '[May] the man who is setting out to your piety be found worthy to embrace [Paphnutius] also with [his] very eyes.'[96] Unlike hearing or smell, sight was believed to be able to translate the object of sight directly to the person seeing,[97] without any interference. Its purity was emphasized in contrast to the other physical senses. For Christians in late antiquity, sight was considered to be a link to God.[98] Georgia Frank draws attention to this in relation to pilgrimage. One of the reasons why Christians travelled far to see ascetic holy men was the hope that by gazing upon the monk, who had a special connection to God, they would see God and gain true knowledge of him.[99] Such conceptualizations of sight demonstrate the negative associations of blindness for Romanos' audience. Blindness disables a pure way of understanding the world and a true connection to God.

[93] Nelson (2000), 152. See also James (2004), 528. And see further in Chapter 4.

[94] Bartsch (2006), 62.

[95] See Bartsch (2006), 59–60. Plato's concept of vision is more complex, but involves light flowing from the eyes to the object, as well as light in the object and in the surrounding air. The eyes still have an active role to play. See *Timaeus* 45ff. See also Betz (1979), 53.

[96] Quoted in Frank (2000), 14.

[97] Nelson (2000), 154.

[98] On the power of sight in relation to the cult of the saints and the sanctification of their shrines, see Hahn (1997), 1079–106.

[99] Frank (2000), 86.

Linked to Adam's blindness is the (similarly biblical) image of darkness. Adam is in darkness, Christ is in light. The second Adam brings the first out of darkness and into eternal light (VI.1.4–9):

For him night is no longer, but all is day.
The moment of dawn is born for him,
for it was in the evening that he was hidden, as it is written.
The one who fell at evening has found the illuminating ray.
He was delivered from darkness and hurries towards the dawn,
which has appeared and illumined all things.

οὐκέτι αὐτῷ νύξ,   ἀλλὰ πάντα ἡμέρα·
τὸ πρὸς πρωῒ πρωῒ   δι' αὐτὸν ἐγεννήθη·
δειλινὸν γὰρ   ἐκρύβη, ὡς γέγραπται·
εὗρεν αὐγὴν φωτίζουσαν αὐτὸν   ὁ πρὸς ἑσπέραν πεσών·
ἀπηλλάγη τοῦ γνόφου   καὶ προέφθασε πρὸς ὄρθρον
τὸν φανέντα   καὶ φωτίσαντα πάντα.

Romanos layers image upon image in this passage, associating Christ with light, appearance, illumination, day and dawn, and Adam with being hidden, with darkness, evening and night. Day is a metaphor for sinlessness, for perfection and restoration to paradise; night is a metaphor for sin and separation from God. This is once again about correction and perfection. The faults of the one who 'fell at evening' have been corrected and there is no longer any evening, but only day: Christ has imparted perfection to the human race. Perfection in this metaphor is restoration of a very physical thing: sight. Romanos argues that the physical creation is good and worth perfecting. Romanos also alludes to the illumination which takes place in baptism by his use of forms of 'illumine' (lines 7 and 9).[100] Believers come to 'see the light' through baptism.

The Senses

While sight is prominent in the *kontakia*, Romanos also uses all the other senses. *On the Nativity II* Romanos presents a 'sensory awakening'.[101] In this *kontakion*, while Mary murmurs to the Christ-child, her ancestor Eve awakes. Eve straightaway recognizes the significance of Christ's birth and tries to wake her husband, Adam. Adam is not very responsive. He distrusts the voice he hears – it led him astray once before! Eventually he wakes himself up and acknowledges that his wife was right, but not before Romanos

---

[100] On φωτίζω as enlightenment through baptism, see definition 4.b.viii in Lampe (1961), 1509.
[101] I am indebted to Frank (2005), 167–8. For an analysis of this *kontakion*, see Barkhuizen (2008b), 1–22.

has taken him through the different senses, waking them up one by one (II.5.1–10):

Adam, on hearing the words which his wife wove,
straightaway putting aside the burden from his eyelids
shakes his head as from sleep,
and, opening his ear, that which he silenced through an unwillingness to
       hear, cries out thus:
'I hear a sweet-toned noise, a delightful warbling,
but the voice of the song now does not delight me,
for it is the woman whose voice I fear,
I am in a trial, therefore I fear the feminine.
The sound enchants me since it is sweet-toned, but the instrument terrifies me,
lest, as of old, it leads me astray, bringing disgrace …'

Ἀδὰμ ἀκούσας τοὺς λόγους,   οὓς ὕφανεν ἡ σύζυγος,
    ἐκ τῶν βλεφάρων τὸ βάρος   εὐθέως ἀποθέμενος
ἀνανεύει   ὡς ἐξ ὕπνου,
    καὶ οὖς ἀνοίξας,   ὃ ἔφραξε παρακοῇ,   οὕτως βοᾷ·
'Λιγυροῦ ἀκούω κελαδήματος,   τερπνοῦ [[δὲ]] μινυρίσματος·
    ἀλλὰ τοῦ μελίσματος   νῦν ὁ φθόγγος οὐ τέρπει με·
γυνὴ γάρ ἐστι   ἧς καὶ φοβοῦμαι τὴν φωνήν·
    ἐν πείρᾳ εἰμί·   ὅθεν τὸ θῆλυ δειλιῶ·
ὁ μὲν ἦχος θέλγει με   ὡς λιγυρός,   τὸ ὄργανον δὲ δονεῖ,
    μὴ ὡς πάλαι με πλανήσῃ   ἐπιφέρουσα ὄνειδος …'

The sensory focus of this strophe is sight and hearing. Initially Adam hears the words (line 1). Then Romanos shifts to sight: Adam's eyes are burdened, but he puts aside this burden because of what he has heard (2). In line 4 he opens his eyes, but now his ears are closed (*parakoē*), a word associated with disobedience: Adam refuses to hear, or he is unwilling and resistant to hearing. Line 5 contrasts those following it. He does hear, but thinks it unwise to listen (6–8). In fact, he is afraid to use his senses. The reason becomes clear in the last few lines: the senses led him astray before. He is enchanted by the sweetness of the sound, but recognizes the instrument which makes it and recalls that that voice led him to sin and to be thrown out of paradise. Therefore he distrusts the senses. Adam does not yet realize that his senses (his humanity) have been renewed by what he is about to see and hear.

In reply to her husband's unwillingness to listen, Eve says (II.6):

'Be fully assured, my husband, by the words of your wife,
for you will not again find me advising you of bitter things.
For the old things have passed away,
and Christ the son of Mary makes all things new.

Smell his scent and straightaway bloom
like an upright ear of corn. For the spring has overtaken you.
Jesus Christ breathes out like a sweeter breeze.
Through whom, escaping the harsh burning heat,
come, follow me to Mary, and take hold of her undefiled
feet with me now, and straightaway she will have mercy,
the highly favoured one.'

Πληροφορήθητι, ἄνερ,   τοῖς λόγοις τῆς συζύγου σου·
    οὐ γὰρ εὑρήσεις με πάλιν   πικρά σοι συμβουλεύουσαν·
    τὰ ἀρχαῖα γὰρ παρῆλθε,
        καὶ νέα πάντα   δείκνυσιν ὁ τῆς Μαριὰμ   γόνος Χριστός·
    τούτου τῆς νοτίδος ὀσφράνθητι   καὶ εὐθέως ἐξάνθησον
        ὡς στάχυς ὀρθότητι·   τὸ γὰρ ἔαρ σε ἔφθασε·
    Ἰησοῦς Χριστὸς   πνέει ὡς αὖρα γλυκερά·
    τὸ καῦσος οὗ   ἀποφυγὼν τὸν αὐστηρόν,[102]
        δεῦρο ἀκολούθει μοι   πρὸς Μαριάμ,   καὶ τῶν ἀχράντων αὐτῆς
        ποδῶν ἄψαι σὺν ἐμοὶ νῦν,   καὶ εὐθέως σπλαγχνισθήσεται
    ἡ κεχαριτωμένη.

Eve recognizes the renewal of their senses: the senses are associated with
sweetness and spring imagery. She contrasts bitter and sweet: the old creation is bitter, the new is sweet. Eve implores Adam to listen (1), explaining to him that things have changed, that womankind has been redeemed
(2) and that the senses which led him astray will not do so again, since
Christ and Mary have renewed everything (3–4). This includes, although
Eve does not explicitly say so, the senses which Adam was afraid to use in
the previous strophe. Eve then tells Adam to use his sense of smell, to catch
the scent of Christ (5). Catching this scent is then followed by a few different physical images: of growth and flourishing, of feeling the sweet wind
that Christ breathes out, and escaping the heat of hell. Adam and Eve will be
restored to pleasant sensations and to abundant life. Finally, Eve mentions
touch (and perhaps by implication sight as well): they will go and see Mary
and grasp hold of her (9–10).

Adam replies, acknowledging his renewed senses (II.7),

'I recognise, O wife, the spring and I perceive the delight,
from which we fell long ago. For I also see another new paradise:
the Virgin, bearing in her bosom
the tree of life itself, which holy thing at some point

---

[102] I have followed the SC edition here, since it seems to make more sense than the reading
offered by the Oxford edition. The Oxford edition prints τὸ καῦσος οὗ ἧς ἀποφυγὼν τὸ
αὐστηρόν.

the Cherubim protected so that I did not touch it.
But now this untouched thing I see growing,
I perceived a breeze, wife, a life-making one,
which gave me breath, me being dust and breathless clay.
Now, being strengthened by its fragrance,
I am carried towards the blooming flower of our life,
the highly favoured one.'

Ἔγνων, ὦ γύναι, τὸ ἔαρ   καὶ τῆς τρυφῆς αἰσθάνομαι,
        ἧς ἐξεπέσαμεν πάλαι·   καὶ γὰρ ὁρῶ παράδεισον
    νέον ἄλλον τὴν παρθένον
        φέρουσαν κόλποις   αὐτὸ τὸ ξύλον τῆς ζωῆς,   ὅπερ ποτὲ
Χερουβὶμ ἐτήρει τὸ ἅγιον   πρὸς τὸ μὴ ψαῦσαί με·
        τοῦτο τοίνυν ἄψαυστον   ἐγὼ βλέπων φυόμενον
ᾐσθόμην πνοῆς,   σύζυγε, τῆς ζωοποιοῦ,
        τῆς κόνιν ἐμὲ   ὄντα καὶ ἄψυχον πηλὸν
    ποιησάσης ἔμψυχον·   ταύτης νυνὶ   τῇ εὐοσμίᾳ ῥωσθεὶς
        πορευθῶ πρὸς τὴν ἀνθοῦσαν   τὸν καρπὸν τῆς ζωῆς ἡμῶν,
τὴν κεχαριτωμένην.

This strophe is full of words related to seeing and perceiving. Adam's eyes have literally been opened by the incarnation, and now he is able to see Mary, who is the new paradise, the new Eden, who holds within her the new Tree of Life: Christ. After the Fall, the Cherubim guarded the Tree of Life against Adam. In lines 5 to 7 he refers to Christ as the untouchable one who has now become visible (and therefore touchable), as a result of the incarnation. Adam also feels a breeze which he associates with the life-giving breath of the first creation: the new creation mimics the first. Finally, Adam draws attention to smell: the fragrance of Christ sustains and strengthens him. In fact, sweet fragrance here is even more powerful – it carries Adam along to meet Mary and her child.

Throughout these three strophes of *On the Nativity II*, Romanos sets up an extended awakening of Adam's senses. The physical senses Adam mistrusts initially become the way in which God in Christ is revealed to him, once again emphasizing the goodness of God's creation. The senses were all part of the originally perfect creation of human nature. As they are healed and made perfect anew, human nature is remade again to be fit for heaven. The perfected senses are once again vehicles for human–divine interaction. Through the second Adam, human nature is corrected and perfected, recreating the bond between God and humanity.

Thirst and Hunger

The brokenness of humanity is also figured by thirst and hunger, and their cure is a metaphor for the perfection of humanity. In *On the Nativity I*, Mary relieves the thirst of Adam and David because she has given birth to Christ (I.1.5–8):

There [i.e. in Bethlehem] is found an undug spring,
from which David once desired to drink.
There a virgin, giving birth to a child,
straightaway stops the thirst of Adam and David.

ἐκεῖ ηὑρέθη   φρέαρ ἀνόρυκτον,
οὗ πιεῖν Δαβὶδ   πρὶν ἐπεθύμησεν·
ἐκεῖ παρθένος   τεκοῦσα βρέφος
     τὴν δίψαν ἔπαυσεν εὐθὺς   τὴν τοῦ Ἀδὰμ καὶ τοῦ Δαβίδ·

This passage alludes to 2 Samuel (23:13–17), in which David wishes to drink at the well of Bethlehem. Three of his men break through the Philistine camp and bring back some water, but David refuses to drink it, saying that it is the blood of the three men who risked their lives to get it. Lifeblood is for God alone, so David pours it out as a sacrifice.[103] This is a type for Christ's sacrifice on the cross: Christ is the well and the 'blood' is Christ's which, through the crucifixion and eucharist, quenches the thirst of Adam, David and all human-ity. Christ's thirst-quenching ability is reminiscent of the story of the Samaritan woman (cf. John 4 and Romanos' *kontakion* IX), in which Christ offers the woman water which will quench her thirst forever. He is this living water.

As we have seen, a key feature of Romanos' imagery is its excess. This passage also resonates with the story of the Israelites thirsting in the desert (Exodus 17:1–7). The Israelites complained of unbearable thirst; God caused water to come forth from a rock to save them. This was also an 'undug spring' which quenched the thirst of David's ancestors when they desired to drink. The image of Mary as the 'undug spring' also recalls the passage from Song of Songs (4:12) which refers to a locked garden and a sealed fountain. The excess of resonances represents the overflowing excess of God's saving actions for humanity.

The reference to Adam is again a reference to all broken humanity, and thirst a metaphor for human need, which can only truly be met by Christ. In fact, Christ *stops* this need. By becoming the second Adam he enables the divinization of humanity, and so renders human bodily needs irrelevant.

---

[103] Robinson (1993), 280.

Similarly, hunger is human sin in *On the Beheading of John the Baptist* (XXXVIII.18.8–11):

> And we are Christ's,
> who willingly fasted and so took away from us
> the ancient hunger, which Adam craved for
> as a transient pleasure.

> ἡμεῖς δὲ Χριστοῦ
> τοῦ νηστεύσαντος βουλήσει   καὶ ἀφελόντος ἡμῶν
> τὴν πεῖναν τὴν ἀρχαίαν,   ἣν ἐπείνασεν Ἀδάμ
> διὰ τέρψιν τὴν πρόσκαιρον.

The transient pleasures of Adam, bodily delights connected with sin, rightfully come to an end in Christ's redemption of humanity. Romanos contrasts Christ's obedience and holiness with Adam's disobedience and excess. Christ's fasting recapitulates Adam's excessive physical hunger, transforming it into a spiritual hunger for God.

Writing

The perfection and correction of humanity is fundamentally achieved in God's forgiveness of human sin. We have seen that, in *On the Adoration of the Cross*, Romanos makes the cross into an inscription, a royal pardon for the good thief (XXIII.11.1–2, 5–6). In *On Peter's Denial*, Romanos refers to that forgiveness as a legal written pardon, inscribed on Christ's body. Christ says to Peter (XVIII.7.5–10):

> For taking a pen in this [hand], I begin to write
> forgiveness for all who come from Adam.
> My flesh which you see will become like papyrus for me,
> and my blood [like] black [ink],[104] where I dip [my pen] and write,
> allotting the perpetual gift to those who cry,
> 'Hurry, holy one, save your flock.'

> ταύτῃ γὰρ κάλαμον λαβὼν   ἄρχομαι γράφειν
> συγχώρησιν πᾶσι   τοῖς ἐκ τοῦ Ἀδάμ·
> ἡ σάρξ μου ἣν ὁρᾷς ὥσπερ χάρτης   γίνεται μοί,
> καὶ τὸ αἷμα μου μέλαν,   ὅθεν βάπτω καὶ γράφω
> δωρεὰν   νέμων ἀδιάδοχον τοῖς κράζουσι·
> 'σπεῦσον, σῶσον,   ἅγιε, τὴν ποίμνην σου.'

---

[104] Literally 'black', but I think ink is what is meant here. See Lash's translation of this hymn: Lash (1995), 132.

God as the Word inscribes his pardon of humanity upon his own flesh. Romanos makes a clever intertextual word play when he chooses *kalamos* (the word for the stick used to strike Jesus and to give him sour wine) as his pen.[105] Christ's flesh is a metaphor for his death, for the crucifixion. By his death on the cross, Christ obtains a universal pardon for human sin. In line 8 Romanos has Christ talk about his blood, with which he will write the pardon on his flesh. It is through this bloody ink that Christ allots the perpetual gift of salvation. As Krueger points out, this passage also has smatterings of legal vocabulary associated with pardoning.[106] 'Forgiveness' here is *synchōrēsis*, the word for a legal pardon, and 'allotting' (*nemōn*) was used of judges dealing out punishments or pardons. The legal metaphor makes it more vivid for the congregation, who may well have been familiar with such vocabulary from civic duties or imperial decrees. Pardoning suggests correction of wrongs and perfection of humanity, bringing humans into a different relationship with God.

Another important referent in this metaphor is the eucharist. Through references to flesh and blood Romanos makes his congregation recall their participation in the eucharist and that it is through the eucharist (which is itself a participation in Christ's death and resurrection) that they are saved.[107]

Doctoring and Illness

Just as he uses legal imagery to appeal to certain groups in his congregation, so Romanos also makes use of medical metaphors.[108] The doctoring or surgery of Christ (Christ's redemptive actions) is contrasted with the ill-health (sin and brokenness) of Adam. Medical healing was closely associated with spiritual healing in Byzantium and therefore, as Krueger points out, medical imagery was not uncommonly used in theological writings.[109] Romanos fits into this tradition.

In *On the Crucifixion,* Romanos makes Christ's body into a surgery from which he heals Adam's illness (XXI.1.1–3):

[105] Krueger (2003), 5, (2004), 161.
[106] Krueger (2003), 5.
[107] Romanos may also be making use of the belief that the writings of a holy man were sacred. On which, see Rapp (2007), 194–222.
[108] On the use of medical imagery in Romanos, and its significance in Byzantine society more generally, see Krueger (2010), 119–30. See also Barkhuizen (1993), 45–7, Mulard (2011), 290–377, Schork (1960).
[109] Krueger (2010), 121–8. Ephrem the Syrian, for example, associated Christ with medical healing: Murray (2006), 200.

Seeing the surgery of Christ opened
and from it health gushing forth for Adam
the devil suffered – he was stung ...

τὸ τοῦ Χριστοῦ ἰατρεῖον   βλέπων ἀνεῳγμένον
    καὶ τὴν ἐκ τούτου τῷ Ἀδὰμ   πηγάζουσαν ὑγείαν
ἔπαθεν, ἐπλήγη ὁ διάβολος ...

The devil watches the crucifixion and sees the body of Christ as a doctor's rooms. Christ's body is opened – pierced by the staff – and salvation gushes out for Adam. Romanos uses a medical metaphor to talk about the recurring theme of Christ's correction and perfection of human life, his redemption of broken humanity. Christ corrects Adam's sin: sin is sickness, and it is healed by Christ's crucifixion and resurrection. This is also the perfection of human life, restoring humanity to the image of the divine. We also see imagery of redemption and punishment again: Adam is redeemed (cured) and the devil is punished (stung, wounded).

This type of medical imagery is used extensively in *On Mary at the Cross*.[110] In strophes 9 and 10, Christ explains to Mary why he must die: because of Adam's sickness (XIX.10.1–6):

Because of profligacy, because of gluttony,
Adam became sick and was carried down to lowest Hades,
and there he mourns the pain of his soul.
And Eve, having once taught him disorder,
groans with him. For with him she is sick,
so that together they might learn to keep the doctor's orders.

Ὑπὸ ἀσωτίας,   ὑπ' ἀδηφαγίας
    ἀρρωστήσας ὁ Ἀδὰμ   κατηνέχθη ἕως Ἅιδου   κατωτάτου
    καὶ ἐκεῖ τὸν τῆς ψυχῆς   πόνον δακρύει.
Εὔα δὲ ἡ τοῦτον   ἐκδιδάξασα ποτὲ   τὴν ἀταξίαν
    σὺν τούτῳ στενάζει·   σὺν αὐτῷ γὰρ ἀρρωστεῖ,
    ἵνα μάθωσιν ἅμα   τοῦ φυλάττειν ἰατροῦ παραγγελίαν·

Adam and Eve's sin is presented as one of gluttony and it causes physical illness:[111] they gorged themselves on the fruit in the garden and now have terrible stomach aches. Romanos sees their sickness as a means of instruction, a way of teaching them to follow God's precepts. And these orders are the same for all humanity: keep away from sin and live. Living the life of Christ is the healthy way; sin leads to illness, pain and death.

---

[110] See Krueger (2010), 120–1.
[111] Krueger (2010), 120.

Later Christ explains how he will cure the sick Adam and all humanity (XIX.13.2–4):

... I dress like a doctor[112] and come to the place where they lie,
and I treat their wounds,
cutting with a blade their calluses and scabs.

   ... καθάπερ ἰατρὸς   ἀποδύομαι καὶ φθάνω   ὅπου κεῖνται,
   καὶ ἐκείνων τὰς πληγὰς   περιοδεύω,
τέμνων ἐν τῇ λόγχῃ   τὰ πωρώματα αὐτῶν   καὶ τὴν σκληρίαν·

The descent into hell becomes a doctor's visit.[113] The doctoring image makes sin into a callus which should be cut off from the body. The body needs to be purged of the scabrous sin which has become attached to it. Skin diseases were considered particularly representative of human sin in the New Testament. Lepers were ostracized and their sin blamed for their disease. Romanos makes use of this tradition in his presentation of humanity's sin. Through his imagery of disease and healing, Romanos preaches that the actions of humanity are counteracted or 'healed' by Christ.

Romanos' use of metaphor can mirror, embody and explain the restoration of humanity in the person of Christ. The metaphor of Christ as the gate which reopens paradise emphasizes that Christ, as the second Adam, corrects the sin of the first Adam and returns humanity to paradise. By using the metaphor of nakedness for human sinfulness, Romanos highlights the summing up (correcting and perfecting) of human existence which Jesus does in his incarnation. When he assumed human nakedness, Christ took on all the faults and sins of the human race, enabling humans to be reclothed in sinlessness, in the 'God-woven robe'. This metaphor also draws attention to the union of humans with God which takes place in the inauguration of the new creation and its consummation. The metaphors of blindness and the senses, as well as illustrating correction and perfection, generally signal the renewed goodness of the new creation: God has not rejected his creation but comes to redeem it. This is also evident in the use of hunger and thirst as metaphors for sinfulness. Through Christ human sin is corrected and human bodily needs are perfected; bodily hunger is replaced by spiritual hunger which is fed by Christ. Perfection in particular is emphasized by both writing and doctoring metaphors: Christ pardons and redeems humanity; Christ heals sick Adam.

---

[112] Literally 'as a doctor I strip off'. Lash suggests doctors may have been naked in some cases. See Lash (1995), 148 n. 28.

[113] Krueger (2010), 120–1.

Conclusions

Romanos' account of the restoration of humanity by Christ the second Adam resonates with many strands of the earlier Christian tradition. It is grounded in biblical arguments and imagery, most fundamentally drawing on Paul. But Romanos' use of biblical images also comes from the Gospels and continually draws on Old Testament narratives to interpret and add meaning to New Testament metaphors while displaying the consistency of God's promises throughout salvation history. The great exchange – that God became human that humans might become God, seen clearly in Paul, elaborated on by Irenaeus and foundational for thinkers including Athanasius, the Cappadocians and contemporary homilists – pervades Romanos' *kontakia*. Romanos follows this tradition in claiming that God became human in the person of Jesus Christ in order to correct human wrongs and perfect the human race; his emphasis on salvation in employing this connection between Adam and Christ also demonstrates his concern to proclaim established orthodoxy about the nature of Christ.

Romanos uses typology to link Adam with Christ and Eve with Mary, demonstrating that the latter corrects and fulfils the former. Adam and Eve are made perfect through Christ (and, to a lesser extent, Mary). Similarly, the cross on which Christ was crucified is linked, typologically, to the tree in paradise, either redeeming the sin associated with the tree (of knowledge), or restoring those taken away from the tree (of life) to their rightful place. Typology rhetorically performs the summing up of humanity in the second Adam and the consequent healing of human nature, since its two parts are matched and mirrored without being made equivalent. In a similar way structural and linguistic comparisons allow Romanos to demonstrate the exchange which takes place.

The way metaphor operates also mimics this exchange, since it puts one thing in terms of another while always preserving an excess of meaning which maintains the transcendent gap between the saving God and healed humanity. If metaphor is a speech act which creates the otherwise unspeakable or unimaginable, the incarnation similarly is, for Romanos, an event in human experience which alters human reality. Here, as elsewhere, the form of metaphor performs the reality of the second Adam's salvific acts. Romanos makes use of multiple metaphors: opening, clothing, blindness, the senses more generally, thirst, writing and healing. The correction of human sin is figured in the image of reopening paradise which had been closed by sin, in Christ's assumption of human nakedness, in the blindness of Adam which Christ turns into sight, in the written pardon of human sins, in Christ's healing of Adam's illness. These are inextricably linked with the perfection of humanity, to which Romanos draws attention perhaps especially in the redemption of Adam's senses, the cure of human thirst and the cure of human sickness. It is through Christ's incarnation that the correction and perfection of humanity are effected, and this is the inauguration of the new creation. God did not abandon his first creation, but comes to redeem and renew it. The reopening of paradise emphasizes this – the new creation is open to humanity. Likewise, Romanos develops this theme through the metaphors of clothing, in which the reclothing of humanity enables the restoration of proper relations between God and humanity; blindness and the other senses, through which Romanos accentuates the goodness of God's creation; writing, in which the 'perpetual gift' signals a new reality. Once again, these are closely connected to the concept of the consummation of the final kingdom. Romanos argues that the final consummation of the new reality is still to come and urges his congregation to watch and be ready for it. The time before then is still a time of mourning, according to the clothing metaphor, because of the separation between God and humanity. But Christ will return to strip humanity of its garb of mourning and reclothe them in the 'God-woven robe'.

3 | The Second Creation: A New Reality for Christians

So if anyone is in Christ, there is a new creation:
everything old has passed away; see, everything has become new.

2 Cor. 5:17

In his second epistle to the Church of Corinth the apostle Paul argued that creation had been renewed through the incarnation, life, death and resurrection of Christ.[1] Christ overcame sin and death and, through the resurrection, Christ recreates creation.[2] He has reconciled the world to himself (2 Cor. 5:19), so humans have a new relationship with God; there is a new covenant, a new creation.[3] This is a consistent Pauline theme. In the letter to the Romans (6:4) Paul writes:

Therefore we have been buried with him by baptism into death, so that, just as Christ was raised from the dead by the glory of the Father, so we too might walk in newness of life.

This 'newness of life' is the changed world in which Christians are called to participate. And the life they participate in is Christ's life.[4] Christians are all too obviously not in paradise,[5] but Paul demands this new way of living in the new reality before paradise.[6] The old creation and covenant are connected with death, whereas the new creation is life (Romans 7:5–6).[7]

This concept of a second creation, a renewal of the old, was crucial for Christian theology from the earliest theologians.[8] Irenaeus argued that as a result of the incarnation humans are now able to participate in paradise, in incorruption.[9] God became human for this reason. The invisible became visible so that humans might see it and be part of it. The idea

---

[1] See also Galatians 6:15, Romans 7:6 and Ephesians 4:24.
[2] Best (1987), 54.
[3] Barnett (1997), 298.
[4] Savage (1996), 177.
[5] Paul believed there would only be a short period between Christ's resurrection and his second coming: Fredriksen (2000), 128.
[6] Byrne (1996), 190.
[7] See also Byrne (1996), 212.
[8] See, for example, Justin Martyr's *Dialogue with Trypho* XI, XXIV.
[9] *The Proof of the Apostolic Preaching* section 31. See further Chapter 2, above.

of new creation is bound up in that of new covenant for Irenaeus. The covenant God made with the Hebrew people (the Law) is the old covenant, and it has been surpassed by the new (Christian life as set out in the Gospels), which renews and revitalizes the earth and human existence.[10] God has made a fresh start, a new beginning, through the death of his son on the cross.[11]

The themes of new creation, renewal and new identity in Christ also colour the writings of theologians closer in time to Romanos. Cyril of Alexandria explored such themes in his commentaries on Isaiah, various other Old Testament prophets, the Gospels and the letters of Paul. For Cyril, the new reality exists because of Christ, who has transformed the old. In his commentary on the Gospel of John, Cyril argues that Paul was right to claim that there is a new creation in 2 Corinthians 5:17:[12]

For he [Christ] renews us, and restores us to a certain newness of life, which is untrodden and not worn out by others.[13]

ἀνακαινίζει γὰρ ἡμᾶς, καὶ ἀναπλάττει τρόπον τινὰ πρὸς καινότητα ζωῆς, ἀστιβῆ δὲ καὶ τοῖς ἄλλοις οὐ τετριμμένην

Cyril's belief in the new creation also informs his exegesis: God becoming man is a world-changing event. Consequently, it makes no sense to interpret the past without reference to the incarnation. For Cyril, in common with other early Christians, a christological interpretation of the Old Testament is the only coherent one. So Old Testament figures like Abraham, Joseph and Moses in different ways prefigure Christ and events from the New Testament. The life of Christ is the fulfilment of all past events, which have been looking forward to his coming.

Ephrem the Syrian speaks of the new covenant in his poem *The Paradoxes of the Incarnation* (*Res.* 1.11.3–5):

From His own mouth He gave a new imprint,
giving us the New Covenant.
Blessed is its Giver![14]

ܡܢ ܦܘܡܗ ܐܛܒܥ ܛܒܥܐ ܚܕܬܐ
ܕܝܬܒ ܠܢ ܕܝܬܩܐ ܚܕܬܐ
ܒܪܝܟ ܝܗܘܒܗ

---

[10] See *Against Heresies* 4.9.1 and 5.33.1. See also Osborn (2001), 88.

[11] Osborn (2001), 102.

[12] See also Wilken (2003), 19–20.

[13] *Commentary on John* 2.384, lines 13–15. See also Young (2003), 61. Young argues that Cyril saw recreation as absolutely central to Paul's theology.

[14] Translation taken from Brock and Kiraz (2006), 87.

In Genesis, the creation of the world is a speech act: God spoke and it happened. Ephrem fashions the new creation in the same way. And many of Ephrem's other compositions demonstrate the changes which have taken place because of Christ, focusing either on the incarnation or the crucifixion.

The new creation is also mentioned in the Akathistos hymn, which has been variously dated to between the fourth and the sixth centuries (13.1–2):[15]

The Creator, having appeared, has revealed a new creation
to us, who were brought into being by him.[16]

Νέαν ἔδειξε κτίσιν ἐμφανίσας ὁ κτίστης
ἡμῖν τοῖς ὑπ' αὐτοῦ γενομένοις[17]

In these lines the new creation is both Christ himself, who reveals himself when he appears on earth, and a new order instituted when the Creator appeared on earth as Jesus Christ.

All of these Christian thinkers believe that a radical change in reality took place at the incarnation. There is a new creation. And yet they also wait expectantly for the second coming of Jesus, which will change reality again and restore humanity to paradise. Basil, among others, therefore argued for three 'creations': creation from nothing, when God brought the universe into being; the new creation instituted at the incarnation, when God made reality better than it had been; and the final new creation, the resurrection of the dead.[18]

From this necessarily brief excursus into early Christian thought, it should be clear that there was a considerable tradition upon which Romanos could draw for his conception of the new creation. For Romanos, the inauguration of a new reality, a second creation, means a fundamental change in reality. The incarnation, crucifixion and resurrection are events which transcend normal temporal boundaries. The Old Testament world-view was governed by prophecies, looking forward to the coming Messiah; the Old foretells the New through typology. Now that the Messiah has come, in Christ, the time of prophecy has come to an end. All previous history led up to the advent of Christ: Christ fulfils and surpasses the old.

[15] There is considerable debate over the date of this famous hymn. Most recently, Leena Mari Peltomaa dates it to before 451, arguing that the descriptions of the incarnation, virgin birth and the use of the term Theotokos are Ephesian in character and are clearly pre-Chalcedonian: Peltomaa (2001), 100–1, 14. Against Peltomaa and in favour of the post-Chalcedonian date, see Constas (2005), esp. 357–8.

[16] See also 1.15–16.

[17] Text used is Peltomaa (2001), 10.

[18] *Epistle 8*. See also Wilken (1971), 164.

In *On the Epiphany,* key themes are paradise and renewal (VI.16):

He utterly obscured gloomy night and revealed everything as noon.
He shone upon the inhabited world, the light without evening,

Jesus our saviour.

The land of Zebulun is prosperous and imitates paradise,
for a torrent of luxury waters her,
and an ever-living river swells in her
which the first [people] did not find, although they dug
a well of the oath, the well of Sychem, but not the source of life.
But in Galilee we see the living spring:
the One who appeared and illuminated everything.

Νύκτα ἠφάνισε τὴν ἀμειδῆ   καὶ ἔδειξε μεσημβρίαν τὸ πᾶν·

   κατηύγασε τὴν οἰκουμένην   τὸ ἀνέσπερον φῶς,

Ἰησοῦς ὁ σωτὴρ ἡμῶν·

χώρα Ζαβουλωνία   ἔστιν ἐν εὐθηνίᾳ   καὶ μιμεῖται παράδεισον·

   ποτίζει γὰρ αὐτὴν   τῆς τρυφῆς ὁ χείμαρρους,

   καὶ βρύει ἐν αὐτῇ   τὸ ἀείζωον νᾶμα,

   ὃ οἱ πρῶτοι   οὐχ εὗρον ὀρύξαντες

φρέαρ τοῦ ὅρκου, φρέαρ τῆς Συχέμ,   ἀλλ' οὐ πηγὴν τῆς ζωῆς·

   ἐν δὲ τῇ Γαλιλαίᾳ   φλέβα ζῶσαν θεωροῦμεν

τὸν φανέντα   καὶ φωτίσαντα πάντα.

This passage establishes Christ's new reality as a second creation. This creation is marked by transformation. The world was in perpetual darkness, perpetual night, until Christ came along (lines 1–2). Christ transformed the night into day, just as God separated night and day in the first creation (Genesis 1:1–5). The first creation is a type for the second. The metaphors of perpetual night (i.e. sinfulness) and everlasting day (i.e. redeemed perfect life) signal a fundamental change in reality: Christ has transformed the world from one reality to its exact opposite: night is hidden away and the eternal day is revealed. This change is symbolic of other significant changes which take place in the new reality.

The change from sinfulness to perfection, symbolized by the transformation from darkness to light is emphasized by the reference to Zebulun's land.[19] Zebulun was one of the sons of Jacob and Leah (Gen. 30:20), and it was prophesized that he would settle by the sea and his land would be a haven for ships (Gen. 49:13). His land was part of Galilee. Isaiah (9:1–2) prophesies the glorification of Galilee, making reference to Zebulun:

But there will be no gloom for those who were in anguish. In the former time he brought into contempt the land of Zebulun and the land of Naphtali, but in the

---

[19]   Romanos refers to the same prophecy in *On the Baptism of Christ* (V.1).

latter time he will make glorious the way of the sea, the land beyond the Jordan, Galilee of the nations. The people who walked in darkness have seen a great light; those who lived in a land of deep darkness – on them light has shined.

In Matthew's Gospel (4:13–16), and for Romanos in the passage above, Christ is the fulfilment of Isaiah's prophecy:

He left Nazareth and made his home in Capernaum by the sea, in the territory of Zebulun and Naphtali, so that what had been spoken through the prophet Isaiah might be fulfilled: 'Land of Zebulun, Land of Naphtali, on the road by the sea, across the Jordan, Galilee of the Gentiles – the people who sat in darkness have seen a great light, and for those who sat in the region and shadow of death light has dawned.'

Romanos' reference to Zebulun recalls the prophecy and its fulfilment in Christ and links these passages strongly through Christ's role as the light which conquers the darkness. Romanos draws on this prophecy for a *kontakion* celebrating the feast of the epiphany because of the imagery of light and dark – it fits well with the revelation of Jesus as God which took place at his baptism. Christ destroys the darkness which envelops the land of Zebulun and makes that which was previously in contempt and gloom into a blossoming paradise. The dry and barren land is transformed into a land of luxurious abundance, watered by Christ.

This abundance or plenty is also a quality of the first creation. In the first creation God tells the first man and woman: 'See, I have given you every plant yielding seed that is upon the face of the earth, and every tree with seed in its fruit; you shall have them for food' (Genesis 1:29); and 'You may freely eat of every tree in the garden' (Genesis 2:16). There is a sense of abundance and freedom in these images of paradise. And the contrast between Eden and the life for Adam and Eve outside the garden is characterized by barren land and hard work (Genesis 3:17–19):

… cursed is the ground because of you; in toil you shall eat of it all the days of your life; thorns and thistles it shall bring forth for you; and you shall eat the plants of the field. By the sweat of your face you shall eat bread until you return to the ground.

Romanos has these stories in mind when he uses the word 'prosperity' (*euthenia*) to describe the land after the incarnation. His depiction of luxurious and ever-living waters in lines 4 and 5 likewise recalls the descriptions of paradise in Genesis. Water is said to nourish the earth in Genesis 2:6: 'but a stream would rise from the earth, and water the whole face of the earth'. And the river which flows out of Eden becomes the life-giving waters of four great rivers (Pishon, Gihon, Tigris and Euphrates) (Genesis 2:10–14). As a result of God's descent to earth, the earth looks more like paradise. In Christ we have the truly everlasting spring, the 'source of life'.

But it is not quite paradise yet. Romanos says that the land 'imitates paradise' (3). Romanos uses his *kontakion* to proclaim a dramatic change inaugurated by the incarnation, but recognizes that he still lives in a broken world. He acknowledges his own brokenness and sinfulness in a number of his hymns (e.g. LVI.7.1–3), and talks about the sins of the people and the wrath of God explicitly in *On Earthquakes and Fires* (e.g. LIV.11.4; 13.1–5). The world has been transformed by Christ's incarnation, but it is not yet paradise. Romanos lives rather in a period of anticipation of paradise and the confirmation of its promise. Present time is a confirmation of the glories of paradise and this confirmation is brought about through imitation and anticipation. The land 'imitates paradise' by awaiting the final consummation of the new creation. This is a time in which prophecies are fulfilled and the people of Christ are called to participate in his life, but the last judgement is still to come. Romanos and his congregation are still awaiting the second coming of Christ.[20] This will be the focus of Chapter 4.

Lines 6 and 7 of our passage are about the Jews. The Jews did not find the ever-living water, even though they dug the well of Sychem (or 'Sychar'). In John's Gospel, Jesus meets the Samaritan woman in the city of Sychar, at Jacob's well (John 4:5–6). When Jesus tells the woman he will give her living water, she says 'Sir, you have no bucket, and the well is deep. Where do you get that living water? Are you greater than our ancestor Jacob, who gave us the well …?' (John 4:11–12). Jesus responds that the water he gives is eternally thirst-quenching, unlike the water of Jacob's well (John 4:13–14). John illustrates Christ's fulfilment and perfection of past events: Jacob gave water, but Christ gives ever-living water. Romanos alludes to this story to set up a comparison between Jews and Christians. Jews rely on ordinary water from the well of Jacob; they do not recognize the 'source of life'. But Christians, following the example of the Samaritan woman, realize that the well of Sychem is nothing in comparison to the living water offered by Christ.

These themes are developed in Romanos' hymn *On the Samaritan Woman*, when he has the woman declare the arrival of the new creation (IX.10.6–8):[21]

Let what has grown old be idle and the new things flourish.
Let momentary things pass by, for the moment has come[22]

---

[20] Romanos describes what he thinks will happen at the last judgement in his hymn *On the Second Coming* (XXXIV). On Byzantine apocalyptic literature, see Alexander (1985).

[21] Hunger suggests that it is the newness of Christianity, which the woman talks about in this passage: Hunger (1981), 42. This seems to miss the point. Christianity is new and Judaism old, but it is the fact that Christians are part of the new creation and Jews are not which is important here.

[22] In order to maintain the word play in the Greek, I have followed Grosdidier de Maton's translation: Grosdidier de Matons (1965), 339.

for the water which you have.
Let this [water] abound and water me ...

ἀργείτω τὰ γηράσαντα   καὶ ἀνθείτω τὰ νέα·
παρέλθῃ τὰ πρὸς ὥραν·   καὶ γὰρ ἦλθεν ἡ ὥρα
                                                τοῦ ὕδατος οὗ ἔχεις·
τοῦτο βρυέτω   καὶ ἀρδευέτω   ἐμοὶ ...

The woman recognizes that a significant change has taken place and that now is a time for new things. The water of Jacob which sufficed for so long is now one of the things which pass by. It has been surpassed by the water of Christ. There are baptismal overtones in 'water me' which link baptism with paradise.

And Christ not only *offers* 'the living water', he *is* this water. In line 8 of our passage from *On the Epiphany* Romanos says that 'we' (i.e. Christians) see the 'living spring' in Galilee: Christ. 'Spring' (*phleps*) can also refer to a vein or artery, and so carries with it the sense of 'life-force'. Christ is the living life-force. This reference to water also recalls the baptism of Christ, which is celebrated on the feast of the epiphany. At his baptism, Christ entered the depths of human sin – represented by the descent into the waters of the Jordan – and brought light to that place of darkness. Christian baptism is therefore an entry into Christ's life and into the new creation.

This passage ends with a look back to its beginning. Romanos' statement that Christ has illuminated everything (9), recalls the first two lines (e.g. 'he revealed everything as noon', 1). Partly this reflects the focus on light in this hymn, *On the Epiphany*, which celebrates the revelation of Christ as the Son of God. The epiphany of God is figured using a plethora of light imagery, drawing on the strong metaphorical connections in Greek literature between light, illumination, sight and knowledge. The hymn also has a cyclical pattern to it which might reflect Romanos' view of time after the incarnation. As we will see in greater detail in the next chapter, time is changed after the incarnation: events no longer occur in a linear fashion and significant events in the life of Christ are re-presented in the liturgical year. But the point is not that time is cyclical rather than linear. Instead, Romanos makes the present time understood christologically, so that present experience is shaped by liturgical time which is generated by christology and which insists on the new creation.

From this brief analysis of one passage, we get a picture of Romanos' thought in relation to new creation. The incarnation is a world-changing event; the world pre-incarnation is a very different place to that post-incarnation. As we will see shortly, he uses various rhetorical techniques, primarily paradox, to illustrate how miraculous and world-changing the incarnation is, in its fullest sense. For Romanos, the incarnation, understood as the life, death and resurrection of Christ, is the point at which the new creation begins, the fulfilment of all preceding history. Prophecies from the Old Testament are fulfilled in Christ. And indeed all the time which the Old Testament represents pointed towards a Messiah and in Christ this period is fulfilled and surpassed. All history has led up to the point of Christ's descent to earth.

Paradox

The concept of new creation is bound up in paradox for Romanos, who is connected to earlier traditions of liturgical poetry and theology. Themes and images apparent in the hymns of Ephrem the Syrian will help to situate Romanos' distinctive proclamation of the new creation through paradox, and point to shared concerns. Ephrem the Syrian particularly emphasized paradoxes of the incarnation and virgin birth. He wrote hymns entitled *On the Paradox of Mary's Birthgiving* (*Nat.* 11) and *The Paradoxes of the Incarnation* (*Res.* 1),[23] which focus on the miracle of God becoming human. To take an example from the latter (*Res.* 1.9, lines 1 and 4):

Mary bore Him as a child …
heaven bore Him as God.[24]

ܛܥܢܬ݂ ܠܗ ܡܪܝܡ ܐܝܟ ܝܠܘܕܐ…
ܫܡܝܐ ܛܥܢܬܗ݂ ܐܝܟ ܐܠܗܐ…

Ephrem heightens the paradox by using the same construction and verb (*t'n*). The lowliness of the child Mary bears is contrasted with the greatness of a God who dwells in heaven.

Similarly, in *On the Paradox of Mary's Birthgiving*, Ephrem sings (*Nat.* 11.6),

Your mother is a cause for wonder: the Lord entered into her
and became a servant; He who is the Word entered
– and became silent within her; Thunder entered her
– and made no sound; there entered the Shepherd of all,
and in her He became the Lamb, bleating as He came forth.[25]

---

[23] Texts and translations of these two hymns can be found in Brock and Kiraz (2006), 39–45, 79–95.
[24] Translation modified from Brock and Kiraz (2006), 87.
[25] Translation taken from Brock and Kiraz (2006), 45.

ܐܟܣܪܝܐ ܣܪ, ܐܡܟ ܝܟ ܠܐ ܚܠ ܟܪܝܐ
ܘܚܡܐ ܟܪܝܟ ܝܟ ܠܐ ܚܠܝܠܗ
ܘܟܠܝ, ܟܝܚܘ ܝܟ ܠܐ ܚܡܝܢܘܪ
ܘܟܝܐ ܠܗ ܟ ܝܟ ܠܐ ܚܪܝ ܟܪ ܗܐܠ
ܐܪܝܟܪ ܗܡ ܗܐ ܟܪ ܢܣܐ ܗ ܟܗܪ ܐܚܪ

In this passage, Ephrem uses a repetitive structure and enjambment to emphasize the paradoxical nature of the incarnation. The final phrase of each line (beginning with the preposition *'al*) is connected to the first phrase of the next line by a connecting particle. The enjambment in particular strengthens the contrast being made: the Lord became a servant, the Word is silent, Thunder makes no sound, Shepherd becomes the Lamb.

For Romanos, as for Ephrem, paradox is an appropriate device to demonstrate the change in reality occasioned by the incarnation. Divine and human – previously mutually exclusive – now exist in a strange sort of harmony. In *On the Presentation in the Temple*, Romanos has angels express the paradoxical nature of what they are seeing (IV.1.4–6):[26]

Now we see marvels and paradoxes, incomprehensible, unspeakable.
For the one who created Adam is lifted up as a child.
The uncontainable is contained in the arms of the old man.

Θαυμαστὰ θεωροῦμεν νυνὶ καὶ παράδοξα,

ἀκατάληπτα, ἄφραστα·

ὁ τὸν Ἀδὰμ γὰρ   δημιουργήσας   βαστάζεται ὡς βρέφος·
ὁ ἀχώρητος χωρεῖται   ἐν ἀγκάλαις τοῦ πρεσβύτου·

The assonance, alliteration and use of cognates in this passage emphasize the disbelief of the angels and highlight the paradox. The incarnation has combined realities which even the heavenly beings thought incompatible. On this paradox, see further below.

As we have seen, paradox is not merely a descriptive tool, it is actually a vehicle for this changed reality.[27] Romanos uses paradox to enact the change by bringing two incompatible things together. His use of paradox, by joining together things irreconcilable before the incarnation, dynamically performs the change which has taken place as a result of God's incarnation. For instance, in *On the Nativity I*, Romanos unites two incompatible truths: 1. God is the Father of Mary; 2. He became the son of Mary (I.2.1):

The Father of the mother of his own accord became her son.

Ὁ πατὴρ τῆς μητρὸς   γνώμῃ υἱὸς ἐγένετο·

---

[26] On the increasing importance of angels in late antique homiletics, see Allen (1998), 210.
[27] See Chapter 1 above.

The physical impossibility that these two statements could be simultaneously true exercises Romanos here. He combines the contradictory statements in the one line, paradoxically juxtaposing them just as Father and Son are paradoxically one in God and Mary is both daughter and mother of the one God.

Likewise, in *On the Mission of the Apostles* (XXXI.3.3–4):

Those who were fishermen before Christ are also fishermen after Christ,
those who did converse with the sea, now gush out sweet words …

οἱ πρὸ Χριστοῦ   ἁλιεῖς καὶ μετὰ τὸν Χριστὸν ἁλιεῖς,
οἱ ἅλμῃ   συνομιλοῦντες   καὶ γλυκὺ ῥῆμα νῦν ἐρευγόμενοι

Fishermen are now able to speak beautifully! Christ gave the most poorly educated and least erudite of society the ability to speak 'sweet words'. Pre-incarnation fishermen never had this ability, but only 'conversed with the sea' – we can imagine the slang and coarse language of ill-educated seamen – but because of Christ their speech has been transformed: they now preach the Gospel. The fishermen 'gush out' the sweet words just as the sea gushes out foam or fish.[28] Romanos uses Jesus' fishing metaphor for proselytizing (Matthew 4:19), while opposing 'before Christ' with 'after Christ': the men are still fishermen, but before Christ they fished for fish, whereas after Christ they fish for people. The paradox drives home the changed reality.

Romanos follows this paradox up with another, later in the hymn: 'and Athenians will be defeated by Galileans' (καὶ ἡττῶνται Ἀθηναῖοι Γαλιλαίοις) (XXXI.16.3). The 'Athenians' are pagans and the Galileans Christians, but the former could have multiple specific referents: those teaching in the philosophical and rhetorical schools in Athens, those educated in the same schools, or particular important philosophers. In any case, these Athenians represent the best-educated and most well-spoken people in the empire, and they are beaten in speech by lowly, uneducated Galileans.[29]

The most important paradoxes for Romanos are those related to the most miraculous events in the Christian story: the incarnation, the crucifixion and the resurrection. The incarnation initiates the new creation. A dramatic change took place in the incarnation: God became man. The joining of these two fundamentally different things changes everything. Romanos emphasizes this paradox by focusing on the physical impossibility of the incarnation and on various characters' lack of comprehension.

---

[28] Carpenter (1970), 340 n. 12.

[29] Averil Cameron sees this as an opposition between Christian simplicity and corrupt classical eloquence. See Cameron (1991a), 190. This becomes a topos in Christian writing from Paul onwards.

In *On the Annunciation I*, Romanos puts paradoxical language into the mouth of the archangel Gabriel, as he struggles to understand what is about to take place (XXXVI.2.3–10):

And [Gabriel], coming to Nazareth, to Joseph's hut, was amazed
that the Most High desired to join with the lowly ones.
'All heaven', he said, 'and the fiery throne do not contain my Lord,
so how will this mere woman receive him?
He is awe-inspiring above, and how will he be seen below?
It is altogether as he wills it. So why do I stand and not rush
and say to the girl,
"Hail, unwedded wife"?'

καὶ ἐλθὼν εἰς Ναζαρὲτ   πρὸς τὴν σκηνὴν
                                                           τοῦ Ἰωσὴφ ἐξεπλήττετο,
     ὅτι πῶς ὁ ὑψηλὸς   τοῖς ταπεινοῖς ἀγαπᾷ συνεπάγεσθαι.
"Ὅλος', φησίν, '[[ὁ]] οὐρανὸς   καὶ ὁ πύρινος θρόνος
                                                           οὐ χωρεῖ μου τὸν δεσπότην.
καὶ ἡ εὐτελὴς αὕτη   πῶς ⟨αὐτὸν⟩ ὑποδέχεται;
     ἄνω φρικτὸς   καὶ κάτω πῶς ὁρατός;
     πάντως ὡς βούλεται·   τί οὖν ἵσταμαι   καὶ οὐχ ἵπταμαι
καὶ τῇ κόρῃ φθέγγομαι·
     "χαῖρε νύμφη ἀνύμφευτε";'

The incomprehensibility of the incarnation is foregrounded by the fact that the archangel, one of the highest celestial beings, does not understand it. Gabriel is puzzled for a while, but in the end accepts that he cannot understand the will of God entirely and that he need not. It is enough for him that God has asked him to do this: Gabriel is not God, even though he is a celestial being; his lack of comprehension sets him below the Father, who has sent him on this mission. The magnitude of the change is highlighted by its physical impossibility. God is uncontainable (line 5), yet Mary somehow will 'contain' him in her womb (line 6). God is likewise unbearable to look upon for the heavenly beings above (line 7), yet humans are about to see him on earth (line 7).

These paradoxes draw attention to the great chasm of difference between the divine and the human, which God bridges at the incarnation. God is the Most High, yet he chooses to associate with the humble and lowly and deigns to send one of his archangels to the flimsy tent of Joseph. This line (4) is a reference to Romans 12, in which Paul instructs the faithful in the ideal Christian life (12:16): 'do not be haughty, but associate with the lowly' (μὴ τὰ ὑψηλὰ φρονοῦντες ἀλλὰ τοῖς ταπεινοῖς συναπαγόμενοι). Romanos uses the same word for lowly (*tapeinoi*) and Paul's word for 'haughty' is

Romanos' word for 'Most High' (*hupsēlos*). In this way, Romanos reworks the Pauline passage to make it about the divine descent to earth, which was prompted by God's love (*agapa*, line 4, related to Paul's 'associate': *sunapagomenoi*) for his creation, and uses it to emphasize the perfection of humanity in Christ which restores humanity to God: Christ's association with the lowly reinforces that he is the perfect Christian.

The paradoxes in this passage also reflect the sixth-century (Chalcedonian) concern to reinforce the unity of the Trinity as well as the two natures of Christ and their relation to each other. In his letter *Against the Monophysites*, the emperor Justinian also contrasted the lofty heights of the divinity with the lowliness of humanity, although without Romanos' clear Pauline reference, while stressing that the Son is not separate from the Father: 'How has it come to pass that he who exists on high has been seen in meekness and humility, without descending from the heights?' (πῶς τὸ ὑψηλὸν ἐν τῶι ταπεινῶι γενόμενον καὶ ἐν τῶι ταπεινῶι καθορᾶται καὶ οὐ καταβαίνει τοῦ ὕψους;).[30] Justinian's answer is that Christ was both perfect man and perfect God, and that both natures are essential for human salvation.[31] Romanos' construction of the annunciation is informed by contemporary debates. Gabriel's anxiety about the immensity of God being contained highlights that Christ is still God even though he has entered humanity.

We see the same concerns, again foregrounded by angelic beings, in *On the Nativity II*. The speaker is the Christ-child (II.13.9–11):

> The one whom the Cherubim do not look upon,
> behold you see and carry and soothe me as a son,
> you, the highly favoured one.

> ὃν οὐχ ὁρᾷ Χερουβίμ,
> ἰδοὺ βλέπεις καὶ βαστάζεις　καὶ ὡς υἱὸν κολακεύεις με,
> ἡ κεχαριτωμένη.

Romanos joins the divine kingship of God with the humble humanity of the Christ-child in this paradox. The two natures of Christ are paramount: the heavenly Christ is so great and powerful that even the Cherubim hide their eyes from him, yet Mary sees him, holds him in her arms and speaks soothing words to him (the point is emphasized rhetorically with an ascending tricolon). Christ's two natures are also made prominent by having the Christ-child as the speaker: the babe in arms speaks with the authority of the divine creator.

---

[30] *Contra monophysitas* 3. For the text of this letter, see Albertella et al. (1973), 6–78. For the translation, see Wesche (1991), 30.
[31] *Contra monophysitas* 3.

The paradox does not stop with the moment of the incarnation. Christ is a living paradox while he is on earth. In *On the Marriage at Cana*, for instance, God reclines in a mortal's house (VII.2.4–6). One *kontakion* in which this is a particularly important theme is *On the Baptism of Christ*, since Christ's baptism was the event at which he was revealed as God by the voice from heaven (Matthew 3:16–17; Mark 1:10–11; V.16.4–5):[32]

How did I have the power to baptize the boundless one, being clay,
unless I first received and took power from above?

πῶς ηὐτόνουν βαπτίσαι   τὴν ἄβυσσον,   πήλινος ὑπάρχων,
            εἰ μὴ πρῶτον   ἐδεξάμην   καὶ ἔλαβον   δύναμιν ἐξ ὕψους;

John the Baptist's reference to 'clay' recalls the creation narrative in which Adam was created out of the earth (Genesis 2:7). The incarnation is here figured as a second creation of a new humanity which transcends mortal, earth-bound bodies of clay.

All further paradoxes flow from the fundamental paradox of God becoming human. The incarnation generates the paradoxical discourse of Romanos' poetry. The virgin birth is one such paradox, combining two impossible realities as a result of God's decision to become human. It is one which seems to be particularly important to Romanos. The well-known first line of his most famous hymn, *On the Nativity I*, draws attention to this: 'Today the Virgin gives birth to the one who is beyond being' (ἡ παρθένος σήμερον τὸν ὑπερούσιον τίκτει) (I.Pr.1). The virgin birth is proof of the change in reality which takes place in the incarnation. Cyril of Alexandria in particular argued that the virgin birth demonstrated Christ's divinity and thus the reality of the incarnation.[33] He claimed that Christ could not have become flesh and thereby saved humanity without having been born from the Virgin.[34] This was part of his argument for the term *Theotokos*.[35] In his opening line, Romanos draws attention to the paradoxical elements of the incarnation: that the one who is beyond being is also brought into being. Never before had God become human. Romanos uses the juxtaposition of 'beyond being' and 'gives birth' to emphasize this paradox.

On the Annunciation I is similarly full of incarnation paradoxes. One which runs throughout is the refrain: 'hail, unwedded wife' (χαῖρε, νύμφη

[32]   See also John 1:29–34.
[33]   Cf. also Irenaeus *Against Heresies* 3.21.10. See Behr (2000), 63.
[34]   *Five Tomes against Nestorius* I.17: Russell (2000), 133–4.
[35]   Atanassova (2008), 105–25, Boss (2007), 53, Price (2008), 96. See also Chapter 2 above.

ἀνύμφευτε).[36] Mary herself expresses doubt about the possibility of this impossible event taking place (XXXVI.5.5–10):

For he said 'you will bear and give birth to a son',
                              yet I know no man.
Perhaps he does not know that I am sealed?
Can he not know that I am a virgin?
I am really not persuaded.[37] If he did not know and have full knowledge,
he would not have come to me saying,
'hail, unwedded wife'.

εἶπε γὰρ ὅτι· 'υἱὸν   βαστάζεις καὶ τίκτεις'·
                              καίτοι ἄνδρα οὐ γινώσκω.
τάχα οὐκ ἔμαθεν   οὗτος ὅτι ἐσφράγισμαι;
   ἆρ' ἀγνοεῖ   ὅτι παρθένος εἰμί;
   ὄντως οὐ πείθομαι·   εἰ μὴ ἔμαθε   καὶ κατέμαθεν,
οὐκ ἂν ἦλθε λέγων μοι·
   'χαῖρε νύμφη ἀνύμφευτε.'

This paradox also contributes to the dramatic tension through rhetoric. Romanos makes the stanza quite repetitive: verbs of knowing dominate the passage.[38] Mary also talks about her virginity in three different ways (lines 5, 6 and 7). The repetition nicely mimics Mary's confused and frightened state. This accentuates Mary's humanity, once again bringing the incarnation to the fore: God enters the world through a *human* woman, not through some divine being. In line 5 'give birth' is juxtaposed with 'and yet I know no man' to highlight the physical impossibility of a virginal birth. The rhetorical questions of lines 6 and 7 make ridiculous the idea that the divine messenger would not know Mary's virginal state.

In many such passages Romanos employs alliteration, rhyme or repetition to emphasize the paradox. Impossible connections made by the paradox are made closer by literary devices such as alliteration and assonance: k and g sounds connect 'suckle' and 'milk' in 'not by chance do I suckle the one who supplies my milk' (οὐκ εἰκῆ **γ**αλουχῶ τὸν **χ**ορη**γ**ὸν τοῦ **γ**άλακτος (I.23.2)); p-alliteration and assonance strengthen the paradox in 'in order that they might see rich poverty, honourable beggary' (ἵνα ἴδωσι | **π**ενί̲α̲ν̲ **π**λουσί̲α̲ν̲, **π**τωχεί̲α̲ν̲ τιμί̲α̲ν̲ (I.7.2–3)). Likewise, in *On the Presentation in the Temple* (IV.1.6), the paradox of the incarnation is made prominent

---

[36] Unfortunately, the cognate and paradox are not easily rendered in English ('hail, unwedded wife' might be the closest), but José Grosdidier de Matons comes closer in the French edition: *Salut, épouse inépousée.* See Grosdidier de Matons (1965), 21ff.

[37] Colloquially, we might render this as 'I really don't get it.'

[38] On the erotic connotations of this *kontakion*, see Arentzen (2013).

by cognates: 'the **uncontainable** is **contained** in the arms of the old man' (ὁ ἀχώρητος χωρεῖται ἐν ἀγκάλαις τοῦ πρεσβύτου). These devices, which support the paradoxes, help to set up the divide between human and divine which has been bridged in the incarnation.

Paradoxes taken from natural imagery, probably drawn from Old Testament narratives, make the new reality all the more striking: 'There an unwatered root has appeared, bringing to light forgiveness. There is found an undug spring …' (ἐκεῖ ἐφάνη ῥίζα ἀπότιστος βλαστάνουσα ἄφεσιν, | ἐκεῖ ηὑρέθη φρέαρ ἀνόρυκτον …) (I.1.4–5), and 'we observe a dewy fire' (πῦρ δροσίζον θεωροῦμεν) (I.13.9). The 'unwatered root' is a reference to Isaiah 53:2, which foretells that the Messiah will grow up like a root out of dry ground; the undug spring may be a reference to King David's desire to drink from the well at Bethlehem (2 Samuel 23:13–17; 1 Chronicles 11:17–19); and the dewy fire could refer to the fiery furnace of Daniel (Daniel 3:19–30). These paradoxes are metaphors for the virgin birth; they are possible if the virgin birth is possible. (We will look at their typological significance shortly). The whole of the cosmos is altered by the incarnation: fire can be wet, roots grow without water, springs burst forth without being tapped into, and so on. These natural paradoxes are confronting because they mean changes to everyday things and make extraordinary phenomena out of the ordinary. The future paradise can be near at hand, in everyday life. This claim is what drives Romanos' extensive exhortations to his congregation to participate in the world of fulfilled prophecy.

The incarnation also means the rehabilitation of womankind. In *On the Annunciation II*, Romanos' paradox changes the state of women. After being told by the archangel that she will give birth to the saviour of humanity, Mary responds: 'How does woman, who previously introduced death to mortals, now bring forth life?' (γυνὴ ἡ πρὶν τὸν θάνατον προξενήσασα βροτοῖς πῶς ζωὴν νῦν βλαστήσει;) (XXXVII.11.3). Mary's obedience to the call of God corrects the disobedience of her ancestor, Eve. As we saw in Chapter 2, Romanos presents Mary as a second Eve who rehabilitates the first, correcting her wrongs and thus perfecting womankind.

The incarnation is a fundamentally paradoxical event which Romanos explores through paradox. God and human previously did not co-exist in the one being, but after the incarnation such things can and do happen. Romanos makes this clear to his congregation through his use of paradoxes, which draw together the previously irreconcilable realities that the incarnation unites.

Romanos often couches the crucifixion in similar terms to the incarnation. At the incarnation God became human for the sake of humanity. At the crucifixion God died a human death for the sake of humanity (XXIV.1.1–3):

Life unto the tomb; unto death, God;
and unto Hades, Hades' destroyer –
he the lawless crowd once handed over.[39]

Τὴν ζωὴν τῇ ταφῇ, τῷ θανάτῳ θεὸν
   καὶ τῷ Ἅιδῃ τὸν Ἅιδην σκυλεύσαντα
   παρέδωκε ποτὲ   τῶν ἀνόμων λαός,

Alliteration and juxtaposition emphasize the paradox of God dying on the cross.[40] The first line is finely balanced: 'life' and 'God' sandwich 'tomb' and 'death', and 'God' and 'death' are alliteratively linked. The repetition and juxtaposition of 'Hades' brings home the incongruity of the event. Word order is used to communicate this incongruity. Romanos deliberately starts the strophe with 'life' and the paradoxes concerning God and then moves to the actions of the crowd in line 3. The most important figure begins the strophe.

In *On the Resurrection V*, the paradox of the transcendent and yet incarnate God is set beside a statement of God's sacrifice on the cross to make another paradox (XXVIII.3.6–7):

Unseen above, you are, [yet] seen below by all,
and you accepted bodily suffering for our sakes.

ἄνω ἀόρατος, γέγονες, κάτω ὁρώμενος πᾶσι·
   σωματικῶς δὲ τὸ πάθος ὑπὲρ ἡμῶν κατεδέξω

As in the paradoxes of the incarnation and virgin birth discussed above, Romanos focuses on the divine and human natures of Christ, increasing the sense of the miraculous. Christ is God and unseen, but human and visible to all. Such paradoxes hold the two natures of Christ together in an acceptably Chalcedonian fashion, reinforcing Christ's divinity despite his becoming truly and *perceptibly* human. And as this living paradox Christ enacts another: willingness to suffer for the sake of humans.

---

[39] I have tried to follow the word order in my translation to illustrate my point. A more grammatical translation might look like this: Once the crowd of lawless ones handed over Life to the tomb, God to death and the one who destroyed Hades to Hades ...

[40] For an analysis of the narrative structure of this hymn, see Barkhuizen (1986b), 17–28.

Romanos foregrounds the paradox of Christ's suffering for humans through word play. At XXVIII.11.7:[41]

He suffers (*paschei*) willingly, in order that he may destroy the passions (*pathē*).

αὐτὸς δὲ πάσχει θελήσει,   ἵνα τὰ πάθη συντρίψῃ

Likewise, in *On the Entry into Jerusalem* (XVI.2.1–2):

Behold our King, the one who is meek and quiet sitting on the colt,
has come in haste to suffer (*pathein*) and wound passions (*pathē*).

Ἰδοὺ ὁ βασιλεὺς ἡμῶν   ὁ πρᾶος καὶ ἡσύχιος   τῷ πώλῳ καθήμενος
σπουδῇ παραγίνεται   ἐπὶ τὸ παθεῖν   καὶ τὰ πάθη τεμεῖν·

Christ's sacrifice is human deliverance from enslaving sins.[42] Romanos' word plays in these passages enable him to put the passion of Christ in the same category as human passions, creating a two-way paradox: Christ suffers to remove human suffering; Christ takes on human sin to remove human sins. The double meaning of *pathos* allows this paradox. It can refer both to 'suffering' and to 'emotion' or 'passion'. Passions (*pathē*), in the sense of irrational or uncontrolled emotional movements connected with sensuality, were mostly viewed negatively in late antiquity (although some theologians identified both natural (or 'pure') and unnatural passions and viewed the unnatural ones as sinful).[43] The passions therefore become associated with sin; they are the irrationality which prevents humans from being the truly rational beings God intended them to be. In this sense, they are something from which Romanos wants to be 'set free'. Romanos' word play thus strongly highlights the direct link between Christ's death on the cross and human salvation from sin.

While paradox mainly accentuates the wondrous new perfections and harmonies of the new creation, the understanding of new creation can also be used to exclude social groups from this perfect reality. For example, in the fifth resurrection hymn, and in various others, Romanos uses paradox to talk about the Jews (XXVIII.7.4–5):

And those who thought by their deeds they were honouring the Law
handed over the one who fulfils their Law to be crucified in the flesh.

---

[41] See also XXVI.Pr.1.

[42] See also LIX.1.2, in which Romanos gives the suffering of martyrs the same efficacy as the suffering of Christ: it removes general human suffering.

[43] Hinterberger (2010), 127. Smith sets one early Christian conceptualization of the passions (Gregory of Nyssa's) in the context of classical views: Smith (2004), 89–92. The Stoics in particular argued that one should attempt to eliminate the passions in order to lead a virtuous life. Cf. Nussbaum (1994), 359–401. Sorabji has traced the movement within early Christian thought from 'Stoic agitation to Christian temptation': Sorabji (2000). See also Knuuttila (2004).

νόμον δὲ τιμᾶν   διὰ τῶν ἔργων δοκοῦντες
  τὸν τοῦ νόμου αὐτῶν πληρωτὴν
        σταυρωθῆναι σαρκὶ παραδέδωκαν

The Law-keepers are really Law-transgressors. Romanos believes that Jews, whom he blames for Christ's crucifixion and who have rejected Christ and the teachings of the Christian church, are excluded from the new creation. In fact, they have excluded themselves by their actions and lack of belief. In their blind allegiance to the Law, they have not recognized its fulfilment in Jesus Christ. We will look further at Romanos' exclusion of the Jews shortly.

Romanos strongly argues for a change in the nature of death as a result of the resurrection of Jesus. The paradoxes he uses fall into two basic categories: the destruction (or 'death') of death; and the deification of humanity. In this section from the second resurrection hymn Hades laments the ramifications of Christ's resurrection for him (XXV.7.1–3):

Behold I, the master, am a prisoner and having just been King I am a slave,
and I, the Fearsome One, am caught and am an object of ridicule for all.
I am completely naked, for he has snatched away everything from me.

Ἰδοὺ πέλω δεσμώτης ὁ δεσπότης
        καὶ δουλεύω ὁ πρώην βασιλεύων.
καὶ γεγένημαι   ὁ ἐπίφοβος ἐπίληπτος
        καὶ πᾶσιν εἰς [γέλωτα]·
παντόθεν γυμνητεύω,   τὰ γὰρ πάντα μου ἀφήρπασεν·

Romanos uses word placement and alliteration, assonance, and rhyming endings to emphasize the paradox here: the alliterative words 'prisoner' (*desmōtēs*) and 'master' (*despotēs*) are juxtaposed, as are 'fearsome' (*epiphobos*) and 'caught' (*epilēptos*), and the choice of vocabulary allows Romanos to use sounds (in bold here) to heighten the contrast. In a few *kontakia*, Romanos has Christ call for the rescued souls to mock Hades. At XXV.11, Hades says the people hit him with their hymns and songs, and in *On the Resurrection IV* Jesus tells the people he is rescuing from hell to trample on Hades (XXVII.6.6) and strike his face (XXVII.7.1).

The normal circumstances and events surrounding death are overturned in the death and resurrection of Christ. Hades points out these paradoxes (XXV.5.1–7):

        And who would not have been deceived,
seeing him wrapped in cloth and put in the tomb?
Who, as if a dumb animal, would not have thought that he had died,
when an unguent of myrrh and aloes anointed him

and he was brought to me?
Again, who says a man is not dead, seeing the stone there,
                                                on which he is lying?
Who would have thought such things, or who would ever have hoped
                                                to cry, concerning him,
'The Lord is risen'?

καὶ τίς ἄρα οὐκ εἶχε πλανηθῆναι
θεωρῶν αὐτὸν   τῇ σινδόνι ἐνειλούμενον
                              καὶ τάφῳ διδόμενον;
τίς οὕτως ἦν κτηνώδης   μὴ νοῆσαι ὅτι τέθνηκεν,
ὁπότε σμῆγμα σμύρνης   καὶ ἀλόης ἐπεχρίετο
                                            πρὸς ἐμὲ πορευόμενος;
τίς εἶπε πάλιν μὴ νεκρὸν   βλέπων λίθον ἐπικείμενον,
                              οὗ ἦν οὗτος κείμενος;
τίς τοιοῦτον ἐνόησεν,   ἢ τίς ποτε ἐπήλπιζε
                              βοῆσαι περὶ τούτου·
'ἀνέστη ὁ κύριος';

By using a repetitive structure of rhetorical questions in this passage, Romanos characterizes Death as distressed and confused by the resurrection of Christ. This characterization, through a powerful personification, further accentuates the paradox of the resurrection. When did all the signs of death not point to death before Jesus? It is only in the new reality that such paradoxes are realized.

Romanos also ignores conventional temporal limits to bring together in his hymns people who could never have met, revealing Romanos' conception of the altered nature of time. Events past, present and future converge in the incarnation and post-incarnation events. So, in *On the Nativity II*, Mary is able to meet and talk with her oldest ancestors, Adam and Eve (II.8–11). Mary's hymn to Christ miraculously reaches Eve's ears (3.3), and she manages to wake Adam only by revealing the wonder of the incarnation and its effect for their salvation (4ff.). Adam is strengthened by the life-giving breeze (a reference to Ezekiel 37) (7.7–8) and only then is he able to speak to Mary (7.9–10; 8).[44] These biblical figures and events converge in the light of the incarnation.

Similarly, in *On the Massacre of the Innocents*, Rachel becomes Mary's contemporary. She is a witness to the slaughter of the sons of Israel (III.1.3–6):

Jacob exults, and why does Rachel mourn?
Joseph is recognised, and why does Rachel groan?

---

[44] On Adam's spiritual and literal awakening in this hymn, see Frank (2005), 167–8. See also Chapter 2 above.

Benjamin is lifted up, why does Rachel cry?
So come, let us see the lament and the sadness.

 … Ἰακὼβ ἐπαγάλλεται, καὶ Ῥαχὴλ τί ὀδύρεται;
Ἰωσὴφ ἀνεγνωρίσθη, καὶ Ῥαχὴλ τί στενάζει;
 Βενιαμὶν ὑψώθη, τί κλαίει Ῥαχήλ;
δεῦτε οὖν ἴδωμεν τὸν ὀδυρμὸν καὶ τὸ πένθος·

Old Testament figures are brought forward in time to be contemporaries of Mary and her baby. Rachel is presented as mother of all Israel's children: her own sons, Joseph and Benjamin, were restored after both seemed to be lost, but in this story she mourns for her descendants. And, once again, Romanos calls for participation in this event. The congregation is called upon to witness the 'sadness': the slaughter of the innocent children.[45] In this new reality, past, present and future converge in the anticipation of heavenly glory.

Paradox and Typology

For clarity, I have divided my analysis so far into sections on different rhetorical devices, which might leave the false impression that each is quite separate. But Romanos uses paradox and typology together, again underscoring the novel temporality of the new creation. In *On the Three Children*, Shadrach, Meshach and Abednego in the fiery furnace (Daniel 3:19–30) become types for the virgin birth, using the paradox of a 'bedewed' fire in the Old Testament as a type for the paradox of the incarnation (XLVI.26.9–12):

Just as he recently sprinkled the furnace with dew,
so, like rain on the virgin, he is about to
        sprinkle those who sing
'Hurry, merciful one, and since you have pity hasten
to our aid, because you are able to do what you will.'

καθάπερ καὶ ἄρτι τὴν κάμινον ἐδρόσισεν
οὕτως μέλλει ὡς ὑετὸς εἰς τὴν ἄγαμον
        καταρδεύειν τοὺς ψάλλοντας·
'τάχυνον, ὁ οἰκτίρμων, καὶ σπεῦσον ὡς ἐλεήμων
εἰς τὴν βοήθειαν ἡμῶν, ὅτι δύνασαι βουλόμενος.'

Typology and paradox unite, connecting an Old Testament paradox (dew in the fiery furnace) to a New Testament one (the virgin birth). The reference

---

[45] We will look at this in more detail in Chapter 4.

to 'rain' on the virgin also recalls the image of the dew on the fleece (Judges 6:36–8) (on which, see further below). Multiple biblical paradoxes are combined in this passage, demonstrating Romanos' analogical mode of thinking, which connects the Old and New Testaments and makes time converge (on which, see further in Chapter 4 below).

The typology also makes Romanos' congregation part of the two paradoxes. God is about to sprinkle the singers of the final two lines of the stanza, the refrain. The singers are Shadrach, Meshach and Abednego, whom God rescued by sprinkling with water in the fiery furnace. But, at the same time, the refrain is the section in which the congregation took part.[46] The congregation is thereby linked to the three in the furnace with whom they share the singing of the refrain.[47]

There is an interesting temporal reversal in this passage. I have suggested that the furnace is a type for the incarnation, but this passage actually reverses the order of the two events. The Old Testament event, which happens 'now' or at least 'recently' (ἄρτι), seemingly looks 'back' to the virgin birth, presenting it as a type for the three who are unharmed by the fiery furnace. We are presented with a multivalent paradox. Each story is paradoxical by itself, but the relationship of the two events is similarly confusing and difficult to ascertain. The link to Romanos' congregation gives a clue. Romanos argues for a 'liturgical time', in which biblical events transcend normal temporal boundaries and actually take place 'now': the day on which they are commemorated in the liturgical calendar. The virgin birth is such an event. Romanos' use of Shadrach, Meshach and Abednego as antitype of the virgin birth in the liturgical drama of his *kontakion* makes the Old Testament story present too.

In a similar way, the second annunciation *kontakion* combines metaphor and paradox (XXXVII.1.1–5):

What I see I cannot understand,

> for it is beyond the human mind.

How does grass bear fire and not burn?

---

[46] It is possible that Romanos is also preparing the congregation to be sprinkled with holy water in the service or in a forthcoming service. This *kontakion* is ascribed in some manuscripts to 17 December, the day which commemorates Daniel, and in others to another Sunday leading up to Christmas: Grosdidier de Matons (1964), 343–5. There is no evidence that the congregation was sprinkled with holy water in the weeks leading up to Christmas. However, such a sprinkling did sometimes occur on the Feast of the Theophany (6 January) and Romanos may be looking forward to that event. There is evidence of the Great Blessing of the Waters from the ninth century and the sprinkling the congregation is attested in an eleventh- or twelfth-century service book. See Gerstel (2010), 118–19.

[47] We will look at how Romanos uses the refrain to make his congregation participate in biblical events (and therefore in the new creation) in Chapter 4.

A lamb bears a lion, a swallow an eagle,
            and a slave-girl her master.
In a mortal belly, as has not been circumscribed,
Mary bears God, my willing saviour …

Ὅπερ ὁρῶ   νοῆσαι οὐ χωρῶ·
                    ὑπὲρ νοῦν γὰρ ὑπάρχει ἀνθρώπινον·
πῶς πῦρ φέρων ὁ χόρτος οὐ φλέγεται;
ἀμνὰς βαστάζει λέοντα,   ἀετὸν δὲ χελιδὼν
                    καὶ δεσπότην ἡ δούλη·
γαστρὶ θνητῇ θεὸν   ἀπεριγράπτως
    Μαρία ἐμὸν σωτῆρα   ἑκόντα φέρει …

Multiple metaphors and images highlight the miraculous nature of the incarnation and its transformative power. A world in which a human can give birth to God is one in which normal order is reversed and miraculous things can and do take place. Prey looks after predator, the small and weak care for the big and strong. Paradox joins two existing creatures in an entirely new way, transforming the two realities into a new, single, paradoxical reality. These images could also be a different take on Isaiah 11:6, which uses the picture of predator and prey (wolf and lamb, leopard and goat, lion and calf) lying down together as a symbol of paradise: the incarnation heralds the new paradise.

The paradox of the incarnation generates and is performed by the paradoxical discourse of Romanos' *kontakia*. This distinctive feature of Romanos' poetic discourse arises from his theological investigation and proclamation of christology. God became human and was brought into the world by a virgin mother. The rhetorical device of paradox by its very form combines realities which could not previously have existed in harmony, thus enacting the paradoxical nature of the new creation. Paradox reflects Romanos' conceptualization of the new creation and its transformation of reality. When joined with typology, the novelty and transformational nature of event or person highlighted by the type, and the consequences for the experience of a new temporality, are emphasized.

Typology

The large range of types employed by Romanos enables him to explore this new, christologically mediated temporality, and to present and elucidate associated interpretations of time and history. The radical transformations

which the incarnation inaugurated are the fulfilment of all history: all previous reality foreshadowed and now converges on Christ. Old Testament
figures and events, across numerous generations, prefigure the one event in
the life of Jesus.

Types for Christ

In *On the Massacre of the Innocents,* Romanos compares the infants Moses
and Christ (III.15.10–12):

And he reached the fruit-giving Nile,
not as Moses in the river, thrown into a marsh and guarded in a basket,
but rather having hurled down all their idols there.

τὸν Νεῖλον δὲ κατέλαβε   τὸν καρποδότην πέλοντα,
οὐχ ὡς Μωσῆς ἐν ποταμῷ   καὶ τῷ ἕλει προσριφεὶς
                                                        καὶ ἐν θίβει φυλαχθείς,
μᾶλλον δὲ ρίψας ἐκεῖ   ἅπαν εἴδωλον αὐτῶν

Romanos draws on well-known narratives from the apocryphal infancy
Gospels about the flight into Egypt. In these stories Egyptian idols acknowledge Jesus as the Son of God and fall down from their pedestals when Jesus
enters Egypt.[48] Unlike the infant Moses who, although he turned out to be
one of the greatest men in Jewish history, was hidden in a basket to save
his life (Exodus 2:3), Jesus is an active figure from the first. The canonical
Gospel of Matthew suggests that the trip to Egypt was to save Jesus from
Herod and his soldiers (Matt. 2:13–15), but this apocryphal narrative suggests otherwise. Jesus is not like Moses; he does not have to be hidden away
for protection. From infancy, Jesus is presented as an active protector of the
faith and destroyer of idolatry.

The most significant events in the life of Christ were his birth, death and
resurrection. The actions which led to his death were likewise prefigured by
the Old Testament. In *On Judas,* Romanos uses Joseph as a type for Christ
(XVII.19.5–7; Genesis 37:28):

Joseph was a type for Jesus, whose price you [i.e. Judas] took,
and, taking it, you received a hanging-noose and Hades.

Ὁ Ἰωσὴφ ἐκεῖνος   τοῦ Ἰησοῦ ἦν τύπος,
                                            οὗ τὴν τιμὴν λαμβάνεις·
καὶ δι᾽ αὐτῆς καταλαμβάνεις Ἅιδην   τὸν βρόχον ἔχων †ἀγχόνην†.

---

[48] *The Gospel of Pseudo-Matthew* 23: Elliott and James (1993), 96.

Joseph was betrayed by those closest to him, his brothers, and therefore is a type for Christ, whose close companion, Judas, betrayed him. There is sufficient ambiguity in the Greek to allow for the impression that the money Judas took was the same money taken by the betrayers of Joseph. Literally, the price is Jesus', but Joseph is another masculine singular noun to which the relative pronoun could refer, strengthening the connection between type and antitype. Once again, antitype outweighs type: Joseph becomes powerful in Egypt and his brothers are not greatly punished for their betrayal, whereas Jesus dies on the cross and Judas hangs himself. The betrayal of Jesus is the more significant and has more serious consequences for the betrayer. In *On Joseph I*, Romanos uses Joseph's brother Judah as a type for Jewish treachery in the New Testament, and perhaps particularly Judas' betrayal, playing on the similarity between the names (XLIII.7). As discussed above in relation to paradox, typologies for the Jews or Jewish treachery seem designed to illustrate that the Jews are not part of the new creation. Their treachery has not lessened but rather increased as a result of the incarnation because they have turned away from the Messiah. All of the Jewish scriptures are to be interpreted christologically – for Romanos, it is part of Jewish sinfulness that they do not see this.

In *On Mary at the Cross*, Romanos presents Christ as the serpent of bronze which Moses erected to save the Israelites, drawing on the Gospel of John (3:14). Mary says (XIX.15.7–10):

And Moses said this to Israel,
that 'You are about to see life on a tree.'
Who is the life?
My son and my God.

Μωσῆς δὲ τοιοῦτο   τῷ Ἰσραὴλ εἶπεν
    ὅτι. 'μέλλεις βλέπειν   ἐπὶ ξύλου τὴν ζωήν.'
ἡ ζωὴ δὲ τίς ἐστιν;
ὁ υἱὸς καὶ θεός μου.

God sent the serpent of bronze, through his servant Moses, to save his people from death by hanging on a pole. In this sense the bronze serpent is life, since it restores life to those about to lose it. This is a foreshadowing of Christ and the crucifixion, since God sent his son Jesus, through his servant Mary, to save his people from death by hanging on a tree. But Moses' bronze snake only saved the Israelites temporarily – from death by poisonous snakes – it did not save them from death itself. The second 'life on a tree', Christ, brings eternal life to humans who have all been bitten by the sting of death.

Isaac and Jonah are both types of Christ's death and resurrection (XLI.19.1–2, 7–8):[49]

At that time the faithful Abraham disregarded the words of [his] son
and was a forceful executor of the sacrifice …
the child did not squirm, since God was calling him
and he was signalling the things about to happen.

Υἱοῦ μὲν τὰ ῥήματα   τότε παρεῖδε   πιστὸς Ἀβραάμ,
    καὶ τῆς θυσίας   ἦν ἐργάτης ἰσχυρὸς …
    οὐ τέκνου σκιρτῶντος,   τοῦ θεοῦ δὲ καλοῦντος
    καὶ σημαίνοντος αὐτοῦ τὰ μέλλοντα.

As we saw in previous chapters, Isaac's 'sacrifice' prefigures Christ's. The time marker 'then' is opposed to 'the things about to happen'. Romanos reads and interprets the Old Testament with the New in mind, and assumes that God did too: the omniscient God, knowing what was to happen to him (in Christ) on the cross, made Isaac a type for his sacrifice. For Romanos, the primary importance of the Old Testament is to point forward to Christ. For the writer of Genesis, Isaac's sacrifice was a way for God to test the faith of his servant Abraham, but for Romanos, Abraham's faith is not in question – Isaac was sacrificed to prefigure the ultimate sacrifice.[50]

Like Isaac, Jonah, who is swallowed by the fish and then regurgitated after three days (Jonah 1:17), was used as a type for the resurrection in the Gospels (Matthew 12:40) and in very early Christian iconography. Second-century wall paintings in the catacombs of Rome witness to this.[51] In Romanos' third resurrection hymn, he has the character of Hades make the connection (XXVI.9.1–2):

Thus the big fish vomited up Jonah on the third day,
And now I vomit up Christ and all Christ's beings.

Οὕτως Ἰωνᾶν τριταῖον   τὸ κῆτος ἐξήμεσε·
    νῦν κἀγὼ ἐμέσω Χριστὸν   καὶ πάντας τοὺς ὄντας Χριστοῦ·

God forces Death to 'vomit up' Christ and all humanity on the third day, just as he forced the fish to vomit up Jonah after three days (Jonah 1:17; 2:10). Here the emphatic 'and now I' strengthens the comparison: previously it

[49] Joseph similarly prefigures the resurrection in the hymn *On Joseph I*, because his father thought he was dead and then he was restored to him (XLIII.37.7–10; Genesis 45:25–8).
[50] In this, as we saw in Chapter 2, Romanos follows the tradition of Christian interpretation of Isaac against contemporary Jewish interpretations. See Kessler (2004), 131–7.
[51] On early Christian iconography, including depictions of early resurrection images like Isaac and Jonah, see Jensen (2000).

was only a fish, but now it is Death himself. It is worth noting that in the Old Testament story, Jonah himself calls the fish 'Sheol': 'Out of the belly of Sheol I cried, and you heard my voice' (Jonah 2:2). Jonah's descent into the fish is portrayed as a descent into hell, so his release from the fish is a figure of Christ's resurrection. But even with this underworld typology for the fish in mind, it is clear that the second 'vomiting' is the more drastic of the two. It is not just Christ who is being released from Hades, but all his 'beings' (all humanity).

The importance of these two Old Testament figures for Romanos is that they represent and foreshadow the crucifixion and resurrection; the Old Testament is fundamentally christological. The lives of Isaac and Jonah are prophecies of the death and resurrection of Jesus Christ and Christ is the fulfilment of their stories. The fulfilment of these foreshadowings signals a change in reality. The period of prophecy has come to an end and Romanos recognizes a period of confirmation of prophecy and anticipation of the second coming. Through these Old Testament types, Romanos enacts the new reality.

In *On Elijah* (XLV.33.1–3), the prophet Elijah's ascent into heaven (2 Kings 2:11–12) is a type for Christ's ascension (Luke 24:51):

See, Elijah is a type of things to come,
> after he was made ready he was received into the heavens.
For the Thesbite was taken up in a fiery chariot, as it was written.
And Christ was taken up amongst clouds and powers [i.e. angels].

Ἰδοὺ τύπος Ἠλίας τῶν μελλόντων
> ἐν τῷ ὕψει στελλόμενος ἐδείχθη·
ὁ Θεσβίτης γὰρ   ἀνελήφθη ἐπὶ ἄρματος
> πυρός, καθὼς γέγραπται·
Χριστὸς δὲ ἀνελήφθη   ἐν νεφέλαις καὶ δυνάμεσιν·

Elijah is Christ's type but not his equal. The clouds and angels ('powers') which accompany Christ's ascension outdo Elijah's fiery chariot.

Elijah's gift of the mantle (2 Kings 2:13) prefigures Christ's sending of the Holy Spirit (XLV.33.4–7):

And [Elijah] sent his mantle to Elisha from the heavens,
> but Christ sent down
to his apostles the Holy Paraclete whom we all received,
having received baptism, through which we are made holy ...

ἀλλ' οὗτος Ἐλισσαίῳ   μηλωτὴν ἐξ ὕψους ἔπεμψεν,
> ὁ Χριστὸς δὲ κατέπεμψε

τοῖς ἀποστόλοις τοῖς ἑαυτοῦ   τὸν παράκλητον καὶ ἅγιον

ὃν πάντες ἐλάβομεν

οἱ τὸ βάπτισμα ἔχοντες,   δι' οὗ ἁγιαζόμεθα ...

But Jesus' gift far outweighs that of the prophet. Elijah sent down his mantle to Elisha, bestowing a valuable gift of power on one man; Jesus sent down the Holy Spirit which is a gift to all people and for eternity. Romanos uses Elijah as a type for Christ, demonstrating that the Old Testament has been fulfilled in Christ. This fulfilment signals that there is a new creation.

Romanos uses Old Testament people, images and events as typologies for Christ, his crucifixion, resurrection and ascension, and to illustrate the significance of these events in the divine plan of salvation. The wealth of Old Testament typologies for Christ underscores his view of a transformed and christologically informed temporality. Through his use of typology, Romanos argues that he lives in a period of confirmation of prophecy, in which the past is shown to be fulfilled in the present and the future. All of the Old Testament is fulfilled in Christ, and is conflated and comes together in him.

Types for the Incarnation

The typologies Romanos uses for the incarnation and the virgin birth are as diverse as those for the person of Christ. In these typologies, instead of using particular figures or one single event as a type, Romanos often uses a proliferation of Old Testament imagery. Miracles and paradoxes from the Old Testament foreshadow the miraculous event of the incarnation. The number of Old Testament miracles used for this purpose helps to illustrate the extent to which the incarnation surpasses these miracles.

Romanos pulls out all the stops in his descriptions of the incarnation and virgin birth. A multitude of different Old Testament miracles foreshadow it. Mary is the bedewed furnace from Daniel 3:49–50 (XLVI.26), the fleece on which Christ is the dew (Judges 6:36–8) (XXXVII.Pr.), and Aaron's flowering rod (Numbers 17:8) (XXXVII.Pr.). The incarnation is foreshadowed by the parting of the Red Sea (Exodus 14:26–9) (XXXVI.8), and the manna from heaven (Exodus 16:4) (XIX.6). And there are various types for Mary's virginity in particular (e.g. XXXVI.8, 9, 10; XXXVII.6; I.9).[52]

As we have already seen, one type for the virgin birth which recurs in the *kontakia* is the burning bush (Exodus 3:2):[53]

There the angel of the Lord appeared to [Moses] in a flame of fire out of a bush; he looked, and the bush was blazing, yet it was not consumed.

[52] On Marian typology more generally in early Christianity, see Capelle (1954).
[53] Hannick (1999), 214–15.

Gregory of Nyssa seems to have been the first to use the burning bush as a type for the virgin birth in his *Life of Moses* (II.21).[54] For Gregory, the analogy is to the 'flower' of Mary's virginity, which is not 'consumed' just as the bush is not consumed. But Romanos does not focus on Mary's perpetual virginity here (although he does elsewhere). Rather, the growing foetus is the fire and Mary's whole body is the bush which miraculously does not burn. In *On the Nativity II*, Mary herself explains the typology (II.11.3–4):

There is a fire inhabiting my belly
and it does not consume me, the lowly one.

πῦρ ὑπάρχων ᾤκησέ μου
τὴν γαστέρα   καὶ οὐ κατέφλεξεν ἐμὲ   τὴν ταπεινήν·

The burning bush in Exodus was a miraculous revelation of God and a type for God's revelation in the incarnation. God reveals himself in the pregnancy of Mary, both through her virginal conception and by the impossibility of containing the immortal God within a mortal being. Romanos performs the revelation and thus the new creation through his fire typology.

This imagery is vividly employed by the character of Joseph in *On the Annunciation I* (XXXVI.15.3–5):

O radiant one, I see a flame and fire encircling you.
Because of this, Mary, I am terrified.
                    Protect me and do not burn me.
Your blameless belly is suddenly a vessel full of fire.

Ὦ φαεινή,   φλόγα ὁρῶ
                    καὶ ἀνθρακίαν κυκλοῦσαν σε·
διὰ τοῦτο, Μαριάμ,
                    ἐκπλήττομαι· φύλαξόν [[με]] καὶ μὴ φλέξῃς με·
κλίβανος πλήρης πυρὸς   ἐγένετο ἄφνω
                    ἡ ἄμεμπτος γαστήρ σου.

Romanos uses alliteration and assonance in line 4 to draw attention to Joseph's fear (*phlexēs*) and plea for protection (*phulaxon*). Interestingly, in the Exodus story, there is no thought of Moses fearing the burning bush. When he sees the bush he says to himself, 'I must turn aside and look at this great sight, and see why the bush is not burned up' (Exodus 3:3). It is only when

---

[54] 'From this we learn also the mystery of the Virgin: The light of divinity which through birth shone from her into human life did not consume the burning bush, even as the flower of her virginity was not withered by giving birth': Malherbe and Ferguson (1978), 59.

the voice of God speaks to him from the bush that he is afraid (Exodus 3:4–6). Comparing the two stories, Moses seems somewhat foolhardy, or Joseph more enlightened. Moses has to be warned that he is on holy ground (Exodus 3:5), whereas Joseph is well aware of the holiness of the fire dwelling in Mary. This may be part of Romanos' concern to show that post-incarnation reality is more enlightened than pre-incarnation reality. As we will see in the next chapter, even great prophets from the Old Testament are unable to see God in the way that ordinary people can after the incarnation.

We find another example of burning bush imagery in the proem to hymn XXXVII, *On the Annunciation II* (XXXVII.Pr.):

Joseph was terrified, seeing this supernatural thing,
and in your unsown pregnancy, *Theotokos*,
he understood the rain on the fleece,
the bush unconsumed by fire,
the budding rod of Aaron.
And when he testified, mindful of you and as your guard,
he cried to the priests,
'A virgin gives birth and after the birth remains still a virgin.'

Κατεπλάγη Ἰωσὴφ   τὸ ὑπὲρ φύσιν θεωρῶν,
  καὶ ἐλάμβανεν εἰς νοῦν   τὸν ἐπὶ πόκον ὑετὸν
  ἐν τῇ ἀσπόρῳ κυήσει σου,   Θεοτόκε,
  βάτον ἐν πυρὶ   ἀκατάφλεκτον,
    ῥάβδον Ἀαρὼν   τὴν βλαστήσασαν·
    καὶ μαρτυρῶν ὁ μνήστωρ σου καὶ φύλαξ
                    τοῖς ἱερεῦσιν ἐκραύγαζεν·
  Ἡ Παρθένος τίκτει καὶ μετὰ τόκον   πάλιν μένει παρθένος.'

These three images (rain on the fleece, burning bush, Aaron's rod) all describe a wondrous connection between the divine and the mortal. The unsown pregnancy and the name of *Theotokos* (God-bearer) are placed within the list of other miracles to which the incarnation is likened. Yet in this one miracle, Joseph sees the summation of the entire Old Testament: three Old Testament miracles converge in the one event. For Romanos, the most miraculous historical events cannot capture the incarnation.

The discourse is marked by excess, generated by the overflowing and uncontained miracle of the incarnation. Romanos grasps at all available imagery and finds it wanting. The excess and proliferation of his imagery, like his use of paradox, is a function of his theological claims about the excess and abundance of the new creation. Theological concerns generate the distinctive poetic discourse of the *kontakia* even as that discourse performs the theology. Through this abundant imagery, Romanos connects significant moments in history in which God has achieved something impossible and this one, world-defining moment which is both the fulfilment of the others and truly surpasses them. He also acts out the change in reality which marks the new creation by drawing together so many Old Testament images into one eschatological event.

The three images which Romanos here associates with the incarnation and Mary's virginal conception all have different connotations. We have already discussed those of the burning bush type. The image of the rain on the fleece is a reference to the story of Gideon in the book of Judges (6:36–8):

> Then Gideon said to God, 'In order to see whether you will deliver Israel by my hand, as you have said, I am going to lay a fleece of wool on the threshing floor; if there is dew on the fleece alone, and it is dry on all the ground, then I shall know that you will deliver Israel by my hand, as you have said.' And it was so. When he rose early next morning and squeezed the fleece, he wrung enough dew from the fleece to fill a bowl of water.

Dew on the fleece is evidence of God's intention to save Israel. Romanos uses this image as a type for the virginal conception, accentuating its implications for human salvation. Just as the dew on Gideon's fleece was proof that God would save the Israelites in battle, so the virginal conception is proof of God's incarnation, through which he will eternally save humanity. Importantly, for the typology of the virgin birth, the fleece is seen to remain pure and uncorrupted despite being sprinkled with dew.[55]

The budding rod of Aaron is evidence of the power of God. God can make dead wood bring forth buds, blossoms and almonds (Numbers 17:8). In the same way, God can make a virginal womb fruitful. By using this type for Mary's conception, Romanos emphasizes the miraculous power of God. The budding rod in the book of Numbers stands as a warning for those who might doubt or rebel. Romanos' use of this typology therefore fits nicely with the reference to Joseph's fear at the beginning of the strophe and his testimony of Mary's perpetual virginity at the end (after the rod type).

Mary's virginal conception, pregnancy and birth-giving to the immortal God is a miraculous set of events which is foreshadowed by but supremely surpasses Old Testament miracles. This excess is, for Romanos, both a defining characteristic and important evidence of the reality of the new creation. He works to enact that new reality, using typology to show the overflowing fulfilment of the past in the 'present' incarnation.

---

[55] John Chrysostom seems to have been most influential in such an interpretation of the dew on the fleece. Through this image he emphasizes the gentleness of Christ's descent to earth. See Ladouceur (2006), 25–6. Ladouceur also draws a link between Chrysostom's interpretation of this image and its use in Marian hymnography: Ladouceur (2006), 26.

Types for Paradise

Paradise typology is harder to quantify than types for Christ or for the virgin birth, since Romanos saw the incarnation as the inauguration of the new paradise. Therefore, many of the images and typologies we have already seen, like the reawakening of the senses, the types for the tree of life, the multiple types for the virgin birth, are all metaphors for or typologies of paradise too. In *On Baptism*, the sacraments of eucharist and baptism are symbols of the new creation and ways in which humans enact that creation. After the resurrection of Christ, the world is renewed and even Adam can partake of these sacraments. Satan recognizes the change (LIII.4.5–10):[56]

The lump of earth [i.e. Adam] has been renewed, the dust made divine.
The poor and least called and washed, even the one who faltered as he entered.
He is drawn to the meal, he dares to eat
and has the courage to drink the one who created him.
And who granted him this? Surely it was
your resurrection.

ὁ χοῦς ἀνενεώθη,   ἡ κόνις ἐθεώθη·
    ὁ πένης καὶ ἐλάχιστος   ἐκλήθη καὶ ἐλούσατο
                            καὶ εἰσελθὼν ἀνέπεσεν·
[[καὶ]] πρὸς δεῖπνον ἕλκεται,   φαγεῖν ἐτόλμησε
    καὶ πιεῖν ἐθάρρησεν   αὐτὸν τὸν ποιήσαντα·
καὶ τίς τούτῳ δέδωκεν; πάντως
ἡ ἀνάστασις ὑμῶν.

Satan emphasizes the lowliness of Adam and the great daring he shows in even approaching the table, let alone eating and drinking his God. The image of the lowly earth eating the one which created it highlights the generosity of God and the dramatic reversal of norms which followed the incarnation, death and resurrection of Jesus Christ. Adam's baptism and communication at the eucharist are evidence that there is a new creation right now, that humanity has been restored to relationship with God and that humans continue to live out that new creation through the sacraments.

In a few *kontakia*, Romanos connects paradise explicitly with Christian virtues or values. Purity is paradise in *On Joseph II*, in which Joseph likens the advances of Potiphar's wife to Eve convincing Adam to eat the forbidden fruit (XLIV.16).[57] Purity and paradise are both associated with sweet smells and abundance (line 5) and purity makes mortals shine like angels

---

[56] On Satan's role in this *kontakion*, see Frank (2013a).
[57] For an analysis of this *kontakion*, especially the image of the athlete, see Barkhuizen (1990c), 91–106. See also Barkhuizen (1990b), 1–31.

(7). Joseph is a type of Christ and Christ-like behaviour. In *On Fasting* (LI.4.3–6), paradise is gained by fasting, again contrasting the behaviour of the first couple: Adam's rejection of fasting (his gluttony in tasting the forbidden fruit) is the cause of his death.[58] Adam is the figure Christians should strive not to imitate, who represents all the sin which Christ came to remove. Through Christ-like living, enacting his purity and self-control, Romanos argues that Christians participate in a present paradise.

And yet paradise also refers to the eschaton, the final consummation of the new reality which God began at the incarnation. Romanos interprets the story of the flood (Genesis 7:1–8:19) as a prophecy of the eschaton in *On Noah*. The hymn is full of images of sin and destruction and refers many times to the final purification of humanity by fire. Noah says (XL.10.9–11):

in this I will now be a prototype of the resurrection of the whole world,
in which you will save your righteous ones from the fire just as you save me
from the midst of the impious, in the wave of evils, snatching me away.

ἐν ταύτῃ προτυπώσω νῦν   τὴν πάγκοσμον ἀνάστασιν,
   ἐν ᾗπερ τοῦς δικαίους σου   σῴζεις πυρὸς καθάπερ κἀμὲ
ἐκ μέσου   ἀσεβῶν ἀφαρπάσας σῴζεις με   ἐν κλύδωνι κακῶν

Romanos' Noah recognizes his importance as a sign of future salvation. In fact, in this passage all time is future – Noah's salvation and that of the righteous – to emphasize the summation of all reality in Christ.[59] Earlier in this strophe the ark is connected both with a womb and a tomb, from both of which Noah can emerge only at God's command (lines 1–8). But the image in these few lines is of the ark as the church: those in the ark/church will be saved and those outside will perish.

Through his use of typology, Romanos argues that paradise is partly to be lived now, in the example of Christ, within the church and following Christ's precepts. But it is also to be anticipated, looking forward to the final consummation of God's promises in the eschaton.

Prophecy

In the changed post-incarnation world which anticipates paradise there is no need for prophecy: all prophecies looked forward to Christ's

---

[58] See also stanzas 21 and 22 in this *kontakion*.

[59] The flood and Noah's salvation from it were very early images of Christ's resurrection and the general resurrection. On these images in catacombs and early Christian art, see Jensen (2000), 82–4.

incarnation, death and resurrection.[60] Just as he uses typology to show that the Old Testament looks forward to and is fulfilled by Christ's life, Romanos refers to a number of different prophecies that have been fulfilled in Christ.[61] In *On the Massacre of the Innocents,* Romanos claims the fulfilment of Isaiah's prophecy in the birth of Christ (III.2.3–9):

And the very thing which [Herod] was not expecting,
          he learnt, paying attention to what the prophet said,
for Isaiah said 'A child has been born for us,
and a son has been given to us.
He is the father of all and the lord of all ages.
He has authority on his shoulders
and his name will be called
Messenger of Great Counsel.'

καὶ ἅπερ οὐκ ἤλπιζε   μελετήσας ἐξέμαθε
                      τὸν προφήτην τὸν λέγοντα·
φησὶ γὰρ Ἡσαΐας·   'Παιδίον ἐγεννήθη
  ἡμῖν καὶ οὕτως υἱὸς   ἐδόθη ἡμῖν·
πάντων πατήρ ἐστι   καὶ τῶν αἰώνων δεσπότης·
  ἐπὶ τῶν ὤμων   τὴν ἀρχὴν ἔχει·
  τὸ ὄνομά δε   αὐτοῦ καλεῖται
μεγάλης βουλῆς ἄγγελος'.

This is almost a word-for-word quote from the Septuagint translation of Isaiah 9:5(6):

A child has been born for us, and a son has been given to us, authority has been set upon his shoulder, and his name will be called Messenger of Great Counsel.

παιδίον ἐγεννήθη ἡμῖν, υἱὸς καὶ ἐδόθη ἡμῖν, οὗ ἡ ἀρχὴ ἐγενήθη ἐπὶ τοῦ ὤμου αὐτοῦ, καὶ καλεῖται τὸ ὄνομα αὐτοῦ Μεγάλης βουλῆς ἄγγελος·

In Matthew's Gospel (2:1–6), when Herod is visited by the wise men from the East, he calls together priests and scribes to inform him about prophecies regarding the Messiah's birth. The passage they quote is not this one, but rather one from the prophet Micah (5:2) which foretells the birthplace of the Messiah. Romanos' congregation probably heard this reading from Matthew (2:1–12) in the week before (on the Feast of the Nativity) and he is counting on it being fresh in their minds. He breaks their expectations by quoting from Isaiah, and thereby gives more dramatic power to the fulfilment of this prophecy in Christ. Romanos

---

[60] See MacCormack (1982), 292.
[61] I do not quote all of them here. See also IV.9, XXVIII.6 and XXX.12.

uses Isaiah to show how pointless is Herod's massacre of the innocent children: if God is as powerful in the person of Jesus Christ, even as an infant, nothing Herod can do will change what God has planned to accomplish.

Romanos makes clever dramatic use of prophecy in *On the Resurrection II*, depicting a succession of prophets in Hades speaking to Adam to declare the fulfilment of their words (XXV.10):

In a sublime voice Sophonias cried out to Adam, 'This is the one,
whom you awaited until the day of resurrection, as I proclaimed to you.'
And Nahum, after him, proclaimed good news for the poor man, saying,
'He has risen from the earth, breathing upon your face,
he who sets free from affliction',
and Zacharias crying out in joy, 'You have come, our God,
with your holy [saints]',
and David singing the good omens thus: 'Power has woken up
and as if from sleep
the Lord is risen.'

Ὑψηλῇ τῇ φωνῇ ὁ Σοφονίας τῷ Ἀδὰμ ἀνεβόα· 'οὗτός ἐστιν,
  ὃν ὑπέμεινας εἰς ἡμέραν ἀναστάσεως, ὃν τρόπον προεῖπόν σοι'·
Ναοὺμ δὲ μετὰ τοῦτον τὸν πτωχὸν εὐηγγελίζετο,
  'ἐκ γῆς ἀνέβη', λέγων, 'ἐμφυσῶν σου εἰς τὸ πρόσωπον,
[[ὁ]] ἐξαιρούμενος θλίψεως',
καὶ Ζαχαρίας χαριεὶς κράζων· 'ἦλθες ὁ θεὸς ἡμῶν
μετὰ τῶν ἁγίων σου',
καὶ Δαβὶδ ψάλλων εὔσημα ὡς· 'δυνατὸς ἐγήγερται
καὶ ὥσπερ ἀπὸ ὕπνου
ἀνέστη ὁ κύριος.'

This passage, and the whole *kontakion*, shows similarities with the apocryphal Gospel of Nicodemus (Part B), in which Christ's harrowing of hell is described in detail.[62] In this text, patriarchs and prophets proclaim that Jesus is the awaited Messiah, and Isaiah stands up and declares his prophecy fulfilled (18.1). Romanos draws on this tradition, and perhaps on the wider (classical and then Christian) tradition of descents into the underworld, as he places four prophets side by side (often closely quoting from

---

[62] For introduction, text and translation, see Ehrman and Plese (2011), 465–89. See also the French translation and commentary: Gounelle and Izydorczyk (1997). On the motif of Christ's descent into hell more broadly, see Gounelle (2000). Gounelle argues that Romanos uses this motif to emphasize the victory and miracle of the resurrection, so that his focus is on Christ's departure from the underworld with all the saints rather than Christ's entry into the underworld: Gounelle (2000), 222–5.

the Septuagint text). The prophets speak directly to Adam, showing the fulfilment of their own words and pointing out the significance of the crucifixion for him and all humanity. Line 2 is a close quote from Sophonias (or 'Zephaniah') 3:8, which refers to the final judgement day, the day on which God will restore the fortunes of his people (see also Zeph. 3:14–20). Line 4 is almost an exact quote from Nahum 2:1 (LXX), a text which was often interpreted as a prophecy of the advent of the Holy Spirit at Pentecost, the occasion in which Christ breathed his spirit upon his disciples.[63] Romanos follows earlier theologians in interpreting Nahum's words as a prophecy of the renewal of life which Christ inaugurates: in the beginning God breathed life into Adam and now he comes to renew that life, again breathing on the face of the first man. In line 5 Romanos makes reference to a passage from Zacharias (or 'Zechariah') (14:5) which again foretells the events of the eschaton, declaring the advent of God with all the saints. The final prophecy is taken from the book of Psalms (77[78].65: 'Then the Lord awoke as from sleep, like a warrior shouting because of wine'; καὶ ἐξηγέρθη ὡς ὁ ὑπνῶν Κύριος, ὡς δυνατὸς κεκραιπαληκὼς ἐξ οἴνου) and Romanos reworks the line to incorporate his refrain.[64] In the psalm, this line is the culmination of Israel's history and the moment at which God angrily awakes and eternally destroys his adversaries. In this passage, Romanos presents a parade of prophets, all declaring their apocalyptic prophecies to be fulfilled in Christ, in his crucifixion and descent into hell.

Humans are not yet in paradise, but the old world in which prophecies are made has passed away. Romanos claims the fulfilment of Old Testament prophecies to emphasize the new creation which the incarnation brings. All prophecies are therefore interpreted christologically, since it is through and in Christ that the transformation of the world has taken place.

Anti-Judaism: the Boundaries of the New Creation

Yet this transformation appears to have its limits. As we have seen, anti-Jewish passages in the *kontakia* suggest that Romanos believed the Jews were excluded from the new creation. We have noted the potential for Romanos' imagery to be socially damaging, but it is worth exploring this aspect of his thought in more detail here.

---

[63] Cyril of Jerusalem, *Catechetical Lectures* 17.12. See also Ferreiro and Oden (2003), 184.
[64] Although Romanos attributes this prophecy to David, the psalm is one of Asaph. 'David' is a generic term for 'psalm' in Romanos.

Two translators of Romanos' hymns differ over his treatment of the Jews. R. J. Schork claims Romanos' work includes 'frequent and virulent anti-Jewish polemic' which he attributes to 'ethnic and sectarian bias – or to the exaggerated zeal of a recent convert'.[65] Romanos uses the word 'Jews' (*Ioudaios*) only nineteen times in his fifty-nine *kontakia*, so, at least at first sight, calling his attack on the Jews 'frequent' seems to be an exaggeration. In stark contrast, Ephrem Lash writes:

Romanos' moderation towards the Jews, despite the mood of the day, was one of the reasons cited by the great classical scholar Paul Maas, a Jewish emigrant from Hitler's Germany, for thinking that Romanos was himself of Jewish stock.[66]

Lash argues that Romanos believed God had a special plan for the Jews, who would be saved at the eschaton.[67] If Romanos did believe this, he would have had modern theological opinion on his side, but would have been extremely unusual in the sixth century.

Despite the problems with both of these opposing views, the fact that each exists points to a difficulty in understanding Romanos' opinions about the Jews. In general, Romanos seems to think that Jews are not included in the new creation, in particular that their rejection of Christ excludes them, as Jews, from paradise. Yet he does not completely condemn them to eternal punishment: there is one passage, as we will see, where Jews are made to see the truth of Christianity in the eschaton.

Romanos uses typology to show that Christians are now God's chosen people, receiving this right from the Jews (XLII.19.1–10):

So, friends, observe these things precisely,
for all these things are proclaimed and inscribed in types.
Esau is a type for the Jews,
and Jacob is presented as an image of Christians,
since he deservedly received his brother's blessing,
through his mother's advice, foretelling [God's] grace to me.
And Rebecca is clearly presented to me
as a type of Christ's church
for, like her, the church also
brings its sons to the father of all.

Ὑμεῖς οὖν ταῦτα ἀκριβῶς κατανοήσατε, φίλοι·
τὰ πάντα γὰρ ἐν τύπῳ προερρέθη καὶ ἐγράφη.

---

65 Schork (1995), 5.
66 Lash (1995), xxvi. Unfortunately Lash does not cite Maas precisely, so I have been unable to verify this statement.
67 That is, Lash thinks Romanos was not a supersessionist. See Lash (1995), 222 n. 12, 224 n. 24.

Ὁ Ἡσαῦ μὲν τύπος   τῶν Ἰουδαίων ὑπάρχει,
Χριστιανῶν δὲ   Ἰακὼβ εἰκόνα προέφερεν,
    ὡς τὴν εὐλογίαν   τὴν τοῦ συγγόνου
    ἔλαβεν ἀξίως   τῇ συμβουλίᾳ τῆς μητρός
                τὴν χάριν προσημάνας μοι·
τύπος δὲ   τοῦ Χριστοῦ   τῆς ἐκκλησίας
    καὶ ἡ Ρεβέκκα μοι   σαφῶς προδέδεικται·
    καθάπερ γὰρ αὕτη   καὶ ἡ ἐκκλησία
    υἱοὺς προσάγει πατρὶ τῶν ὅλων·

Esau is a type for the Jews because he is the first born but both his birthright and the blessing of his father (and God) go to his younger brother, Jacob, who represents Christians. In Genesis, Esau gives up his birthright for food, considering the immediate concerns of his body more important than his position in the family, and is cheated out of his position and his father's blessing, both of which are bestowed on Jacob (Genesis 25:29–34; 27:18–36). Rachel and Jacob are presented as schemers, using trickery to obtain their goal. The result is the murderous anger of his brother, and Jacob is forced to flee (Gen. 27:41–5). Although Jacob is blessed by God, who promises to protect him (Gen. 28:13–15), he is still seen as a usurper. By contrast, the Jacob of Romanos' *kontakion* 'deservedly' received Esau's blessing. Romanos makes Esau a type for the Jews because they gave up their birthright in ignoring the Messiah and therefore do not deserve God's blessing. Christians are represented by Jacob because they receive the birthright and the blessing, which were originally intended for the Jews. Jacob foreshadows God's benevolence to Christians when he receives the inheritance Esau rejected and grasps Esau's blessing. The church, represented by Rachel, is the means by which Christians receive this inheritance.

By the sixth century, Romanos' interpretation of this Old Testament story was standard in Christian theology. Drawing on Paul (primarily Romans 9:6–13), early Christian theologians saw the struggle between an older and a younger brother as prophetic of the strife between Jews and Christians, and the blessing of the younger as proof of God's choice of Christians over Jews.[68] In contemporary Jewish exegesis, however, Esau represents Rome and therefore Christians, and Jacob is Israel.[69] While Romanos' exegesis is traditional within Christianity, the fact that contemporary Jews were employing an opposed (and no less traditional) typology may suggest discursive competition between the two communities.

[68] See, for example, Justin Martyr, *Dialogue with Trypho* 134, and Irenaeus, *Adversus Haereses* 4.21. See Dunn (1998), 133–41.

[69] Yuval (2006), 10–12.

The image of the Jews as the older brother also aligns with Romanos' view that Jews remain wedded to the past, refusing to open their eyes to the new creation. They are so fixated with their past glory that in *On the Resurrection V* they believe they are behaving as their ancestors did under the leadership of Joshua; they fail to recognize that they are in fact killing the second Joshua (XXVIII.8.2). Likewise, in *On the Entry into Jerusalem*, Romanos says (XVI.5):

The lawless ones, behaving unfairly, embraced ignorance,
                            and from then on were ignorant
about the one they planned to kill. They did not know him,
                                        the sons of deceit!
What they say is not strange, for they remake the past.
When Moses led them out of Egypt
                        straightaway he was denied by them.
And Christ, who saved them from death, was just now unknown [by them].[70]
Those who knew the calf refused to know Moses,
The friends of Belial denied Christ.
For this reason they did not wish to cry out,
'You are the blessed one who comes to call up Adam.'

Ἀγνωμονοῦντες ἄνομοι   τὴν ἄγνοιαν ἠσπάσαντο,
                            καὶ δῆθεν ἠγνόησαν
    ὃν κτεῖναι ἐσκέπτοντο·   οὐκ ἠπίσταντο   οἱ τοῦ ψεύδους υἱοί·[71]
    οὐ ξένον ὅπερ λέγουσι·   τὰ γὰρ πρῶτα καινίζουσι·
Μωσῆς ἐξαγαγὼν   αὐτοὺς ἐξ Αἰγύπτου
                        εὐθὺς ἠρνήθη ὑπ' αὐτῶν·
    καὶ Χριστὸς ὁ σώσας   αὐτοὺς ἐκ τοῦ θανάτου νῦν ἠγνοήθη·
ἠγνόησαν Μωσῆν   οἱ γνόντες τὸν μόσχον,
    ἠρνήσαντο Χριστὸν   οἱ φίλοι Βελίαρ·
    ὅθεν οὐκ ἠθέλησαν βοᾶν·
῾Εὐλογημένος εἶ ὁ ἐρχόμενος   τὸν Ἀδὰμ ἀνακαλέσασθαι.'

Romanos draws on New Testament characterizations when he calls the Jews 'sons of deceit' and 'friends of Belial'.[72] In John's Gospel, Jesus himself accuses the Jews of being the devil's offspring (John 8:44–5):

You are from your father the devil, and you choose to do your father's desires. He was a murderer from the beginning and does not stand in the truth, because there is no truth in him. When he lies, he speaks according to his own nature, for he is a liar and the father of lies. But because I tell the truth, you do not believe me.

---

70   With the sense of 'refusing to know'.
71   I have followed the punctuation in the SC edition here.
72   On the charge of deicide laid against the Jews, see 1 Thessalonians 2:14–16.

For the Gospel writer, the sins of the devil stem from his untruthfulness. Romanos taps into this characterization: the sins of the Jews (lawlessness, deceit, deliberate ignorance, denial) are all outcomes of their rejection of truth.

But Romanos does not leave it there. He sets up a comparison between the Exodus narrative and Christ's crucifixion. Moses is a type for Christ; Old Testament saviour is a type for the ultimate saviour. The Jews rejected their first saviour and now they reject the second. Romanos presents them as an unchanged people; they behave much as their ancestors did in the escape from Egypt. But their fault is greater now: before they rejected a temporary saviour, but now they reject the one who eternally saves them from death; before they worshipped idols, but now Romanos presents them as friends of the devil.

In *On the Crucifixion,* Satan encourages the Jews to be part of his plan to crucify Jesus (XXI.8):[73]

Behold I see the Sanhedrin of the Jews
discussing it amongst themselves and being engrossed.
Do they perhaps want what I am planning?
So, approaching I will say, 'Be men,
because you anticipate my plan.
So since you are very serious about it,
what do you say now, so that he might suffer,
the one who is everywhere, filling all things?'

Ἰδοὺ δὴ τῶν Ἰουδαίων   τὸ συνέδριον βλέπω
    καθ' ἑαυτὸ ἀδολεσχοῦν   καὶ ἀπησχολημένον·
τάχα ἃ λογίζομαι βουλεύονται;
ἐγγίσας οὖν εἴπω·   'ἀνδρίζεσθε,
    ὅτι τὴν βουλήν μου   προλαμβάνετε·
ἐπειδὴ οὖν   σπουδαιότεροι ἐστέ,
    τί λέγετε νῦν, ἵνα πάθῃ
ὁ πανταχοῦ τὰ πάντα πληρῶν;'

Satan makes use of the Jewish hatred of Jesus to further his aims, but the Jews are by no means unwilling partners. Romanos makes the Jews into demons by giving them shared aims with the devil, even to the extent of anticipating his plans. In the next strophe they report back to Satan about their actions (XXI.9.3–8):

Put your mind at rest.
We have accomplished what you had planned.

73 See also XXII.2.6–8.

Let nothing worry you. Be carefree.
Jesus has been handed over and denied,
bound, given to Pilate,
[Jesus] who is everywhere, filling all things.

> … Ἀπόθου τὴν φροντίδα σου·
> ἃ εἶχες τελέσαι ἐτελέσαμεν·
> μηδέν σοι μελήσει· ἀμερίμνησον·
> παρεδόθη καὶ ἠρνήθη Ἰησοῦς,
> ἐδέθη, ἐδόθη Πιλάτῳ
> ὁ πανταχοῦ τὰ πάντα πληρῶν.

Short phrases in this passage make the actions of the Jews seem business-like and complete. The use of cognates (line 4: *telesai etelesamen*) reinforces the link between Satan and the Jews. The Jews characterize Jesus as passive and beaten by their actions by their repeated use of passive verb forms, but Romanos makes sure to undercut this in the refrain, which emphasizes that Jesus cannot be confined. By giving this line to the Jews, spoken perhaps as if they were mocking Jesus, Romanos ensures that the Jews themselves become the mockery.

Romanos then uses the Old Testament stories of manna in the wilderness (Exodus 16) and the golden calf (Exodus 32:1–10) to characterize the Jews as lawless, fickle betrayers of God: after eating the manna God provided, the Israelites then betrayed him and worshipped a golden calf (XXI.10). In this case, Romanos puts the words into the mouth of Satan, who sees this as evidence that the Jews are trustworthy partners of the devil (XXI.10). Satan believes that the Jews only pretended to hate him, using words against him but actions against God (XXI.11).

The devil also establishes the character of the Jews as bound by the Law and yet lawless (XXI.12):[74]

I see that you uphold the letter of the Law of Moses
but you do not bind fast these things within your spirit.
You carry them about on your tongue and not in your thought.
You lift up the books in your hand,
but you touch them not at all in your heart.
Let him call you and believe you to be
readers and not understanders of the Scriptures,
the one who is everywhere, filling all things.

> Ῥητὰ τοῦ νόμου Μωσέως βλέπω ὅτι κρατεῖτε,
> ἀλλὰ μὴ σφίγξητε αὐτὰ ἐντὸς τῆς διανοίας·

---

[74] On the Jews as lawless and their leaders as hubristic and stupid murderers, see also III.12.7.

γλώσση καὶ μὴ γνώμη περιφέρετε·
χερσὶ τὰ βιβλία   βαστάζετε,
   φρεσὶ δὲ μηδ' ὅλως   αὐτῶν θίγετε·
ἀναγνώστας   καὶ μὴ γνώστας τῶν γραφῶν
   καλείτω ὑμᾶς καὶ ἡγείσθω
ὁ πανταχοῦ τὰ πάντα πληρῶν.

These words have greater force coming from the character of Satan. Not only does Romanos say the Jews merely pay lip service to the Law, but he makes it a compliment from the devil. Their behaviour makes the Jews the perfect partners for Satan in all his actions, but particularly in his plans to destroy the second Adam.

Finally, in *On the Massacre of the Innocents*, a *kontakion* all about the fate of the children in Herod's vicious campaign, Romanos uses the image of fertility to denigrate the Jews: the land of the Jews is barren and not filled with good (III.15.8), so the child Jesus leaves it behind (7) and goes to Egypt, where the river Nile makes the land fruitful (9). Fruitfulness is associated with Jesus but also with places external to Israel.

Most of the references to the Jews in Romanos' *kontakia* fit into this mould. The Jews participate in the crucifixion of Christ and so not only reject the Messiah but actively help to kill him. These actions, which Romanos says are just a continuation of their behaviour in the Old Testament, where they frequently turn their backs on God, fit them to be allies of Satan and exclude them from God's second creation. Their choices have made their land barren and isolated them from the flourishing paradise to which they were originally called.

There is one passage, however, which would seem to cast doubt on Romanos' belief in the complete exclusion of Jews from the new paradise (XXXIV.3.4–9):

And when things in heaven and on the earth and those under the earth altogether glorify and worship Christ the crucified one
and clearly confess that he is God and the creator,
then the Jews, lamenting, will look upon the one whom they pierced.
The just will shine, crying out, 'Glory to you,
Most Just Judge.'

ὅτε καὶ τὰ οὐράνια καὶ τὰ ἐπίγεια   ἅμα καὶ καταχθόνια
   δοξολογήσει καὶ προσκυνήσει   Χριστὸν τὸν σταυρωθέντα
   καὶ σαφῶς ὁμολογήσει   ὡς θεός ἐστι καὶ κτίστης·
τότε Ἰουδαῖοι   ὄψονται θρηνοῦντες   εἰς ὅνπερ ἐξεκέντησαν·
   οἱ δίκαιοι λάμψουσι   κραυγάζοντες· 'Δόξα σοι,
κριτὰ δικαιότατε.'

The phrase about the Jews is a reference to a passage from the prophet Zechariah (12:10, 13:1):

And I will pour out a spirit of compassion and supplication on the house of David and the inhabitants of Jerusalem, so that, when they look on the one whom they have pierced, they shall mourn for him, as one mourns for an only child ...
  On that day a fountain shall be opened for the house of David and the inhabitants of Jerusalem, to cleanse them from sin and impurity.

Reference to this passage suggests that Romanos believes the Jews will be redeemed at the eschaton, and points again to the centrality of an analogical reading of the Old Testament, which transforms it into a Christian frame without eliminating it. But their lamentation is meant to imply a recantation: the Jews will acknowledge their mistake in crucifying Christ and repent and, having become Christians (by being baptized in the fountain), they will be redeemed.[75] This passage might imply that Romanos believed in universal salvation. The revelation of Christ as God at the eschaton would cause all non-believers to believe. All people, including Jews, would thus become Christians at the end of time and would therefore be redeemed. However, the key thing for our purposes is that Romanos does not allow Jews to retain their identity as Jews in paradise: all will be made Christian.

How should we understand Romanos' views about the Jews in the context of wider Jewish–Christian relations? Many late antique Christian writers, for whom the continuation of Judaism was a threat to their theology and world-view, engaged in vehement anti-Jewish polemic. Such sentiments also pervade other Christian writings which were not specifically written against Jews and Judaism. Romanos fits into this latter category.

There has been debate in recent scholarship about the extent to which early Christian and late antique anti-Judaic polemical texts reflect real situations and the extent to which 'the Jew' in such texts is a mere figure, a straw man set up to aid Christian theological argument.[76] But these ideas seem to be too polarized. The anti-Judaism of these texts is neither entirely about real conflicts nor entirely divorced from such conflict, making use of a 'hermeneutic Jew'.[77] As we have seen throughout this book, there is no such thing as 'mere rhetoric'; the 'hermeneutic Jew' can be a hermeneutic of violence. Rhetoric is performative and, in the case of anti-Judaism,

---

[75] Romanos seems to use this passage from Zechariah in the same way as the writer of the Book of Revelation (1:7). See Harrington (1993), 47.

[76] On this debate and against the 'straw man' argument, see, for example, Carleton Paget (2010), 43–5, Jacobs (2004), 200–6.

[77] Jacobs (2004), 207ff. For 'the hermeneutic Jew' see Cohen (1999).

Christian polemics perform both their hatred of and the power they have over the Jews living in their Christian empire.[78]

Judaism was a threat to Christians on many levels. From apostolic times on, there were competitions between Jewish and Christian groups over converts, liturgy and ritual practices.[79] Jewish and Christian communities continued to live side by side for centuries, so there was naturally some interaction between the two groups.[80] Many theologians and preachers recognized that Judaism had a certain cultural appeal to their flock, so that we hear of 'Judaizing' Christians who, although Christian, still celebrated Jewish feasts, maintained certain Jewish rituals or viewed the synagogue as a particularly sacred or mystical place.[81] This practice, which blurred the distinction between the two religions and so threatened the truth claims of Christianity, was troubling to preachers like John Chrysostom and Ephrem the Syrian.[82] Chrysostom calls Judaizing practices a sickness, labelling Judaizers as 'half-Christians'.[83] Their illness consisted in observing the practices of a religion which was a perversion, a rejection of God and his Son.[84] Ephrem characterizes the Jews as blind, stubborn and shameful, and paints them with the blood of Christ.[85] He emphasizes circumcision as a defining characteristic of the Jews to support his argument that the categories of 'Jew' and 'Christian' are mutually exclusive.[86] Just as Chrysostom does, Ephrem links contemporary Jews with their ancient forebears, arguing that their wilful and persistent rejection of Christ has lost them the covenant relationship with God.[87]

We can see that the 'stubbornness' of Jews in maintaining their faith was a puzzle for Christians, who believed that the advent of Christ should have meant the end of Judaism and the complete conversion of all Jews to Christianity.[88] So continuing Jews became a symbol of sin and separation

---

[78] Jacobs (2004), 207.

[79] Carleton Paget (2010), 55–6, Fredriksen and Irshai (2006), 988. Early polemics on both sides are also part of self-definition: Boyarin (2007), 71–2.

[80] Fredriksen (2007), 61–2.

[81] On which phenomenon, see Gager (1983), 117–33, Wilken (1983). There were also 'Jewish Christians' who were essentially Jewish but incorporated elements of Christianity into their worship. See Frankfurter (2007), 134–5.

[82] Sandwell (2007), 82–4.

[83] Sandwell (2007), 83–4.

[84] Sandwell (2007), 85.

[85] Shepardson (2008), 34, 47, 50–1.

[86] Shepardson (2008), 38.

[87] Shepardson (2008), 48–59, 81, 85–6.

[88] It is for this reason that Judaism was sometimes referred to as a heresy. See Cameron (2007), 357.

from God and therefore a blot to be wiped out before the second coming of the Messiah. One reading of the history of God's action in the world is that after Jesus, God's promise to Israel is replaced or superseded by a promise to Christians (supersessionism). While such a reading may not be true to Paul, it was normal in the sixth century.[89]

Romanos may well have been responding to conflict between Jews and Christians in the sixth century. The emperor Justinian had interfered in Jewish religious matters by legislating that the scriptures must be read in Greek (or the local language) in the synagogue.[90] Justinian also excluded several laws protecting Judaism and the rights of Jews, even removing the statement of Judaism's legality, in his codification of the law.[91] Malalas mentions rioting amongst Jews, Samaritans and Christians in Palestine in 529 and 556 (18.35; 18.119). Procopius refers to the forced conversion of Jews and the re-sanctification of synagogues as churches (*Buildings* 6.2.21–3).[92] This all points, at the very least, to an ongoing animosity between the two groups. From the other side, anti-Christian polemic marks much contemporary Jewish hymnography.[93] Romanos' theological claims about the sin of the Jews in the time of Christ helped his congregation glory in the new creation but it would also have resonated with such sixth-century conflicts. Romanos' listeners would certainly have been aware of the contemporary situations and his comments would therefore have played into existing hatred, fear and unease about the Jewish people living in Constantinople.

Conclusions

The idea of new creation permeates Romanos' hymns. The world is a dramatically different place after the incarnation than what it was before. The life of Christ and his death and resurrection are the fulfilment of all history. But Romanos is aware that the world does not look very different, that it is necessary to argue strongly for a changed reality in a still very broken

---

[89] This has been emphasized by the so-called 'new perspective' on Paul, for which see Dunn (2007).

[90] For an interpretation of *Novel* 146 as an attempt by Justinian to eradicate the use of Hebrew in synagogues, see Rutgers (2003). Perczel suggests Pseudo-Caesarius could have been involved in the preparation of this law, based on the anti-Jewish polemic in his *Erotapokriseis*: Perczel (2006), par. 32.

[91] De Lange (2005), 420.

[92] There is some archaeological evidence for this, but also evidence of new synagogues being built. See De Lange (2005), 406.

[93] On anti-Christian polemic in Hebrew poetry, see Van Bekkum (1993).

world. Rhetoric and liturgical experience come to Romanos' aid. He makes his case through the rhetorical devices of paradox and typology. Paradox enacts the new creation by combining conflicting realities. Typology brings together Old and New Testament events, illustrating that the Old Testament is fulfilled and surpassed by the New and that the time of prophecy has come to an end. All prophecies are brought to fruition in Christ. Both these devices are also used to show that the Jews are not part of this new creation.

Yet Romanos recognizes that the world has not ultimately been perfected. His *kontakia* also exhibit a strong sense of anticipation of the final eschatological event: the second coming of Christ. As the final consummation of God's actions in Christ, the eschaton is an event which Romanos wants his congregation to look for with anticipation. But how are they to prepare for this coming event? The following chapter investigates how Romanos makes his congregation participate in this new creation and how he believes they should live in preparation for the final resurrection.

4 | The Second Coming: A Theology of Time and Liturgy

Romanos' conception of the second creation drives him both to encourage participation in it now and to direct his listeners to anticipate its ultimate consummation in the second coming of Christ. Participation in the present new creation means taking part in the life of Christ and in the perfected humanity of Christ. This is also part of anticipation of the second coming. One central way in which this participation takes place is in the liturgy, which regularly makes the events in the life of Christ present realities. The *kontakia* are liturgical texts, probably performed, as we have seen, as part of the night vigil which ended at the Great Church for the Sunday eucharistic service.[1] By drawing attention to the participatory parts of the liturgy, Romanos re-enacts and reinforces liturgical participation through his *kontakia*. Romanos' conceptualization of liturgical time and the dramatic nature of the *kontakia* enable him to draw his congregation into participation in Christ and his new reality and focus their minds on the approaching eschaton. Participation in Christ and his new creation happens in different ways: liturgical participation, participation in the Gospel stories and participation in Christ-like models. The rhetorical techniques of *ekphrasis*, characterization and apostrophe are the important ones here: Romanos brings the biblical narratives to life through such devices, making the congregation eyewitnesses and participants in the events and presenting them with models of behaviour. In these ways, Romanos directs them in Christ-like living in preparation for the second coming.

Liturgical Time

The Divine Liturgy partakes of eternity. In the liturgy past, present and future are telescoped. Liturgical time is time in its fullness, experienced as a simultaneous whole. Worship taking place on earth in Constantinople was considered to be one with worship taking place in heaven and throughout the ages.

---

[1] Frank (2006), 59–78, Koder (2005), 21, Krueger (2005), 297, Lingas (1995), 50–2, Louth (2005), 199–200, McGuckin (2008), 649–50. The setting of the *kontakion* is also discussed in the Introduction to this book.

Past and present events converge, paradigmatically, in the eucharist.[2] John Chrysostom argued that the eucharist makes the incarnation present:[3]

For if we attend [the eucharist] in faith, we will definitely see him lying in the manger; for the table itself fulfils the position of the manger.

καὶ γὰρ, ἂν μετὰ πίστεως παραγενώμεθα, πάντως αὐτὸν ὀψόμεθα ἐπὶ τῆς φάτνης καίμενον· ἡ γὰρ τράπεζα αὕτη τάξιν τῆς φάτνης πληροῖ.

The eucharist makes present at once the incarnate life of Christ. Theodore of Mopsuestia believed that at the eucharist Christ died, rose and ascended into heaven again.[4] This understanding of the sacrament makes sense within liturgical time, time in its fullness, a time which participates in God's eternal comprehension of all historical time.[5] Such a view of time was available to Romanos in contemporary theologians and philosophers, who distinguished eternity as continuing temporal duration from eternity as the simultaneous atemporal apprehension of all time. This latter atemporal eternity was characteristic of divinity. This logical division is conceptually similar to Romanos' view of the fullness of liturgical time, but his poetry does not dwell on the philosophy. Rather, his hymns are partly generated by, and partly seek to deepen the experience of, the liturgy as the place where all time converges by bringing the worshipper into the presence of God. Where Chrysostom had emphasized the alteration of standard temporal succession in the eucharist, Romanos extends this claim to the sermon, and, through wide-ranging injunctions in the hymns, to the rest of the liturgy. Past, present and future converge in the *kontakia*. This convergence is partly performed through, and partly governed by, rhetorical participation.[6] Romanos' hymns encourage worshippers to experience time in a new way in the liturgy and thereby to participate in the divine life.

A similar view of the fullness of liturgical time is evident in the *Christian Topography* of the roughly contemporary sixth-century writer Cosmas Indicopleustes. Cosmas also believed that the incarnation meant a dramatic change in time and history. Citing Matthew 11:13, Cosmas argued that the

---

[2] Schulz (1986), 15.

[3] *Hom. de beato Philogono* 6 (PG 48, 753).

[4] *Commentary on the Eucharist.* See Mingana (1933), 83.

[5] M. S. Champion has analysed a similar 'fullness of time' in the fifteenth-century low countries: M. S. Champion (2014).

[6] The idea of eternal time as opposed to linear, historical time is also used by Cyril of Jerusalem (among others) in his *Mystagogical Catecheses*. In the fourth lecture (*On the Body and Blood of Christ*) he says that the bread of the Old Testament came to an end, but 'in the New Testament there is the bread of heaven' (Section 5). Translation taken from Yarnold (2000), 180.

time of prophecy came to an end with the advent of John the Baptist and that all prophecies were fulfilled in Christ (*CT* II.73).[7] For Cosmas, this has important political implications. The time of prophecy has come to fulfilment, which means that Daniel's prophecy of the fifth and everlasting kingdom must also be fulfilled (Dan. 2:44–5). Since Rome became an empire at the time of Christ's incarnation, the Roman empire must be God's kingdom and the emperor God's regent on earth (*CT* II.66–71).[8] The Roman empire is therefore eternal and time itself is telescoped, so that past, present and future no longer exist and everything takes place 'now'.[9] Cosmas believed that the incarnation occasioned a dramatic change in reality. This does not mean, however, that his eschatology was fully realized; he still awaits the second coming.

The fact that similar ideas appear in two such different but contemporary authors suggests that these concepts were more generally important in the empire in the sixth century. MacCormack has pointed to the importance of new creation for Cosmas' political thought and in particular for later Byzantine political theory.[10] It seems unlikely that politics was Romanos' driving purpose, even if it may have been in some hymns or on some level,[11] but the comparison with Cosmas' work does show some continuity of eschatological ideas throughout the empire in the sixth century and the potential political implications of his theology.

Liturgical Time in Romanos' *Kontakia*

In many of his hymns Romanos talks about the Gospel events as if they are happening right now: 'today the Virgin gives birth to the one above being' (ἡ παρθένος σήμερον τὸν ὑπερούσιον τίκτει) (I.Pr.1); 'today the foundations of the earth trembled' (σήμερον ἐταράττετο τῆς γῆς τὰ θεμέλια) (XX.Pr.1).[12] These statements heighten the drama of the hymns; it is as if Romanos opens a theatrical performance, like an actor reciting the prologue of a play.[13] He simultaneously brings the events to his listeners

---

[7] See also MacCormack (1982), 292.

[8] See also MacCormack (1982), 292–3.

[9] MacCormack (1982), 302. See also Champion (2006), 387.

[10] MacCormack (1982), 302.

[11] See, for example, Varghese (2006). Koder argues that the *kontakia* may have helped increase devotion to the emperor: Koder (2010).

[12] These are just two of many instances.

[13] On the possible existence of theological plays performed in the liturgy, see La Piana (1936), esp. 178ff. Although this idea is appealing, it has long been shown to be fairly implausible. See, for example, Baud-Bovy (1938a), 321, 329, 334.

and his listeners to the events. The congregation is invited not only to view the events of Christ's life as they unfold, but also to take part in the drama of the Gospel stories. Romanos calls on his listeners: 'Let us rush to the God-bearer, we who wish to see her son brought before Symeon' (Τῇ θεοτόκῳ προσδράμωμεν οἱ βουλόμενοι κατιδεῖν τὸν υἱὸν αὐτῆς | πρὸς Συμεὼν ἀπαγόμενον) (IV.1.1–2). It is possible to see many parallels both with ancient drama and with modern narrative techniques in film and literature in these dramatic statements. But, unlike that of the tragedian or the modern film-maker, Romanos' invitation is not simply dramatic; it is most importantly theological. Through it he emphasizes the present reality of the new creation: Gospel events take place 'now' (V.Pr.1–2; VII.4.8–9, my emphasis):

Today you appeared to the inhabited world,
and your light, Lord, was signalled to us;

Ἐπεφάνης *σήμερον*   τῇ οἰκουμένῃ
καὶ τὸ φῶς σου, κύριε,   ἐσημειώθη ἐφ' ἡμᾶς

… and *just now* at the marriage he changes its [i.e. water's] nature again,
the one who made all things in wisdom.

ἐν τοῖς γάμοις δὲ ἄρτι   φύσιν πάλιν μεταβάλλει
ὁ τὰ πάντα   ἐν σοφίᾳ ποιήσας.

As we have seen above, the baptism of Christ and the miracle in Cana (to take the examples of these two hymns) are not merely historical events – they transcend temporality and are present in sixth-century Constantinople. In the first example, taken from *On the Baptism of Christ*, sometimes called *On the Holy Theophany*,[14] Romanos asserts that the revelation of Christ as God at his baptism is not merely a single point in time. It is an event which recurs 'today', the day on which Christ's baptism is celebrated by the church. In this event Jesus was revealed as God to historical figures like John the Baptist and to 'us' at the same moment.

In *On the Marriage at Cana*, before the two lines quoted above, Romanos makes a comparison between Old and New Testament events. He describes the Old Testament miracles in Egypt (Exodus 7ff.) as past events (VII.4.2–7):

He who long ago showed the power of miracles to the Egyptians
                                        and the Hebrews themselves.
For then the nature of water was miraculously changed into blood.
He brought ten-plague-anger against the Egyptians,

---

14   Ephrem Lash uses this title: Lash (1995), 37–47.

he prepared a passable sea for the Hebrews,
which they quickly travelled through as though on dry land.
In the desert he supplied water from a rock for them …

ὁ πρώην Αἰγυπτίοις δείξας
        καὶ Ἑβραίοις αὐτοῖς τῶν θαυμάτων τὴν δύναμιν·
τότε μὲν γὰρ εἰς αἶμα   ἡ τῶν ὑδάτων φύσις
           θαυμαστῶς μετεβάλλετο·
δεκάπληγον ὀργὴν   Αἰγυπτίοις ἐπῆξε,
τὴν θάλασσαν βατὴν   τοῖς Ἑβραίοις παρέσχεν,
ἣν ὡς χέρσον   σπουδαίως διώδευσαν·
ἐν τῇ ἀνύδρῳ ὕδωρ χορηγεῖ   ἀπὸ τῆς πέτρας αὐτοῖς,

The miracles in Egypt took place 'long ago' and 'then'. By contrast, the life of Christ is ever-present: the miracle at Cana takes place 'now'. The similarity of the two miracles creates a typological link between the two events: the changing of water into blood foreshadows the changing of water into wine. Romanos shows continuity between the God of the Old Testament and that of the New; the second miracle is inextricably linked to the first: God changes the nature of water 'again'. Romanos uses the verb 'to change' to refer to both miracles, placing the verb in the same position each time, so that the contrast between what happened in the past and what is a present reality is even more striking.

There is one event which he talks about as a future event, seemingly reverting to a linear idea of time. This is the eschaton, the second coming of Christ and final judgement. In the second hymn on the resurrection (XXV.22.4), Romanos says:

For you will come, my saviour, not as just now from the tomb,
          but from the firmament.

ἐλεύσῃ γὰρ, σωτήρ μου,   οὐχ ὡς ἄρτι ἐκ τοῦ μνήματος
         ἀλλ' ἐκ τοῦ στερεώματος

Once again the New Testament event, the resurrection of Christ, is a present event that has happened 'just now'. But Romanos uses the future tense (*eleusē*) to refer to Christ's second coming, the final resurrection. This may, however, be understood within the general picture of the fullness of liturgical time, past, present and future, in Romanos' *kontakia*. Of course he does not think that he is currently in paradise. In his *kontakion On Earthquakes and Fires*, for instance, Romanos' awareness of human frailty and sin and the devastating effects of natural and man-made disasters is all too obvious (e.g. stanzas 13 and 14). Paradise does not yet exist on earth. So Romanos holds in tension the idea of the present new creation and that of the coming eschaton and final consummation of that creation. The incarnation was an eschatological event, which changed the nature of reality. He accentuates this by the concept of liturgical time: prophecies are fulfilled, all history culminates in the incarnation and we may anticipate the coming paradise by enjoying the divine liturgy now. And yet Romanos still looks for the final consummation of God's promise. In this sense, the period in between the incarnation and the eschaton (in which Romanos lives) is one in which prophecies are confirmed and in which anticipation reigns. The future revelation of divine glory can be experienced as present anticipation.

Participatory Theology

Both the present reality of Christ and the present anticipation of his future advent require Christians to live Christ's life, to participate in his earthly life and his perfect humanity. But how do humans do this? Romanos argues, as we saw in Chapter 2, that Christ corrects and perfects humanity. He draws attention to this changed human nature through the senses. Sight, hearing, taste, smell and touch are such physical human qualities that a change in them is dramatic. In *On the Epiphany* and *On the Nativity II,* Romanos makes explicit the fallen state of humanity before the incarnation and its redemption by God. The first stanza of *On the Epiphany* begins thus (VI.1.1):

For Adam, blinded in Eden, the sun appeared from Bethlehem

τῷ τυφλωθέντι Ἀδὰμ ἐν Ἐδὲμ   ἐφάνη ἥλιος ἐκ Βηθλεέμ

The blindness represents the darkness which Adam inhabits: his fallen state, his humanity, his lack of faith or spiritual understanding, his death. And, since Adam represents all fallen humanity, the blindness is also general human blindness. The physical nature of the affliction makes it easier for the congregation to imagine and relate to it. Christ is the Sun which enables him to see: Adam is brought from the darkness of sin into the light of heaven by Christ's actions. But the literal meaning of blindness is also important, since it highlights the goodness of sight. Lack of sight is associated with darkness and sin, whereas sight is connected with light and the divine. Blindness represents the state of humanity after the Fall, and sight its state after its redemption by Christ. The fruit which in Genesis 3:6–8 causes Adam's eyes to be opened to his nakedness is described by Romanos as 'blind-making' (VI.2.1). By turning away from God and eating the forbidden fruit Adam could only destroy his sense of sight, not improve it. Christ alone can restore Adam's sight.

Yet it is not only the sinful Adam who cannot see; other Old Testament figures in *On the Epiphany* are partially blind. God did not reveal himself to Abraham but appeared like a man (stanza 4), Jacob wrestled with God at night but did not see him (5), Moses only saw God's back (6) and Isaiah saw God only with his spiritual eyes after death and not with bodily eyes (7). Romanos contrasts pre- and post-incarnation figures: those born after the incarnation can truly see God (VI.7.3–5):

The prophet saw in the slumber of his spirit, not with the eyes of his body;
but we, with our fleshly eyes, see
the Lord of Sabaoth ...

εἶδεν ἐν κατανύξει   πνεύματος ὁ προφήτης, οὐκ ἐν ὄμμασι σώματος·
    ἡμεῖς δὲ σαρκικοῖς   ὀφθαλμοῖς θεωροῦμεν
    κύριον Σαβαώθ ...

The senses have been redeemed through the incarnation. Adam's 'blind-making fruit' marred human sight throughout history, even that of the great prophets. But at the incarnation humanity was redeemed – perfected – and so was the sense of sight. Romanos accentuates this redemption through the physical imagery of 'body' and 'flesh': true (perfected) humanness is now the way to know God (VI.8.1–3, 7–8):

The eyes of the earthborn are able to see the heavenly form
The eyes of clay beings behold the immaterial light's beam
                            that cannot be concealed,
which prophets and kings do not see, but desire to see ...
We are not in a dream, but are alert, for we are not of the night.
In the day we see God embodied ...

ἴσχυσαν ὄμματα τῶν γηγενῶν   οὐράνιον θεωρῆσαι μορφήν·
    κατεῖδον βλέφαρα πηλίνων   τοῦ ἀΰλου φωτὸς
                            τὴν ἀκτῖνα τὴν ἄστεκτον,
ἥντινα οἱ προφῆται   καὶ βασιλεῖς οὐκ εἶδον, ἀλλ᾽ ἰδεῖν ἐπεθύμησαν. ...
οὐ φανταζόμεθα, ἀλλὰ νήφομεν·   οὐ γὰρ ἐσμὲν τῆς νυκτός·
    ἐν ἡμέρᾳ ὁρῶμεν   θεὸν σεσωματωμένον ...

Romanos uses variation and repetition to reinforce the miracle: two different words for 'eyes' (*ommata, blephara*) and repetition of 'see' in variant forms. In the incarnation, in God embodied, darkness has given way to light and humans are entwined once again with heavenly things. The dream of the pre-incarnation world is over: humans are now awake and can see God with their perfected human eyes.

Romanos makes the incarnation the central focus of this hymn on the epiphany, using the event that reveals Christ's divinity to show the importance of his humanity: in the incarnation Christ perfects humanity, bringing humans nearer to God: 'He became human so that you might be divine' (ἐγένετο θνητός, ἵνα σὺ θεὸς γένῃ) (VI.3.5).[15] So reality has changed as a result of God becoming human. But what does this mean for Romanos' congregation? How are they to take part in this changed reality?

Liturgical Participation

Romanos' theology of liturgy is central to this question of congregational participation. His understanding of ways worshippers participate in the life of Christ sits within a wider tradition of liturgical participation. So it is worth considering aspects of church architecture and the wider liturgy that inform his poetry. Through this necessarily brief exploration we will gain insight into the sixth-century experience of participation through church attendance.[16] Thus, when we come to explore in detail Romanos' methods of engaging his congregation, we will see how he makes use of the existing tradition and draws on normative conventions and practices to facilitate worshippers' participation in the new creation.

Art and Architecture

In theological tracts, sermons and even secular literature, churches were seen as symbols of heaven and paradise, places in which God himself dwelt.[17] The sixth-century historian Procopius made this claim for the newly rebuilt Hagia Sophia (*Buildings* I.1.61), which epitomized the 'heavenly' church.[18] John Chrysostom characterized churches thus:[19]

For the church is not a barber's shop, nor a perfumery, nor some workshop of men in the agora, but the place of angels, the place of archangels, the kingdom of God, heaven itself.

---

[15] This is a paraphrase of Athanasius' statement in *Festal Letter* 10.8, and is evident elsewhere in Athanasius. See further in Chapter 2 above. By the sixth century, this exchange formula (God became human that humans might become God) was standard theology.

[16] For a discussion of participants' experience of the liturgy, based on their position in the church and what they could see, touch, hear and do, see Caseau (2013), 59–77.

[17] See Taft (1995), 19, Wybrew (1990), 4.

[18] Doig (2008), 68, Taft (1995), 19, (2008), 600. The idea that the place of worship unifies gods and men is not, of course, an exclusively Christian concept.

[19] *Homilia in epistolam primam ad Corinthios* PG 61 col. 313.

οὐ γὰρ κουρεῖον, οὐδὲ μυροπωλεῖον ἡ ἐκκλησία, οὐδὲ ἐργαστήριον ἕτερον τῶν ἐπ' ἀγορᾶς, ἀλλὰ τόπος ἀγγέλων, τόπος ἀρχαγγέλων, βασιλεία θεοῦ, αὐτὸς ὁ οὐρανός.

Three lowly buildings are balanced by three lofty ones, culminating in 'heaven itself'.[20] Chrysostom goes on to say that the things which take place in the church are likewise a heaven: worship on earth partakes in heavenly worship. Church building was therefore based on the idea of the fullness of time and the telescoping of divine and human experience.

This fullness of time was matched by a fullness of space for Theodore of Mopsuestia, who saw particular parts of the church as representing the *loca sancta* (holy places in Palestine where events in Christ's life took place).[21] In his commentary on the eucharist, for instance, Theodore states that the altar (of any church) represents the tomb in which Christ was laid, and that the act of placing the eucharistic bread on the altar therefore symbolizes the placing of Christ's body in the tomb.[22] Through the liturgy, therefore, the 'pilgrim' worshipper is taken on a journey to the Holy Land to experience the events of the Passion first hand.

Churches which were built in the actual *loca sancta* (such as the Church of the Holy Sepulchre in Jerusalem) performed the continuing significance of the events they commemorated – their present reality in the life of believers.[23] The crucifixion and resurrection are eschatological events, events which alter the nature of reality and anticipate the future reign of God. In commemorative churches, worshippers experienced in the present not merely the past historical event but, more significantly, the new creation revealed by these past events. By granting believers access to a past event, therefore, worshippers in fact experienced reality in an anticipatory mode – they anticipated the reign of God by participating in an eschatological space.

Architectural mimesis enabled the *loca sancta* to transcend temporal and spatial boundaries.[24] By designing a church to look like the Church of the Holy Sepulchre in Jerusalem, for example, one could make the Holy Sepulchre present in that church, albeit a long distance from Jerusalem. Pilgrims who had visited the first, or worshippers who had heard it

[20] On the Byzantine image of the imperial court as heaven, see Mango (1980), 151–5.
[21] Meyendorff (1985), 358. On the development of the concept of *loca sancta* in early Christian thought, see Markus (1994). Supporting Markus on the historicization of the liturgy, see Meyendorff (1985), 352. On the art at the holy places of Palestine, see Weitzmann (1974). On the wide reception of Theodore of Mopsuestia, see Becker (2006).
[22] Mingana (1933), 86 (Chapter 5).
[23] On the role these churches played in giving significant events historical and temporal bases, see Loerke (1984), 34. See also Cardman (1982), Frank (2001), 628–9. On the role that *loca sancta* played in helping pilgrims to memorize Gospel narratives, see Frank (2006a).
[24] MacCormack (1990), 28–9.

described, would be transported to Jerusalem when they entered the new church. In this way, the biblical events which were made present at the *loca sancta* could also be made present in the imitative church. Participation in Christ's death and resurrection in Jerusalem could be transported to any similarly designed church in the empire. And, since all Christian churches grant believers access to eschatological events, all Christian churches could to some extent represent these *loca sancta*. All church buildings thus helped to emphasize the role of anticipation in the Christian life.

Liturgical festivals further underscored this sense of participation by anticipation, and also helped to make the fullness of time a lived experience for sixth-century Christians. At the festival of, for instance, the annunciation or the crucifixion, every church became the place of commemoration of the event. This became a more powerful and unified symbol in the sixth century when certain feasts were given fixed and universal dates. Before the emperor Justinian formalized them, the feasts of the annunciation and Christmas were given different dates by different groups of worshipping Christians.[25] Justinian insisted on 25 March for the annunciation and 25 December for Christmas.[26] These festivals helped to shape the liturgical year and, by making them universal, Justinian strengthened their authority and importance, building into the Christian calendar anticipation of the annunciation and nativity of Christ.

Church decoration of the period was also designed to draw the viewers into the action of the event depicted, and, crucially, onwards into the changed reality of divine glory which the event is believed to have achieved.[27] Such artworks therefore also helped the believer to anticipate the divine glory of the new creation. The events are represented symbolically and not exhaustively so that the viewer has to complete the action of the story: viewer becomes participant.[28] The scene in the apse at Sant'Apollinare in Classe, for instance, is only identifiable as a depiction of Christ's transfiguration if one can interpret the symbols. It is not narrative. The viewer needs to recognize the cross in the mandorla as a symbol of the transfigured Christ, and recall the presence of Moses and Elijah at the transfiguration. The viewer participates in the images and thereby in the stories which they depict by decoding their symbols. Liturgical setting is also often a clue to interpreting decoration, and once more draws the viewer into participation in the image. At San Vitale, in Ravenna, four Old Testament characters and stories are depicted in the sanctuary which were considered types of Christ's sacrifice and the eucharist. Once again, the stories are not narrative, and it is

---

[25]   On the anti-Chalcedonian problems with the date of Christmas, see van Esbroeck (1968), 368.

[26]   Allen (2011), 121, van Esbroeck (1968), 371.

[27]   Loerke (1984), 30. On the ability of icons to do this, see Brown and MacCormack (1975).

[28]   Loerke (1984), 30.

partly their link to the crucifixion and the celebration of it in the eucharist which enables the viewer to interpret the images.

Artists played into and expanded these experiences of participation in and anticipation of heavenly reality through colour and light. The Byzantines did not describe colour in terms of hue, but rather in terms of its brightness or dullness.[29] Paul the Silentiary's description of Hagia Sophia, for example, focuses more on the brilliance of the artworks than on their use of particular colours (668–72).[30] John Chrysostom asserts that colour makes an image recognizable: it is a mere outline until someone 'paints the brightness and smears over the colour' (*In epistulam ad Hebraeos*, PG 63, 130A).[31]

Since brilliance was of more importance than hue, mosaicists constructed their artworks so that the light was reflected in different ways, contributing to the mosaic's gleaming qualities.[32] These reflections could help bring a mosaic to life, making it appear slightly different at different times of the day or with fewer or more candles.[33] In this way the mosaics became more participatory, and invited onlookers to engage with them and what they depicted.[34] Crucially, the play of light and colour represented heavenly glory, and thus being drawn into the scintillating light of the mosaics was supposed to draw believers into a present experience of the glory of divine life to which they were being called.

Church buildings combined heavenly and earthly realms, symbolizing the changed creation, and church decoration brought viewers into participation with the events they depicted as well as the glory of paradise. They thus anticipated the future reign of God in their present lives through participation in biblical events and the liturgy of the church. Church art and architecture were designed to facilitate participation in the new reality brought about by Christ's incarnation. They structured Christian experience as active, participatory and anticipatory.

Liturgy

Participation and anticipation are enacted in the liturgy as much as in the architecture and decorative scheme of churches; the liturgy, understood as an image of heaven and a participation in heavenly worship, was most

---

[29] Borsook (2000), 5, James (1991), 68, (2000), 40.

[30] James (2000), 40, 44. Part of the poem is translated in Mango (1972), 80–91.

[31] James (2000), 44. Gregory of Nyssa and others thought similarly. See Frank (2001), 637, James (2003), 227.

[32] Borsook (2000), 9, Demus (1948), 35–7, James (1995), 4–5, (2000), 42.

[33] James (2004), 528.

[34] This light which bounced about the church on mosaics was sometimes considered to symbolize the 'enlightenment of grace': Schulz (1986), 33.

importantly a mode of interaction with the divine.[35] We have already seen how church architecture augments the experience and meanings associated with the eucharist, placing the celebration of the sacrament in a heavenly space:[36]

For whenever you see the Lord sacrificed and lying [on the altar] … do you still consider [yourself] to be among humans and standing on the earth, rather than moving straight to the heavens and throwing away all fleshly thought …?

ὅταν γὰρ ἴδῃς τὸν Κύριον τεθυμένον καὶ κείμενον … ἆρα ἔτι μετὰ ἀνθρώπων εἶναι νομίζεις καὶ ἐπὶ τῆς γῆς ἑστάναι, ἀλλ᾽ οὐκ εὐθέως ἐπὶ τοὺς οὐρανοὺς μετανίστασαι καὶ πᾶσαν σαρκικὴν διάνοιαν ἐκβάλλων …;

For Chrysostom, as for other contemporary theologians, one does not merely see the bread and wine at the eucharist, but Christ crucified. Partaking in the eucharist is not a simple earthly experience, but transports communicants to heaven. In fact, it is God himself who officiates at the eucharist:[37]

But the Father and the Son and the Holy Spirit organize everything. The priest lends his tongue and provides his hand.

ἀλλὰ Πατὴρ καὶ Υἱὸς καὶ ἅγιον Πνεῦμα πάντα οἰκονομεῖ· ὁ δὲ ἱερεὺς τὴν ἑαυτοῦ δανείζει γλῶτταν, καὶ τὴν ἑαυτοῦ παρέχει χεῖρα.

Earthly worship is transformed into heavenly, presided over by the Trinity. Although this idea was current in the fourth and fifth centuries, the sixth century was a period of change and innovation in the liturgy and ceremonies of the church,[38] with growing emphasis being placed on the earthly liturgy's connection to the heavenly.[39] The late sixth century, for example, saw the introduction of the Cherubikon (or 'Cherubic hymn'), a hymn sung at the Great Entrance (i.e. the procession of the elements of bread and wine), which indicated that those bringing forward the elements of bread and wine represented the Cherubim.[40] Further developments in the

---

[35] Theodore of Mopsuestia's fifteenth catechetical sermon (XV.15, 20): Tonneau (1949), 485, 497. See also Bornet (1966), 80–1, Kallistos (1990), 8–9, Meyendorff (1985), 358, Schulz (1986), 32.

[36] *Sur le Sacerdoce* III, 4. See Malingrey (1980), 142–4. See also *In epistulam primam ad Corinthios*, PG 61, col. 313.

[37] *Homilia in Ioannem*, PG 59, col. 472. See also *Hom. in Matt.* PG 58, col. 507, and Kallistos (1990), 15–16, Schulz (1986), 15.

[38] See, for example, Taft (1995), 14. We have already discussed the introduction of fixed feasts by Justinian. See van Esbroeck (1968), 371.

[39] Krueger (2005), 295.

[40] Kedrenos is the source which dates the introduction of the Cherubikon by Justin II to 573/4: Bekker (1838), 685, lines 3–4. On the deacons as symbols of angelic servants of God, see Theodore of Mopsuestia *Hom.* XV.25: Tonneau (1949), 505. See also Kallistos (1990), 11, Schulz (1986), 35.

liturgy in the seventh century placed even more emphasis on this connection between the earthly and heavenly liturgies. The hymn at the Liturgy of the Pre-sanctified Gifts, for instance, mentioned the powers of heaven which invisibly worship with those worshipping on earth.[41] Yet while these sixth- and seventh-century liturgical changes make the connection between heavenly and earthly worship explicit, they should not be read as signalling a completely realized eschatology or a marked departure from earlier practice. Rather, they heighten the sense, present already in the sixth-century liturgy, that human actions can experience the joys of heaven in an anticipatory way.

This emphasis on the link between earthly and heavenly realms is reflected in contemporary theological writings. In his *Ecclesiastical Hierarchy* (II.3.2), Ps-Dionysius the Areopagite writes:

For, as is declared clearly in the treatise *Concerning the Intelligible and the Perceptible*, sacred things which are perceptible are copies of intelligible things and are the guide and the way to them.

Ἔστι γὰρ, ὡς ἐν τῇ *Περὶ νοητῶν* τε καὶ *αἰσθητῶν* πραγματείᾳ σαφῶς διηγόρευται, τὰ μὲν αἰσθητῶς ἱερὰ τῶν νοητῶν ἀπεικονίσματα, καὶ ἐπ' αὐτὰ χειραγωγία καὶ ὁδός.

Not only does the liturgy partake in heavenly life, it also participates in the Gospel stories and brings them into the present experience of the worshippers, something which the late sixth-century patriarch of Constantinople, Eutychius, was keen to emphasize.[42] Different sections of the liturgy represented different events in the life of Christ.[43] Theodore of Mopsuestia (among others) interpreted the liturgy as focusing on the life of Christ.[44] In this scheme the service moves through the events of Christ's life to culminate in the resurrection, Pentecost and the ascension at the celebration of the eucharist. Old Testament prophecies and Christ's birth are commemorated at the beginning of the service. The Little Entrance represents Christ's baptism, the reading of the Gospel represents the preaching in Galilee, and the Great Entrance symbolizes the entry into Jerusalem and the Passion. This was probably the most prevalent interpretation in the sixth century.[45] For Theodore of Mopsuestia, the liturgy is a representation of Christ's

---

[41] See Kallistos (1990), 11.
[42] Krueger (2005), 293–4. Eustratius' *Life* also participates in this concept of time, by setting Eutychius' life in biblical contexts. See Cameron (1990), 212.
[43] For the following, see Kallistos (1990), 20.
[44] See, for example, *Hom.* XV. 25–6: Tonneau (1949), 503–7. See also Bornet (1966), 80–2.
[45] Another interpretation was put forward in the seventh century by Maximus the Confessor, which focused on the eschaton (*Mystagogia* 8ff.) See also Bornet (1966), 121–3.

Passion and death and communicants are called to be witnesses of the cru-cifixion and resurrection.[46] Thus in the liturgy past, present and future are brought together and events which happened in the Old Testament come together, with New Testament events, into the sixth century. Just as these schemes of the liturgy bring together biblical events, so the liturgical cycle brings biblical events into the present and not only commemorates but also relives these events.[47]

The eucharist is a particularly important means of participation in the transformed reality. Christ is truly present in the eucharist in two ways. First, in the bread and wine, which were believed to become the body and blood of Christ.[48] The strength of this belief is demonstrated by contempo-rary stories of disbelief which result in miraculous visions of a child slaugh-tered and presented to the heretic at the eucharist.[49] Secondly, as we saw earlier, Christ was believed to officiate at the eucharist, through the media-tion of the priest.[50]

Baptism is no less participatory, since it was seen as burial and resur-rection with Christ.[51] In Romans 6:3 Paul stated that 'all of us who have been baptized into Christ Jesus were baptized into his death'. Baptism was also seen by some as a marriage between the initiate and Christ.[52] Many preachers and commentators on the liturgy, following Paul, interpreted the descent into the water at baptism as death and burial and the ascent out of the water (usually on the other side of an inbuilt font) as the resurrection.[53]

In addition to these truly physical sacraments, participation in the liturgy could confer other, more sensual experiences.[54] Smell in particular was seen as a way of bridging the divide between humans and the divine, drawing on a long Greco-Roman tradition where fragrance was associated with the presence of divinity.[55] For Cyril of Jerusalem, the holy oil used to anoint the

---

[46] Barber (1991), 50–1, Tonneau (1949), 461–5. See also Bornet (1966), 82.

[47] Merton (1965), 53–6.

[48] This certainly seems to have been the belief in the sixth century, but it was not formalized until the Council of Constantinople in 1157, which condemned the idea that the eucharist was merely a memorial of Christ's sacrifice. See Kallistos (1990), 16. This was called the doctrine of transubstantiation in the West, but that term was not used in the East.

[49] *Sayings of the Desert Fathers* 18.3.

[50] For example, John Chrysostom, *Homilia in Ioannem*, PG 59, col. 472 (quoted above), and Theodore of Mopsuestia's commentary on the eucharist: Mingana (1933), 83. See also Kallistos (1990), 15–16, Schulz (1986), 15, 17.

[51] John Chrysostom, *Catecheses ad illuminandos* 2.11.

[52] Cyril of Jerusalem, *Procatechesis* 1. See also Harvey (2006), 72.

[53] See, for example, Cyril of Jerusalem, *Mystagogical Catecheses* 2.4 and 3.1. See also the Apostolic Constitutions III.17.1, 3. Cf. Whitaker (2003), 32, 36.

[54] This is still the case in Orthodox liturgy. See Wybrew (1990), 5.

[55] Caseau (1999), 107, Harvey (2006), 65, 72.

senses of initiates at baptism undergoes a change not unlike the bread and wine in the eucharist: the oil imparts the Holy Spirit.[56] John Chrysostom asserts that pleasantly scented oil should remind the congregation of the deeds of holy martyrs;[57] Romanos describes faith as a perfume (XXX.15).[58] Learning to understand and attend to the different scents in the liturgy was considered to increase faith and religious understanding as well,[59] making incense a useful devotional tool.[60]

Participation in Christ through the Liturgy

Romanos was well aware of this tradition of participatory theology and practices, and used his *kontakia* to reinforce and enact it for his congregation. Just as the liturgy implies, Romanos believed that the earthly liturgy participates in that which is taking place in heaven. In *On the Multiplication of the Loaves*, the angels watch and marvel at the liturgy taking place on earth (XIII.1.1–5):

All the angels in the heavens marvel at terrestrial things,
because earthborn men dwelling below
are lifted up in thought and reach the things above,
sharing in Christ, the crucified one.
For together they all eat his body.

Πάντες ἄγγελοι   οἱ ἐν οὐρανοῖς   θαυμάζουσι τὰ ἐπίγ[εια],
   ὅτι ἄνθρωποι γηγενεῖς   τὰ κάτω   κατοικοῦντες
ὑψοῦν[ται] τῇ διανοίᾳ   καὶ φθάνουσι   πρὸς τὰ ἄνω
   μέτοχοι Χριστοῦ   [ὄν]τες τοῦ ἐσταυρωμένου·
τὸ σῶμα γὰρ αὐτοῦ   πάντες ἅμα ἐσθίουσι·

Romanos imagines the angels amazed at what God has granted to lowly humans: by receiving the eucharist, humans reach heaven. Mind and body

---

[56] Cyril of Jerusalem, *Mystagogical Catecheses* 3.3.

[57] *Homilia in martyres*, PG 50, col. 664. See also *Catecheses ad illuminandos* 6.22. Quasten and Burghardt (1963), 101.

[58] On Romanos' use of the senses, see Chapter 2 above.

[59] Harvey (2006), 81, 86.

[60] Caseau (1999), esp. 103, Harvey (2006), 128. Many theologians did not encourage use of the senses to bridge the human–divine divide, but talked about fragrance in a metaphorical sense (as Chrysostom does in relation to sin above). On Ephrem's use of the senses in this way, see Harvey (1998). Clement of Alexandria, for instance, interprets the scented oil which the sinful woman uses to wash Christ's feet as a representation of divine instruction or even Christ himself: *Paedagogus* II.8.253–4. Taste was another important sense which had both positive and negative associations in the early church up to the sixth century. Cf. Frank (2001), 626–8, James (2004), 526.

both extend to heaven through the (bodily) eating of the eucharist. The body is important for Romanos (and for Christians more generally) because God chose it as the vehicle for his salvific plans. In the incarnation, Christ took on human form and perfected it and humans can now participate physically in that perfection through their bodily experience in the liturgy. Bodily imagery is often particularly vivid in the Syriac tradition.[61] Ephrem the Syrian talks about worship both as a means of renewal of the body, and the way in which humans learn how to experience things correctly (i.e. as a true Christian).[62] And in the *Odes of Solomon* we see the complete physicality of worshipping God (40:2–4).[63] Romanos sees the physicality of the eucharist in a similar way.

Yet while humans can, through the eucharist, 'reach' the future reign of God, they remain 'earthborn'. As in Romanos' conception of the new creation, his eschatology is not fully realized. Human experience is anticipatory: Romanos urges his congregation to participate in the new creation although the exuberance of his poetry often emphasizes the attainment of heavenly joys on earth. In *On All Martyrs*, heaven and earth join together to praise God (LIX.2.4–6):

For with us even the angels cry out,
'Truly you are wonderful amongst the saints,
very merciful One.'

μεθ᾽ ἡμῶν γὰρ βοῶσι καὶ ἄγγελοι·
'Θαυμαστὸς ἐν ἁγίοις σου εἶ ἀληθῶς,
πολυέλεε.'

Immortal ranks join with those of mortals to praise God in the liturgy. Earthly and heavenly liturgies take place simultaneously, together worshipping God. Romanos' liturgical hymn reinforces that through the liturgy (and therefore through the *kontakion*) the congregation participates in a cosmic liturgy, joining in with angels and saints and people from all ages. His words are heavenly words. This sense is performed by, and helps to generate, the excess of imagery throughout the *kontakia*.

Romanos creates a picture of the church as heaven in *On Earthquakes and Fires* (LIV.23.6–10):

The very home of the church
is being built with such skill

---

[61] Harvey (1999), 106–8.
[62] Harvey (1999), 115.
[63] Harvey (1999), 113.

that it imitates heaven, the divine throne,
which supplies
eternal life.

ὁ οἶκος δὲ αὐτὸς   ὁ τῆς ἐκκλησίας
  ἐν τοσαύτῃ ἀρετῇ   οἰκοδομεῖται,
ὡς τὸν οὐρανὸν   μιμεῖσθαι, τὸν θεῖον θρόνον,
  ὃς καὶ παρέχει
  ζωὴν τὴν αἰώνιον.

The 'home' probably refers to Hagia Sophia, which was in the process of being rebuilt after the Nika riots.[64] Unlike contemporary descriptions of the dome or decoration of the church, Romanos focuses on the skill with which it is constructed; this skill connects the church's construction to God's creation of the heavens and earth. As far as Romanos is concerned, both the church building and the liturgy are intimately connected with heaven. Entering a church is akin to entering heaven, and participation in the liturgy is participation in that which is simultaneously taking place in heaven.

At times Romanos re-enacts parts of the liturgy in the *kontakia*, simultaneously exploring the purpose of different rituals, reminding the congregation of their participation in the new creation and encouraging them to anticipate its consummation through the liturgy. In *On the Epiphany*, Romanos alludes both to the prayer of the Thrice Holy (Trisagion) and to the Sanctus (VI.7.4–8):[65]

But we see with fleshly eyes
the Lord of Sabaoth and the six-winged ones
and we send up a hymn to him:
Holy, holy one made flesh, holy are you, God.
We hallow you three times, one holy of holies ...

  ἡμεῖς δὲ σαρκικοῖς   ὀφθαλμοῖς θεωροῦμεν
  κύριον Σαβαώθ   καὶ τῶν ἑξαπτερύγων
  ὑμνῳδίαν   αὐτῷ ἀναπέμπομεν·
ἅγιος, ἅγιος ὁ σαρκωθείς,   ἅγιος εἶ ὁ θεός·
  ἁγιάζομεν τρίτον   ἕνα ἅγιον ἁγίων

---

[64] Schork makes this clear in his translation: Schork (1995), 194. This hymn is often described and generally accepted as an encomium to Justinian on the occasion of the rebuilding of Hagia Sophia after the Nika Riots. See Barkhuizen (1995), esp. 16, Topping (1978), esp. 25–32, Varghese (2006), 395.

[65] See also *On Judas* (XVII.23). On the dating of the Trisagion (fifth century, but used at the beginning of the eucharistic service from the sixth century), see Taft (1977), 367–8.

Angels in heaven sing both the Trisagion, which was part of the Little Entrance, and the Sanctus, making it clear that the earthly liturgy participates in the heavenly liturgy:[66]

Holy is God who is carried by the six-winged seraphim, while they make a great noise with their wings and sing the triumphal song, 'Holy, holy, holy Lord of Sabaoth, the favourable one.'

ἅγιος ὁ Θεὸς ὁ τοῖς ἑξαπτερύγοις σεραφὶμ ἐποχούμενος καὶ κροτούντων τὰς ἑαυτῶν πτέρυγας καὶ τὸν ἐπινίκιον ὕμνον ὑμνούντων τὸ ἅγιος ἅγιος ἅγιος Κύριος σαβαὼθ ὁ προσδεχόμενος.

Romanos recontextualizes the Trisagion and the Sanctus, accentuating human connection with God through the incarnation, rather than the angelic praise of God. In the new reality, humans (with their 'fleshly eyes') are able to take the role of the angels in the singing of these hymns. But this passage also looks forward to a time when humans will be with the angels and sing praises to God alongside the seraphim.

Reference to the Sanctus also reminds the congregation of the eucharist. Through such references Romanos explains what the congregation participates in when they receive the elements and encourages them to be mindful of this meaning when they communicate. A direct statement of participation in the eucharist is found in *On the Marriage at Cana* (VII.20.3–6):

And now we all take part in the banquet in the church,
for the wine is changed into the blood of Christ,
and we drink it with holy joy,
praising the great bridegroom.

ἄρτι δὲ ἐν τῷ δείπνῳ   τῷ ἐν τῇ ἐκκλησίᾳ
                    ἀπολαύομεν ἅπαντες·
εἰς αἷμα γὰρ Χριστοῦ   μεταβάλλεται οἶνος,
καὶ πίνομεν αὐτὸν   εὐφροσύνῃ ἁγίᾳ
τὸν νυμφίον   τὸν μέγαν δοξάζοντες·

Romanos points to the approaching mass, presenting it as a wedding feast like that at Cana (John 2:1–11): at Cana Christ changed the nature of the water; at the eucharist he changes the nature of the wine.[67] Romanos weaves his narrative with threads of other Gospel stories, using the marital theme

---

[66] From the liturgy of John Chrysostom: Hammond and Brightman (1965), 313.

[67] This story is often used as a symbol of the eucharist. See Barrett (1978), 189, 191, Dodd (1968), 299–300, Meyendorff (1990), 104. For the interpretations of the church fathers, see Smitmans (1966), 94ff.

of the *kontakion* to name Christ as bridegroom and thereby cast him in the eschatological role of Matthew's bridegroom (25:1–13). And so the eucharistic narrative becomes one of the general resurrection. Participation in the eucharist is participation in Christ's death but also in his resurrection. This apocalyptic story encourages Christians to be vigilant; Christian lives should be ones of expectation and anticipation of the coming kingdom.

Hunger and thirst imagery recalls the eucharist and prompts listeners to remember the taste of the bread and wine. In Chapter 2, we saw how Romanos uses the thirst of the Israelites in the wilderness to refer to the eucharist and to Christ as the thirst-quencher. Physical imagery like this is another means of sensory participation in the life of Christ. Romanos draws on memory of the senses in the liturgy to facilitate his congregation's participation in the new creation: through correct use of the senses humans can know God.[68]

Eucharistic drinking is both revelatory and transformative in *On Doubting Thomas* (XXX.3.5–10):[69]

From there the thief drank and became sober,
from there the disciples watered their hearts,
from there Thomas drew the water of the knowledge which he sought.
So first he drinks, then he gives to drink.
Having doubted for a short time, he persuaded many to say
'You are my Lord and my God.'

ἐκεῖθεν ὁ λῃστὴς   ἔπιε καὶ ἀνένηψεν,
    ἐκεῖθεν μαθηταὶ   ἤρδευσαν τὴν καρδίαν,
    ἐκεῖθεν Θωμᾶς ἤντλησε   τὴν γνῶσιν ὧν ἐζήτει·
πίνει οὖν πρῶτος,   εἶτα ποτίζει·
    ἀπιστήσας μικρὸν πολλοὺς ἔπεισε λέγειν·
'Κύριος ὑπάρχεις   καὶ θεὸς ἡμῶν.'

The wound in Christ's side transforms 'doubting Thomas' into a believer, along with the Good Thief and all the disciples. Interestingly the thief becomes sober, although Christ's side recalls the eucharistic wine. *This wine does not make one drunk*; rather, the thief was drunk before and Christ's side – the eucharistic wine – has restored his sobriety. The repetition in lines 5 to 7 emphasizes that it is a universal thirst-quenching and one which satisfies different sorts of thirst: it cures drunkenness (5), cares and cherishes (6), and satiates the thirst for knowledge (7). Christ's wound

---

[68] On the different ways in which sight was believed to give access to God, see Frank (2000). And on the revelation of God through human senses, see James (2004), 522–37.
[69] On writing imagery, see Chapter 2 above. See also Krueger (2003), 2–44, (2004), 159–88.

is a double reference to the eucharist. In the Gospel accounts blood and water come from his side when it is pierced by the soldiers and this is taken as evidence that Christ is already dead (John 19:33–4). Yet these liquids which signify Christ's death do so because they are his life pouring out. So these 'life liquids' become the life-giving elements of the eucharist. The wound also refers to the whole crucifixion, which the eucharist commemorates and in which it participates. Romanos thus demonstrates the transformative power of the eucharist and encourages his listeners both to communicate at the eucharist and to reflect on their communication in order to receive blessings commensurate with those of Thomas, the thief and the other disciples.

In *On the Prodigal Son* Romanos replays the eucharistic rite, imaginatively reinventing the Gospel story (Luke 15:11–32) as an extended metaphor for Christ's sacrifice.[70] The interest for Romanos lies in what it says about the crucifixion and the eucharist. He calls for congregational participation in the eucharistic feast early on in the hymn (XLIX.2.1), but the metaphor for the eucharist runs throughout. The calf which the father sacrifices to celebrate the son's return is Christ (8.1–6):

But now, for the one who has stumbled, sacrifice, as I said,
the virgin calf, the son of the Virgin,
who has not been tamed by the yoke of sin,
who with eagerness goes towards those who drag him.
For he does not revolt against the sacrifice,
but bows his neck willingly for those who hurry to sacrifice him.

Ἀλλ' ὑπὲρ πταίσαντος λοιπὸν   θύσατε νῦν, καθὼς εἶπον,
    τὸν μόσχον τὸν παρθένον,   τὸν υἱὸν τὸν τῆς παρθένου,
    τὸν μὴ δαμασθέντα   ζυγῷ τῷ τῆς ἁμαρτίας,
τὸν προθυμίᾳ   πρὸς τοὺς ἕλκοντας πορευόμενον·
    οὐ γὰρ στασιάζει   πρὸς τὴν θυσίαν,
    ἀλλὰ τὸν αὐχένα   κλίνει ἑκουσίως αὐτοῖς
                    τοῖς θύειν ἐπισπεύδουσιν·

The calf not only prefigures Christ, it *is* Christ.[71] The whole story becomes a metaphor for the crucifixion: the father in the Gospel account is God the Father and the prodigal son is fallen humanity; the calf is Jesus Christ, whom the Father sends to be sacrificed and who willingly submits to the cross for the sake of humanity. He is the sacrifice for those who have stumbled: Adam and all humanity. The fatted calf of the Gospel (Luke 15:23)

---

[70] Barkhuizen (1996), 39–54.
[71] Barkhuizen (1996), 41.

becomes the virgin calf untouched by the yoke of sin (lines 2–3): Jesus Christ, the son of the Virgin, who was without sin. The parable becomes the service of the eucharist: angels serve the feast (11.1–3) and their singing recalls the sanctus: 'Holy are you, Father ... holy also is your Son ... holy again is the Spirit' (ἅγιος εἶ, πάτερ, ... ἅγιος ἔστι δὲ καὶ ὁ υἱός σου, ... τὸ Πνεῦμα πάλιν ἅγιον ...) (11.5, 7, 11). Romanos once again reinforces for his congregation that their participation in the eucharist unites them with the heavenly realm.

This replaying of a liturgical rite within a Gospel narrative is not uncommon for Romanos and reflects his understanding of post-incarnation time. In *On the Resurrection VI* the events at the tomb mimic the entrances of the sixth-century liturgy,[72] casting the resurrection of Christ in a contemporary mould. Mary's entrance to the tomb in stanza 7 recalls the Little Entrance of the liturgy: her speech is reminiscent of the Trisagion hymn which was sung at this part of the service. Christ reveals himself to Mary (10) and tells her to proclaim what she now knows (12); a command which fits well with the scripture readings and homily which follow the Little Entrance. In stanza 17, Mary brings the women back to the tomb and they sing a hymn in praise of the tomb. The empty tomb is a symbol of Christ's death and resurrection, and so for Romanos becomes a symbol of the eucharist; the women's second entrance to the tomb becomes the Great Entrance, at which the elements of bread and wine were brought forward for the eucharist.

Gospel characters again participate in sixth-century rites in *On the Sinful Woman*. The harlot, whom Romanos upholds as an example of repentance, becomes a catechumen preparing for baptism. She renounces her life of sin in a way which recalls the catechumenal rite of rejecting Satan (by blowing and spitting on him) (X.5.10–11):[73]

In short, by blowing I renounce
the filth of my deeds.

συντόμως ἀποτάσσομαι   ἐμφυσῶσα
τῷ βορβόρῳ τῶν ἔργων μου.

'By blowing I renounce' is repeated in the penultimate stanza of the hymn, where the words are simultaneously put into the mouths of the woman and of the church, again a reference to the liturgical rite of rejection of Satan.[74]

---

[72] Frank (2006b), 64.

[73] See notes in Lash (1995), 245.

[74] See John Chrysostom's *Baptismal Instructions* 2.18, 20 and Cyril of Jerusalem's *Mystagogical Catecheses* (1.4).

So Romanos makes the sinful woman into a catechumen and her repentance part of her baptism. In the following strophe the woman refers to her own cleansing (X.6.6–11):

I will make the house of the Pharisee a place of light,
for there I wash away my sins,
and there I purify myself of my offences.
With weeping, with oil and with perfume I will mix the font
and I am washed and cleansed and I flee
from the filth of my deeds.

φωτιστήριον ποιήσω   τὴν οἰκίαν   τοῦ Φαρισαίου·
ἐκεῖ γὰρ ἀποπλύνομαι   τὰς ἁμαρτίας μου,
   ἐκεῖ καὶ καθαρίζομαι   τὰς ἀνομίας μου·
κλαυθμῷ, ἐλαίῳ καὶ μύρῳ   κεράσομαι κολυμβήθραν
   καὶ λούομαι καὶ σμήχομαι   καὶ ἐκφεύγω
τοῦ βορβόρου τῶν ἔργων μου.

Romanos turns the house of Simon the Pharisee into a baptistery.[75] Alliteration ('ph' sounds) and the symmetrical placement of 'place of light' and 'Pharisee' at either end of line 6 emphasize this transformation. Words of washing and purifying are repeated, highlighting the similarities between the woman's repentance and Christ's forgiveness and the baptismal liturgy of repenting and being purified. Romanos wants the congregation to recall their own baptism and its meaning.[76] The three nouns (weeping, oil and perfume) in line 9 are balanced by the three verbs (washed, cleansed and flee) which bring her out of her sins in line 10. The reference to tears, oil and perfume also recalls the biblical narrative, perhaps especially the Lucan version, in which the woman is said to wash Jesus' feet with her tears and dry them with her hair before she anoints them with expensive perfume (Luke 7:32–8).[77] Christ becomes the font (line 9) through which the woman's purification takes place, recalling the biblical imagery of Christ as source of living water (John 4:14) as well as emphasizing that it is into Christ that the congregation is baptized and through him that they are purified.

For Romanos, there are rites other than baptism and eucharist which are also participatory. As we saw in the introduction, Romanos refers to the night vigil, the probable setting for the *kontakia*, in *On the Man Possessed*

---

[75] As Lash has it: Lash (1995), 79 n. 9.
[76] On memory and baptism, see Frank (2013a).
[77] On the repentant tears of the harlot in Ephrem and his followers, see Hunt (1998).

with Devils (XI.1.1–3). This is a rite for the people, involving singing and processions (XI.25.1–3):

Servants of Christ, who always love
to stand around and sing to his glory,
we have now led the devil in a procession [i.e. triumphing over him] …

Ὑπηρέται Χριστοῦ,   οἱ φιλοῦντες ἀεὶ
παραμένειν καὶ ψάλλειν εἰς δόξαν αὐτοῦ,
οἱ πομπεύσαντες νῦν τὸν διάβολον …

The congregation takes part in the physical movement of this service and vocally in the singing of psalms and hymns. They perform both their love of and service to God and his destruction of the devil at the resurrection. Night vigils which moved through the city often finished at a church in time for the eucharistic service. In this sense, the vigil could be interpreted as a wandering in the desert, during which glimpses of the eschaton are possible and which ultimately culminates in proleptic participation in the eschatological feast: the eucharist.

For Romanos, the liturgy is a participation both in the heavenly liturgy and in the life of Christ. There is a sense of eternal present, in which biblical events occur in sixth-century Constantinople through the liturgy, but always with an anticipation of the eschaton and final consummation of God's promise to his people. Romanos plays out this theology in his *kontakia* by casting biblical events in contemporary liturgical moulds and accentuating the participation which takes place in rituals like baptism and the eucharist.

Participation in Christ through the Gospels and *Imitatio Christi*

As dramatic texts, the *kontakia* enable another form of participation. Through the devices of characterization, vivid description and direct rhetorical address, Romanos draws the congregation into the Gospel stories, making them part of the first-century life of Christ, and presents them with models of Christ-like behaviour, demonstrating how to act as Christians in the new creation and in anticipation of its consummation.

Characterization (*Ethopoeia*)

Characterization has an emotional impact; it can be used to create vividness and invoke pity and fellow-feeling in the listener, but equally hatred and fear, and many other emotions besides. It excites the passions and makes the narrative vivid.[78] Both these purposes are important for Romanos' eschatological theology.

Characterization in Earlier Homiletics

Romanos' use of characterization draws on earlier practices, especially from homiletics. The fifth-century preacher Basil of Seleucia, who has long been claimed as an influence on Romanos' style and thought,[79] uses characterization (or perhaps 'personification' would be the more accurate term) in his homily *On Lazarus*. He creates a monologue for Death (12), who vividly describes the raising of the dead and rather pathetically mourns the end of his reign over humanity:

Alas, for these misfortunes! Even the tombs are faithless to me with regard to the dead and the dead, although putrefying, are leaping out; all in their swathing bands they are dancing, mocking my laugh.[80]

Οἴμοι τῶν κακῶν· ἄπιστά μοι λοιπὸν πρὸς νεκροὺς καὶ τὰ μνήματα, νεκροὶ σεσηπότες ἐξάλλονται, μετὰ τῶν ἐνταφίων χορεύουσιν τὸν ἐμὸν ἐξορούμενοι γέλωτα.

The personification (*prosopopoeia*) of death and the exploration of his character through this speech have the effect of making death into an enemy whom Christ beats decidedly in the battle over human lives. Death is not simply the deaths of all human beings but a monstrous creature who loves power and destruction and who imprisons human bodies beneath the earth. They are a trophy for him. It is easier to imagine the defeat of such a creature than to comprehend the end of all human deaths. So Basil makes the end of all human deaths, which is brought about through the resurrection of Lazarus, and ultimately through Christ's death and resurrection, more imaginable and real through *prosopopoeia*.

The vivid picture this characterization creates draws the audience into the story, making them part of this miraculous event. Basil reinforces this by his assertion that this event transcends time: 'Time had no knowledge of this and the manner <in which it happened> was unknown' (ὁ χρόνος οὐκ οἶδεν, ὁ τρόπος ἠγνόηται).[81] Just as we have seen throughout Romanos' poetry, Basil is also working with a concept of sacred time, in which events are not placed in a linear, chronological sequence, but

---

[78] Schouler (2005), 49.
[79] E.g. Maas (1910a), 291–2, 299.
[80] For both text and translation, see Cunningham (1986), 176, 183.
[81] The translation is Cunningham's: Cunningham (1986), 182.

converge, encouraging Christians to approach reality and experience the world in a new way. The ethopoeic monologue Basil gives to Death enables him to present the raising of Lazarus as a foreshadowing of the general resurrection.[82]

Characterization through speeches was a technique also employed by the fourth-century homilist Ephrem the Syrian. Ephrem explores the characters of Simon and the sinful woman from Luke 7:36–50 in the prose homily attributed to him, *On the Sinful Woman*, through dialogues which function to characterize the actors. This homily, and the tradition to which it belongs, were certainly a major influence on Romanos' own composition on the same theme. The woman's faith is demonstrated by her exchange with the perfume seller who is curious about her change of attire (4) and whom she reprimands for suggesting she is seeking another lover (5):

Hinder me not, O man, and stop me not by thy questioning. … I will go to Him who endures, and will buy that which endures. And as to that thou saidst, about a merchant; a Man has met me today Who bears riches in abundance. He has robbed me and I have robbed Him; He has robbed me of my transgressions and sins, and I have robbed Him of His wealth. And as to that thou saidst of a husband; I have won me a Husband in heaven, Whose dominion stands for ever, and His kingdom shall not be dissolved.[83]

Ephrem creates a determined character through this little speech: the woman has decided to repent and knows exactly how she must do it. Ephrem further emphasizes her faith and determination by inserting a debate between the woman and Satan, who appears to her in the guise of a former lover (7–8). Satan attempts to turn her from her chosen course, but he is not successful. The woman's firm penitence is set up as a model for the congregation, and her conversation makes her a vivid and believable character. Ephrem thus brings the characters to life and makes it easier for the congregation to identify with them.

As these two examples suggest, Greek and Syriac preachers used characterization to make the congregation participate in the new creation. Basil of Seleucia's personification and characterization of death in *On Lazarus* vivifies the narrative, making the effect of Lazarus' (and therefore the general) resurrection all the more obvious for his congregation. In a similar way, Ephrem's vivid characterization of the sinful woman draws the congregation into the Gospel story, bringing the narrative to life before their eyes and making them identify with this Gospel character.

---

[82] Cunningham (1986), 169.
[83] For the translation, see Schaff and Wace (1890), 336ff.

Characterization in Romanos

Romanos encourages his congregation to become participants in the scriptural narratives and draws the biblical stories into the sixth century, both demonstrating his conceptualization of new creation time and helping his audience to become part of Christ's life.[84] He creates vivid models or anti-models of appropriate Christian (Christ-like) behaviour as he points his congregation towards the approaching eschaton.

Romanos creates an archetype of penitence in *On the Haemorrhaging Woman*, exploring her fear and courage through a monologue (XII.5.2–6):

How will I be seen by my all-seeing one,
> bearing the shame of my sins?
If the blameless one sees the flow of blood, he will draw back from me as from one unclean,
and this will be more terrible for me than a blow,
if he turns back from me as I cry to him,
'Saviour, save me.'

Πῶς ὀφθήσομαι τῷ παντεπόπτῃ μου
> φέρουσα τὴν αἰσχύνην πταισμάτων ἐμῶν;
αἱμάτων ῥύσιν ὁ ἀμώμητος   ἐὰν ἴδῃ, χωρεῖ μου ὡς ἀκαθάρτου,
καὶ δεινότερον ἔσται μοι τοῦτο πληγῆς,
ἐὰν ἀποστραφῇ με βοῶσαν αὐτῷ·
'σῶτερ, σῶσον με.'

There is an irony in the first line of this speech in that the 'all-seeing' Christ of the Gospel did not see the woman until she had touched him: Mark says that Jesus was 'immediately aware that power had gone forth from him' and he turned to face the woman and release her from her illness (Mark 5:30–4). In this speech her concern about the omniscient power of God is a demonstration of her great faith. Repetition of first-person pronouns, in various forms, focuses attention on the speaker and her fears and suffering. She is fearful of rejection and somewhat self-pitying, although listeners are themselves moved to pity rather than disgust by the speech. Her fear of rejection is clear in lines 3 to 5. Jewish concern with ritual cleanliness and fear of disease are behind her fear of being branded unclean (line 3). This line is framed by the words 'blood' and 'unclean', highlighting the cause of her fear. Her certainty that Christ will reject her engenders pity in listeners. The refrain also makes the congregation part of this exploration of character;

---

[84] This is a technique Romanos uses throughout his *kontakia*. Barkhuizen observes that Romanos engages his listeners in the biblical world through dialogue, monologue and creative narrative expansion in *On Dives and Lazarus*: Barkhuizen (2008a), 270.

with the haemorrhaging woman they cry out 'Saviour, save me!', acknowledging that they are as much in need of salvation as she. The woman is a
model of repentance and piety for the congregation to imitate. Romanos
uses her as an illustration of proper Christian penitence.

The accentuation of the faith and penitence of this ritually unclean
woman is in stark contrast to the treatment of Abraham in *On Abraham
and Isaac*. In this *kontakion*, Romanos makes the archetype of faith,
the man who would have sacrificed his only son, into a more believable, doubting and fearful man, creating a more human and perhaps ultimately more helpful model of faith. He creates an elaborate dialogue
as a way of expressing the fears of both Abraham and Sarah, neither of
which was expressed in the biblical account of Isaac's sacrifice (Gen.
22:1–14). Romanos acknowledges that Abraham did not question God's
command: 'For this reason you were not doubtful about the demand'
(διὸ πρὸς τὸ ῥηθὲν ἀμφίβολος οὐ γέγονας (XLI.3.3)), but then he creates
a monologue for Abraham, imagining what Abraham might have said to
God if he *had* been doubtful. In this long monologue there is even an
imagined debate between Abraham and Sarah which Abraham presents
to God (XLI.7.1–5):

Sarah will hear all your words, O Lord,
and knowing that this is your will, she will say to me,
'If the one who gives has taken away, why did he give?
You, old man, let me keep my [child] with me.
And if the one who has called you wants him, he will reveal this to me.'

Ἀκούσει τοὺς λόγους σου   πάντας ⟨ἡ⟩ Σάρρα,   ὦ δέσποτα,
   καὶ τὴν βουλήν σου   ταύτην γνοῦσά μοι λέξει·
'εἰ αὐτὸς ὁ διδοὺς ἐλάμβανε,   τί παρέσχηκε;
σύ, πρεσβῦτα,   τὸν ἐμὸν ἔα πρός με·
   καὶ ὅταν θελήσῃ   τοῦτον ὁ καλέσας σε,   δηλώσει μοι.'

Sarah's characterization by Abraham works similarly; the fears that Sarah
expresses are those of an ordinary mother. Through the dialogue the congregation is made to feel her sadness, her hope, her fear and her anger, as
she rails against the reality of God's command (9.4–6):

Alas, my son Isaac, may it not be that I should look down upon
your blood poured out on the ground.
He will kill me first, only then will he kill you.

οἴμοι, τέκνον   Ἰσαάκ, εἰ κατίδω
   σοῦ ἐπὶ γαίας   αἷμα ἐκχυνόμενον·   μὴ γένοιτο·
φονεύσει με πρώτην,   εἶτα οὕτως σε φονεύσει·

This mother's desire to die before her son is reminiscent of Romanos' representation of Mary at the cross (XIX) and certainly plays into ideals of motherhood. Through passages like these Romanos draws the congregation into the biblical events.

Romanos uses characterization to create the fears and doubts of a biblical character whose faith was apparently unfailing in the biblical account. Rhetorical expansion through dialogue creates a new narrative, based on but not the same as the biblical account. The new narrative emphasizes the humanity of Abraham and Sarah and draws connections between their experiences and wider human emotions such as fear, doubt, grief and hope. Through this humanizing, emotional narrative, Romanos encourages the audience to identify with Abraham and Sarah and similarly give over their human uncertainty and emotional turmoil to God.

Romanos also characterizes himself in his *kontakia*, once again through the use of dialogue. In *On the Resurrection II*, as we will see shortly, he uses a 'reporter persona' to draw the congregation into the Gospel events. But Romanos also creates a persona for himself which emphasizes human frailty and which encourages the congregation to behave in particular ways.[85] This penitential persona draws attention to human frailty and sin, but, most importantly, it allows him to offer a model of penitence and piety to his congregation. Romanos uses the first person to make the model more immediate to his listeners and to create a bond of sympathy between preacher and audience. The character he creates for himself is a model for how a Christian should behave in expectation of the second coming of Christ (VI.18.4–9):

I fall down before you, saviour, like the woman with the haemorrhage,
and I grasp your hem and say,
'If I only lay hold [of you], I will be saved.'
So do not let my faith come to nothing, healer of souls.
Uncovering the pain, let me find you as my deliverance,
the one who appears and illuminates everything.

προσπίπτω σοι, σωτήρ,   καθάπερ ἡ αἱμόρρους
ἁπτόμενος κἀγώ   τοῦ κρασπέδου καὶ λέγων·
'Ἐὰν μόνον   κρατήσω, σωθήσομαι'·
μὴ ματαιώσῃς οὖν τὴν πίστιν μου,   ὁ τῶν ψυχῶν ἰατρός·
ἐκκαλύπτων τὸ ἄλγος   εὕρω σὲ εἰς σωτηρίαν
τὸν φανέντα   καὶ φωτίσαντα πάντα.

Romanos associates himself, in this penitential persona, with the woman's faith, but also with her sinfulness. He is not above the sinners in the

---

[85] See Krueger (2006a), 255–74.

Gospels, but is as fallen as the haemorrhaging woman, who is his model of faith and penitence. He is literally 'fallen' in this passage too, since he prostrates himself before God.[86] Romanos uses it again in this context in *A Prayer* (LVI.7.2) and *On Baptism* (LIII.22.6), acknowledging his own sinfulness and begging for forgiveness. By presenting himself, the preacher, in this way, Romanos encourages his congregation to do likewise.

Similarly, at the end of *On the Resurrection VI* Romanos acknowledges his own sins and asks for God's forgiveness (XXIX.24.4–12):

Yes, merciful one, I beg you not to abandon me
who am stained with sins,
for in iniquities and sins my mother conceived me.
My father, holy and compassionate,
hallowed be your name forever
by my mouth and by my lips,
by my voice and by my song.
Grant me grace as I proclaim your hymns, since you are able,
you who grant resurrection to those who are fallen.

ναί, ἐλεήμων,   ἱκετεύω σε μὴ καταλείπῃς με
    τὸν ταῖς πλημμελείαις   κατεστιγμένον·
ἐν γὰρ ἀνομίαις   καὶ ⟨ἐν⟩ ἁμαρτίαις ἐμὲ
                        ἐκίσσησεν ἡ μήτηρ μου·
πάτερ μου,   ἅγιε   καὶ φιλοικτίρμον,
    ἁγιασθήτω σου   ἀεὶ τὸ ὄνομα
ἐν τῷ στόματί μου   καὶ τοῖς χείλεσί μου,
    ἐν τῇ φωνῇ μου   καὶ τῇ ᾠδῇ μου·
δός μοι χάριν   κηρύττοντι   τοὺς ὕμνους σου,   ὅτι δύνασαι,
    ὁ τοῖς πεσοῦσι παρέχων ἀνάστασιν.

This personal plea draws on various liturgical and biblical sources to ground and strengthen the characterization. The word 'abandon' (*kataleipēs*) in line 4 of this stanza recalls Christ's cry to God from the cross: 'Why have you abandoned (*enkatelipes*) me?' (Mark 15:34). This passage also calls to mind other parts of the liturgy by a direct quotation from the Psalms (line 6) and a reference to the Lord's Prayer (line 8). Line 6 is a quote from the Septuagint translation of Psalm 50(51):5: 'For behold, I was conceived in iniquities, and in sin did my mother conceive me' ('Ιδοὺ γὰρ ἐν ἀνομίαις συνελήφθην, καὶ ἐν ἁμαρτίαις ἐκίσσησέ με ἡ μήτηρ μου). This psalm emphasizes the sinfulness

---

[86] In Christian texts 'to fall down' (*prospiptō*) is used of prostration before God. It occurs in the Ephrem Graecus collection in this context, among many others. See, for example, *De passionibus animi* 357.8, and *Sermo paraeneticus* 407.10.

of humanity and human need for forgiveness and redemption. The connection Romanos makes between the prayer, human sinfulness and the generosity and love of God as seen in the crucifixion elucidates the meaning of the Lord's Prayer as praise of God and prayer for forgiveness.

Romanos brings the doubt and fear of the apostle Thomas to life when he likens his own doubt and fear to Thomas' (XXX.18.5–10):

Thomas, by touching [you], now recognizes your glory,
but I am afraid, for I know your counsels,
I know my deeds. My conscience troubles me.
Spare me, my saviour, spare me, merciful one,
so that in deeds and words I may unceasingly cry to you,
'You are our Lord and our God.'

ὁ Θώμας ψηλαφῶν   νῦν ἐπέγνω τὴν δόξαν σου,
    ἐγὼ δὲ δειλιῶ·   οἶδα γὰρ τὰς βουλάς σου·
    ἐπίσταμαι τὰ ἔργα μου·   τὸ συνειδός με ταράττει·
φεῖσαι, σωτήρ μου,   φεῖσαι, οἰκτίρμων,
    ἵνα ἔργοις καὶ λόγοις ἀπαύστως βοῶ σοι·
Ἱ Κύριος ὑπάρχεις   καὶ θεὸς ἡμῶν.'

In the Gospel story, Christ says to Thomas that those who will believe without having touched his wounds are blessed (John 20:29). Romanos creatively expands the Gospel narrative, not only in the dialogue he gives Thomas, but also by parachuting himself into the action. He addresses Christ directly as if he were himself a doubting apostle. Romanos acknowledges the difficulties of believing and thereby encourages the congregation to confront their own doubts. But there is a sense of urgency about the appeal to God which concludes the *kontakion On Doubting Thomas*, perhaps reflecting Romanos' belief in the impending eschaton,[87] but also preparing his congregation to receive the eucharist (XXX.18.1–4):

By grace strengthen me in soul and flesh and save me, Most High,
so that, by touching your side, I might receive your grace,
your blood and your body, and be delivered from my evils,
so that I might find forgiveness of transgressions.

Ὑπὸ χάριτος   ψυχῇ καὶ σαρκὶ   στηρίξας σῶσον με, ὕψιστε,
    ἵν' ἁπτόμενος τῆς πλευρᾶς   λαμβάνω   σου τὴν χάριν
λυτρούμενος τῶν κακῶν μου   τὸ αἷμα σου   καὶ τὸ σῶμα,
    ἄφεσιν ἵνα   εὕρω τῶν παραπτωμάτων·

---

[87]   On sixth-century ideas about the end of the world see Daley (2003), 171–8. Cf. also Alexander (1985), Rubin (1961), Vasiliev (1942–3).

Christ's side, from which water and blood flowed, is the source of the eucharistic wine and Romanos asks for strength to touch it: to receive the sacrament which will be his salvation.

Romanos also uses personal prayer to acknowledge his character's own sinfulness, to model penitential behaviour and to intercede on behalf of the congregation.[88] The prayer at the end of *On the Resurrection VI* (quoted above) is a particularly personal call for forgiveness. Romanos uses his persona to model penitence for his congregation and to act as an intercessor.[89] He creates this persona to guide his congregation towards living out the perfect humanity of Christ in preparation for the second coming.

But Romanos also uses himself as an anti-model, comparing himself with great biblical figures to illustrate his (and general human) comparative sinfulness or weakness. In *On Abraham and Isaac*, he compares himself to Abraham (XLI.1):

I, who am young, wish to emulate you, [Abraham], the old man
going up the mountain, but my feet grow numb.
For even if the spirit is willing, the flesh is weak.
O my soul, have courage now as you look upon
Abraham, who put aside old age and became young.
His feet toiled, but he had courage in his soul.
He did not know the place, but he departed on the way,
being guided by the one who called him.
Because he alone is good, the saviour of our souls.

Εἰς ὄρος ἀναβαίνοντα   σὲ τὸν πρεσβύτην   ὁ νέος ἐγὼ
   ζηλῶσαι θέλω   καὶ ναρκοῦσί μου πόδες·
εἰ γὰρ καὶ τὸ πνεῦμα πρόθυμον,   ἀλλ' ἡ σὰρξ ἀσθενής·
ὦ ψυχή μου,   θάρρησον θεωροῦσα
   τὸν Ἀβραὰμ νῦν   τὸ γῆρας ἀποθέμενον   καὶ νεάζοντα·
οὐ ἔκαμνον πόδες,   ἀλλ' ἠνδρίζετο τῇ γνώμῃ·
   ἠγνόει τὸν τόπον   καὶ ἀπῄει τῷ τρόπῳ
   ὁδηγοῦντος αὐτὸν τοῦ καλέσαντος.
ὅτι μόνος ἀγαθὸς   ὁ σωτὴρ τῶν ψυχῶν ἡμῶν.

Faith gives strength to the old man and makes him young again. Romanos uses the mountain scene to make Abraham into a Christ figure and himself into a sinful disciple. Line 3 is almost a direct quote from Matthew 26:41 in which Jesus returns from praying on the mountain, finds his disciples

---

[88] On final prayers in Romanos, see Barkhuizen (1989), (1991a), Grosdidier de Matons (1980), 197–201.

[89] The audience is heavily involved here, *contra* Barkhuizen (1991a), 93.

sleeping and rebukes them for their weakness. The direct address to his soul (line 4) is also a call upon his listeners – the personal touch encourages them to identify with him; Romanos wants the congregation to see Abraham (and his antitype, Christ) as a model of faith and action.

Self-characterization enables Romanos to make himself a model or anti-model for his congregation, taking on the role of penitent and showing his failings as he seeks to live a Christ-like life.[90] Romanos creates a persona which he hopes appeals to his listeners as they also strive towards imitation of Christ. Romanos also gives his congregation different roles in the biblical narratives through dialogue and the refrain. Dialogue explores and develops the characters of those who are speaking. By making the congregation part of this exploration of biblical characters, Romanos is able to create models of behaviour, explain points of doctrine and generally bring the text to life for his congregation. In a dramatic sense, the congregation becomes part of performing the stories of Christ's life and thereby participates in it. *On the Baptism of Christ* contains a long dialogue between Christ and John the Baptist which has been expanded from the brief conversation in Matthew's Gospel (3:13–15) and which dwells primarily on John's reluctance to baptize Christ. I quote one strophe, in which John is speaking, as an example (V.7):

Why have you appeared at the streams? What do you wish
                     to wash away, or what sort of sins,
you who were conceived and born without sin?
You come to me, but heaven and earth watch [to see] if I will dare.
You say to me, 'Baptize me', but above the angels watch
so that then they might say to me, 'Know yourself.
                        How far will you go?'
So, as Moses said, choose another
to do this, Saviour, which you ask of me.
It is greater than I and I am afraid. I beg you.
For how can I baptize
the unapproachable light?

Ἐπέστης ῥείθροις διὰ τί;   τί θέλων ἀποπλῦναι
                      ἢ ποίας ἁμαρτίας
  ὁ δίχα ἁμαρτίας   καὶ συλληφθεὶς καὶ γεννηθείς;
σὺ μὲν ἔρχῃ πρός με·   οὐρανὸς δὲ καὶ ἡ γῆ
                 τηρεῖ, εἰ προπετεύσομαι·
λέγεις μοι· 'βάπτισόν με'·   ἀλλ' ἄνωθεν   ἄγγελοι σκοποῦσιν,

---

[90] See Krueger (2014), 29–65, Gador-Whyte (2011), 23–37.

ἵνα τότε   λέγωσί μοι·   ʻγνῶθι σαυτόν·[91]
                                μέχρι ποῦ παρέρχῃ;ʼ
ὡς εἶπεν οὖν Μωσῆς,   προχείρισαι ἄλλον
   εἰς αὐτὸ τοῦτο, σωτήρ,   ὃ ἀπαιτεῖς με·
μεῖζον μου ἐστὶ   καὶ δέδοικα· δέομαί σου·
   πῶς γὰρ βαπτίσω
τὸ φῶς τὸ ἀπρόσιτον;

Romanos puts into the mouth of John the Baptist a rhetorically charged stanza as he argues against baptizing Christ. He begins with two rhetorical questions, the answer to the first of which he already knows (Christ has already told him why he is there) and the second of which he answers in the second line (i.e. Christ has no sin to wash away). John presents his dilemma by placing Jesus in opposition to the physical world and the angels, and imagining the angels' response. He appeals to an important authority and precedent: Moses also said no to God and at that time God sent Moses a helper (Aaron) (Exodus 4:13–14). His honest admission of fear and the final rhetorical question are perhaps the most affecting, especially when juxtaposed with the reference to Moses. Although Moses was sent out by God to do a very difficult thing (tell Pharaoh to let the Israelites go free), he did not have to touch the 'unapproachable light'. Moses was only allowed to see God's back (Exodus 33:23): God said to him, 'you cannot see my face; for no one shall see me and live' (Exodus 33:20). If Moses, that great patriarch, was not allowed even to look upon the face of God, how can he, John, possibly baptize God? The style and content of this argument present a vivid picture of an anxious and fearful Baptizer who recognizes the enormity of the task and feels himself inadequate. This portrayal of emotions vivifies the character of John for Romanos' listeners. Their participation in John's story continues in the refrain, through which the congregation plays the characters of both John and Jesus, enacting the drama as it unfolds.

Romanos thus facilitates participation in Christ through vivification of biblical stories and clever characterization of Christ-like models of behaviour. Romanos' conception of time after the incarnation means that sixth-century Christians can participate in the Gospel stories when they reoccur in the liturgy and he uses characterization and the refrain to make this happen in the *kontakia* as well. His own self-portrayal as a repentant sinner draws the listeners into sympathy with him and encourages imitation of his penitential model.

---

[91] γνῶθι σαυτόν is one of the sayings of the Delphic Oracle to which Socrates refers in Plato *Alcibiades 1* 124b and *Hipparchus* 228e. See also *Philebus* 48c.

Vivid Description (*Ekphrasis*)

Emotional engagement with biblical characters and exemplars is an important aspect of Romanos' participatory theology and to this end he augments his characterizations with vivid description, a technique which orators, poets and preachers had long used to elicit certain emotional responses from their audiences.[92]

Ekphrasis before Romanos

As a brief example of the way in which the homiletic tradition before Romanos employed vivid description to engage the audience's emotions and encourage transformation of lives, we turn to the fourth-century preacher, poet and theologian Gregory Nazianzus. In his Oration 14, *On the Love of the Poor* (PG 35.857–909), Gregory uses vivid descriptions to create feelings of pity towards poor lepers in his congregation and then to make his audience feel shame at their comparative wealth (13):

They lie beside each other, horribly united by their sickness, and each one contributing another bit of misery to the general wretchedness. And they are an addition to each other's suffering, piteous in their weakness, more piteous because it is shared suffering. ... They toss about at the feet of men in the sun and in the dust. At other times they suffer in the bitter frost, and in storms, and in tumults of winds. They are not trampled upon only because we are loath to touch them ...

Οἱ μὲν κεῖνται μετ' ἀλλήλων, κακῶς ὑπὸ τῆς νόσου συνεζευγμένοι, καὶ ἄλλος ἄλλο τι τῆς συμφορᾶς πρὸς τὸ ἐλεεινὸν ἐρανίζοντες· καὶ εἰσὶν ἀλλήλοις προσθήκη τοῦ πάθους, ἐλεεινοὶ τῆς ἀρρωστίας, τῆς συμπαθείας ἐλεεινότεροι. ... Οἱ δὲ κυλινδοῦνται πρὸς τοῖς ποσὶ τῶν ἀνθρώπων ἡλίῳ καὶ κόνει· ἔστι δὲ ὅτε καὶ κρυμοῖς ἀγρίοις, καὶ ὄμβροις, καὶ ταραχαῖς ἀνέμων ταλαιπωρούμενοι, παρὰ τοσοῦτον οὐ συμπατούμενοι, παρ' ὅσον καὶ ψαύειν αὐτῶν βδελυσσόμεθα ...

This section gives a taste of the colourful imagery Gregory uses to describe the lepers. Their lot is one of pain and suffering, made worse somehow because there are many of them together; other people cannot bear to touch them. This vivid depiction of lepers in their wretched state is followed (in section 17) by one on 'our' way of life. 'We' live in luxury, sleep in comfortable beds, desire the floor and table to be perfumed, are served by slave boys, eat expensive and indulgent food, drink only the best wine. Gregory uses this comparison to show his congregation that 'we' live in a state of

---

[92] On *ekphrasis* in John Chrysostom, for example, see Ameringer (1921), 86–100.

gluttony and greed, in short, in 'spiritual sickness'. 'We' are the lepers. Thus, the feelings of pity evoked by this earlier *ekphrasis* are then turned around to make the feeling one of self-disgust, or even self-pity. But this suggests inaction. Gregory by no means advocates inactive self-pity; he follows this inversion of roles with clear directions about how his congregation should change their lives: by following the way of God and looking expectantly for the eschaton.

Ekphrasis and Related Techniques in Romanos

Gregory's use of vivid description is deliberately affective; it attempts to use listeners' emotional responses to change their behaviour. Romanos also uses vivid description to elicit emotional responses from the congregation; *ekphrasis* is part of an affective strategy to shape the listeners' modes of behaviour through appeals to emotion.[93]

Romanos' own discussion of leprosy resonates strongly with Gregory's homily. In *On the Healing of the Leper,* Romanos includes a vivid description of leprosy which makes the congregation picture the disease and share in the shame felt by the leper because of his affliction (VIII.5.3–8):[94]

It is more ugly than the other diseases among humans,
since the flesh is fed upon by it as though on fodder.
It attacks all the limbs
as if desiring to make the human appear as the definition of disgraces,
for unclean disease is the kinsman of mutilation
which medical skill is wholly incapable of treating …

τῶν παθῶν ἐστὶ τῶν ἄλλων   δυσειδεστέρα ἐν ἀνθρώποις,
    ὡς ἐπὶ χόρτου βοσκομένης   τῆς σαρκὸς ὑπ' αὐτῆς·
ἐπιτίθεται αὕτη   τοῖς μέλεσι πᾶσιν,
    ὥσπερ ἐπιθυμοῦσα   παραδεῖξαι ὅλον   ὄνειδος τὸν ἄνθρωπον·
τῆς λώβης γὰρ ὑπάρχει   συγγενὴς ἡ ἀκάθαρτος νόσος,
    ἣν τέχνη ἰατρείας   ὅλως οὐ θεραπεύει …

The disease is almost personified; Romanos imagines that the disease 'desires' to disfigure the human, and that it 'feeds' or 'is nurtured' on human flesh, as though it is some horrible animal. It is called both a 'suffering' or 'misfortune' and a 'disease'. The desperate state of the leper is emphasized by the exclusion from society that comes with ugliness and deformity and the lack of any potential cure. This vivid description, and others throughout

---

[93] See Gador-Whyte (2010).
[94] For an analysis of this *kontakion*, see Barkhuizen (1997).

this *kontakion*, urge the congregation to pity the leper, and perhaps identify with him. Even more than this, they may see leprosy as symbolic of human sinfulness generally and themselves as lepers, in need of the healing of Christ.

The personified disease returns in stanza 16 when Romanos says that it was terrified by Christ and so fled the leper (VIII.16.1–4):

The disease of leprosy, having been mortified
                              by the command of the Lord, ran away,
for the sickness shuddered when it saw the one who is creator and redeemer.
And yet the Arians do not thus shudder at the rule of the Lord,
the absolute power of the Word, the Son of God …

Νεκρωθὲν τῇ κελεύσει τοῦ κυρίου
                              δραπετεύει τὸ πάθος [τῆς λέ]πρας·
    ἔφριξε γὰρ τὸ νόσημα   αὐτὸν ἰδὸν τὸν κτίστην
                                        καὶ λυτρωτήν·
καὶ οὐ φρίττουσιν οὐδ᾽ οὕτως   Ἀρειανοὶ τ[ὴν δε]σποτείαν,
    τὴν αὐθεντίαν τὴν τοῦ λόγου   τοῦ υἱοῦ τοῦ Θεοῦ …

It might seem odd that Romanos chooses Arianism to compare with leprosy, since it was not the most recent heresy to beset the church, but he wants to emphasize the divinity of Christ, which the disease recognizes but the Arians do not. The message about heretics can be broadened: heresy is a disease, or even worse than a disease, since heretics do not acknowledge Christ. Rejection of heresy therefore becomes rejection of disease and defilement and assent to the wholesome life of God.

In the final strophe Romanos says (18.2):

Just as you pitied the leper, save [our] suffering by your word …

ὡς τὸν λεπρὸν ἠλέησας   διώξας λόγῳ τὸ πάθος …

Through vivid description Romanos has connected leprosy with general human suffering and sin. He thereby makes his congregation recognize their sin and need for salvation. He also connects disease with heresy, reminding his congregation that correct belief is a necessary part of their life as they prepare for Christ's second coming. Yet this use of *ekphrasis* also has the effect of making the Gospel event, Jesus' healing of the leper, vibrant and present for his congregation. By the pity for the leper that Romanos invokes in them the congregation is drawn into the story and partakes in the action. The Gospel healing of the leper has become a sixth-century event.

Similarly, in *On the Massacre of the Innocents*, Romanos uses *ekphrasis* to facilitate the congregation's participation in the Gospel. He describes the slaughter in graphic detail and over several strophes.[95] Here is an early section of the *ekphrasis* (III.9.1–11):

With a shining cloud spreading over
the Jews and overshadowing them,
Herod brought in the darkest gloom and made all humanity dark.
For the cheerful and laughing nature of children
straightaway he rendered bitter weeping.
Those who shortly before had rejoiced in the child
of the all-undefiled, holy Mary
now are altogether lamenting.
For as a flower which on the same day [it opens] falls down to the earth,
and everyone who sees it laments, [everyone] cries to Rachel,
'Come, weep, Rachel, and mourn together with us [in] a lamenting song …'

Νεφέλης φωτεινῆς   ἐφαπλωμένης
    κατὰ τῆς Ἰουδαίας   καὶ σκιαζούσης,
    γνόφον σκοτεινότατον   ὁ Ἡρώδης εἰσήνεγκε
                            καὶ ἐσκότισεν ἅπαντας·
τὴν ἱλαρὰν γὰρ φύσιν   τῶν παίδων καὶ γελῶσαν
    δεικνύει παραχρῆμα   κλαίουσαν πικρῶς·
τὴν πρὸ μικροῦ ⟨ἔτι⟩   εὐφραινομένην τῷ τόκῳ
    τῆς παναχράντου   ἁγνῆς Μαρίας
    καὶ ἄρτι μᾶλλον   ὀδυρομένην·
ὡς ἄνθος γὰρ αὐθήμερον   ἐπὶ τὴν γῆν κατέπιπτε,
    καὶ πᾶς ὁρῶν ὠδύρετο   καὶ τῇ Ραχὴλ ἐμήνυε·
'Δεῦρο κλαῦσον, Ραχήλ,   καὶ συνθρήνησον ἡμῖν
                            μέλος ὀδυνηρόν.'

Romanos contrasts the happiness and laughter of children with the darkness and gloom of Herod and the Jews. The joyful knowledge of God (the children recognize Jesus as the Christ) is dramatically transformed into lamentation. This is Romanos' creative reinvention of a biblical narrative. There is nothing in the Gospel accounts which suggests that anyone except the Magi (and through them, Herod) was aware of Jesus' birth or its significance, but it makes a nice contrast with those carrying out the slaughter. To this extent, we might see the children as 'Christians', being attacked by the 'Jews', their traditional enemies. Romanos asks his congregation to identify with the innocent children, who knew and rejoiced in the coming of their saviour, in contradistinction to the Jews who refused to acknowledge the truth. He reinforces this request by vivid imagery: the 'darkest gloom' and

---

[95] For a detailed analysis of this *ekphrasis* see Barkhuizen (2007), 29–50, esp. 36–7. On torture as an oft-used topic for *ekphrasis* see Maguire (1981), 99.

'darkening' of line 3 are followed immediately by 'cheerfulness' and 'laughter' in line 4. But darkness returns in line 5, with 'bitter weeping'. Romanos takes his congregation on an emotional rollercoaster and it is their emotional engagement with the story which makes them part of it.

Finally, as we have discussed above, Romanos uses his concept of sacred time to make the narrative more real and immediate for his listeners. The Old Testament figure of Rachel weeps and mourns with 'us' (line 11). Rachel is the matriarch of the faith who cares for her people, but she is also an ordinary mother mourning for her lost son, Joseph. Rachel becomes a contemporary figure, in two times: that of the Gospel event, and sixth-century Constantinople. Time is conflated in the post-incarnation reality: the congregation joins both with Rachel in mourning and with the people of the Gospel story. This multi-layering is reminiscent of some of the contemporary views about holy places investigated above. One holy place could take on multiple layers of significance if an Old Testament narrative was seen to prefigure that event.[96] By visiting this place, the pilgrim could participate in both the precursor of the event and the event itself. And, of course, we have seen that church buildings could themselves be transformed into holy places (*loca sancta*). Similarly, in this *kontakion*, Romanos makes pilgrims out of his listeners, drawing them back to the loss of Rachel which prefigures the first-century loss of life and asking them to participate in both. Romanos continues this layering by associating the innocent children with Abel (12.3), the first innocent to be murdered (Genesis 4:8).

Later in this *kontakion*, Romanos includes a graphic description of the murders (III.14.1–9):

Those who were killed mercilessly with daggers,
as in the way of murder, were blameless children.
Some were tortured indecently and died, and others were cut up.
Others had their heads cut off whilst they were tugging
at their mothers' breasts and drinking milk.
As a result the revered skulls of the infants
hung on their breasts,
and their teats were held back
within the mouths of the infants, in their delicate teeth.

Μαχαίραις ἀνηλεῶς   ἀποκτανθέντα,
   ὡς ἐν σχήματι φόνου,   ἄμεμπτα βρέφη.
     τὰ μὲν ἐκεντήθησαν   ἀπρεπῶς καὶ ἀπέψυξαν,   τὰ δὲ διεμερίσθησαν·
ἄλλα κάρας ἐτμήθη,   τοὺς μασθοὺς τῶν μητέρων

⁹⁶ MacCormack (1990), 26.

καθέλκοντα καὶ γάλα   ποτιζόμενα,
ὡς ἐκ τούτου λοιπὸν   ἐν τοῖς μασθοῖς κρεμασθῆναι
  τὰ τῶν νηπίων   σεπτὰ κρανία,
  καὶ τὰς θηλὰς δὲ   κατασχεθῆναι
ἔνδον αὐτῶν τοῦ στόματος   τοῖς ὀδοῦσι †τοῖς τρυφεροῖς†.

Violence opens the stanza and stands in stark contrast to the images of infancy and caring motherhood. Images of children slaughtered at their mothers' breasts are both revolting and affecting, since they highlight both the innocence of those slaughtered and the heartlessness of the slaughterers.[97] Romanos also figures the children as new Abels, drawing on the earlier characterization of Abel as the blameless victim of murder: 'murder' is juxtaposed with 'blameless' in line 2. Just like Abel, the children are 'revered', beloved of God.

Romanos brings the slaughter to life, making the congregation vividly picture the deaths and the mourning, encouraging them to act out the role of witness to the Jewish soldiers' brutality. Arguably, Romanos is creating a picture of the Jews as barbaric slaughterers, but like Gregory Nazianzus' *ekphrasis* mentioned above, the main point is general human sinfulness. Romanos wants his congregation to recognize the potential for such action in themselves and to turn away from it. By shaping their emotional responses to the biblical event, Romanos directs them towards Christian behaviour.

This vivid description is an appeal to the imagination through sight, encouraging the listener to visualize the event. Romanos also appeals to other senses. References to aroma, anointing, perfume and scent in *On the Sinful Woman* (X.1.1, 4; 3.1; 5.3 and passim) conjure up the scene of her bathing Christ's feet and remind the congregation of beautiful scents associated with the liturgy.[98] Romanos' descriptions are so vivid they are almost *ekphrastic*, in that they bring the scene before the eyes (or perhaps one should say the nose!) of the listeners. Although the passage which follows is a simile, it is one which certainly has the quality of activity (*enargeia*) which is essential for vivid description. At X.1.1–4, Christ's words are sweet-smelling and in stark contrast to the woman's ill-smelling sins:

The once prostitute, perceiving the words of Christ
sprinkled everywhere like spices

---

[97] In line 3 Romanos follows the listing technique considered desirable by theorists like Hermogenes, in the use of τὰ μὲν ... τὰ δὲ to describe the different deaths the children suffered, and the alliteration of ἀπρεπῶς and ἀπέψυξαν emphasizes the indecency in their deaths.

[98] Barkhuizen (1990a), 35–6. On the sinful woman in the Syriac tradition and the use of scent in those homilies, see Harvey (2006), 148ff.

and supplying life-giving breath to all believers,
hated the ill-smelling nature of her deeds.

Τὰ ῥήματα　τοῦ Χριστοῦ　καθάπερ ἀρώματα
　ῥαινόμενα　πανταχοῦ　βλέπων ἡ πόρνη ποτὲ
καὶ τοῖς πιστοῖς πᾶσι　πνοὴν ζωῆς χορηγοῦντα,
　τῶν πεπραγμένων αὐτῇ τὸ δυσῶδες ἐμίσησεν ...

The woman buys an expensive perfume to bathe Christ's feet (X.8), but here it is Christ's words which smell sweet. Romanos draws on the tradition of sensual participation. He takes advantage of the references to perfume in the Gospel story and by developing this theme he makes a link between the incense smelt by the congregation during the service and the words of Christ which he proclaims (and which the congregation have heard in the Gospel reading). He appeals to the congregation's memory of the scent of incense in earlier parts of the liturgy but also to their familiarity with scent as a part of worship more generally. The connection between the words and scent in this passage is assonantly emphasized, as is the effect of the life-giving breath (*pnoēn*) on the woman who was once a prostitute (*pornē pote*).

This passage is also an allusion to 2 Corinthians 2:14–16a:

But thanks be to God, who in Christ always leads us in triumphal procession, and through us spreads in every place the fragrance that comes from knowing him. For we are the aroma of Christ to God among those who are being saved and among those who are perishing; to the one a fragrance from death to death, to the other a fragrance from life to life.

Romanos too desires to spread the sweet smell of Christ among his congregation. The sinful woman spreads 'the fragrance which comes from knowing [Christ]' rather than the stench of her former actions. By appealing to their sense of smell, Romanos draws the congregation into sympathy with the woman and encourages them to mimic her actions.

Christ's sweet scent is life-giving perfume in *On the Raising of Lazarus I* (XIV.12.7–9; Hades speaks):[99]

And the ill smell has left them [i.e. the limbs of Lazarus].
Alas! Truly Jesus has come. He, having sent the smell towards us,
perfumed the foul-smelling [corpse] ...

　καὶ ἀφῆκεν αὐτὰ δυσοσμία·
οἴμοι ὄντως　Ἰησοῦς ἦλθεν·　οὗτος, πέμψας
　　　　　　　　　　　τὴν ὀσμὴν πρὸς ἡμᾶς,
　τὸν ὀζέσαντα εὐωδίασε ...

---

[99]　See Barkhuizen (1994), 101.

Like the foul-smelling deeds of the sinful woman, here Romanos uses scent to make vivid the resurrection of Lazarus and thereby shape his listeners' lives. The stench of the dead is a powerful, physical image which accentuates human sin and separation from God. Romanos explains the resurrection in olfactory terms: Jesus is the means by which Lazarus (and therefore all humanity) becomes sweet smelling again. The despair of Hades is a cause of joy and hope for Romanos' listeners: the advent of Christ has overturned stench (death) and restored humanity to fragrance (life).

Sweet fragrance is a symbol of holiness and the means of salvation in *On the Three Children* (XLVI.3):

So they offered a hymn on behalf of all and from all,
the three-perfumed fragrance supplicating the Lord,
'You who are benefactor in everything and blameless in every way,
do not let this stream of idolatry provoke you
when you see your earth full and stinking everywhere of
demonic sacrifices and transgressions.
For we are like incense in the middle of the filth.
If it seems good to you, Saviour, catch the scent
of your slaves and your true beloved,
the sweet-smelling Daniel whom you love. For with us he cries aloud to you,
"Come quickly, merciful one, and hasten, as the one who has pity,
to our aid, because you are able to do what you will."'

Ὕμνον οὖν ὑπὲρ πάντων   προσέφερον ὡς ἐκ πάντων
     ἡ τρίμυρος εὐωδία   τὸν δεσπότην ἱκετεύουσα·
     'Εὐεργέτα ἐν πᾶσι   καὶ ἄμωμε κατὰ πάντα,
     ὁ τῆς εἰδωλολατρείας   ὀχετὸς μὴ παροξύνῃ σε
ἐκ θυσιῶν δαιμόνων   καὶ ἐκ παραπτωμάτων
     ὁρῶν τὴν γῆν σου γέμουσαν   καὶ παντόθεν ἐξόζουσαν·
ἐσμὲν γὰρ ἐν μέσῳ   βορβόρου ὡς θυμίαμα·
     εἰ δοκεῖ σοι,   ὀσφράνθητι ἡμῶν
     τῶν σῶν δούλων, σῶτερ,   καὶ τοῦ γνησίου φίλου σου
     τοῦ εὐόσμου   Δανιὴλ ὃν ἠγάπησας· σὺν ἡμῖν γὰρ κραυγάζει σοι·
     "τάχυνον, ὁ οἰκτίρμων,   καὶ σπεῦσον ὡς ἐλεήμων
     εἰς τὴν βοήθειαν ἥμων,   ὅτι δύνασαι βουλόμενος."'

Shadrach, Meshach and Abednego become a 'three-perfumed' scent which carries through the stench of human sin to God's nose; their fragrance (as well as their words) draws God's attention and enables their salvation from the fire. Once again, Romanos uses scent imagery physically to repel his congregation from sin ('demonic sacrifices and transgressions') and turn them towards Christ and new creation life. Loaded words like 'idolatry', 'sacrifices' and 'transgressions' make sin into heresy, suggesting that a rejection of true orthodoxy is as deadly as any other offence. Listeners are called upon to imitate the three children by remaining adherents of the true faith and so retain their sweet fragrance by which God will know them at the eschaton.

Ekphrasis and other sensory appeals thus enable Romanos to create new (albeit biblically grounded) narratives which draw his congregation into the Gospel events and into Christ-like living. Through vivid description and imagery, the listeners become witnesses of the events, taking them back to the Gospel events and simultaneously making Gospel events contemporary. Time is reoriented and past events become present realities in the sixth-century liturgy. Thus the congregation participates in these events, and therefore in the life of Christ. Physical appeals to the senses help listeners identify with characters and actions and enable Romanos to shape their modes of behaviour.

Direct Address (Apostrophe)

The final device I focus on is apostrophe, or direct address: the narrator intrudes on the narrative by addressing either the listeners or the characters in the story directly. It is linked to both characterization and *ekphrasis*, since it includes speech or dialogue and creates a similar vividness in the narrative. Its purpose is to shape the listener's response to an event, person or thing by vividly depicting the narrator's response.[100]

Earlier and Contemporary Uses of Apostrophe

Clearly, apostrophe was a signficant and ubiquitous device in earlier and contemporary homiletics.[101] By directly addressing characters or listeners, preachers could build emotional engagement in their audience, strengthen invective or praise, emphasize points of doctrine, and augment and expand biblical narratives; these functions will all be seen in Romanos' use of apostrophe. To take an initial example, from earlier homiletics, in his sermons *On the Judaizing Christians* John Chrysostom apostrophized the Jews, calling out 'You Jews' at the opening of a criticism or attack.[102] Chrysostom

---

100   Block (1982), 8–9.

101   For example, for a discussion of John Chrysostom's use of apostrophe in homily 6, in which he addresses the apostle Paul, see Heath (2004), 396–400. See also Glenthøj (1997), 272.

102   Chrysostom's attack is a singular one: 'You Jew', but refers to all Jews. See Harkins's note in Harkins (1979), 7 n. 28. On these discourses, see, for example, Maxwell (2006), 83ff., Shepardson (2008), 64–5, Wilken (1983). On anti-Judaism in late antiquity and in Romanos, see Chapter 3 above.

addresses the Jewish race, setting before them their iniquity, for the benefit of Christians who envy the ancient traditions and rituals of Judaism and desire to partake in them. Through these apostrophes, which are rhetorically highly charged, Chrysostom characterizes the Jews and encourages his listeners to agree with his portrayal:

Are you Jews still disputing the question? Do you not see that you are condemned by the testimony of what Christ and the prophets predicted and which the facts have proved? But why should this surprise me? That is the kind of people you are. From the beginning you have been shameless and obstinate, ready to fight at all times against obvious facts.[103]

Ἔτι οὖν ἀμφισβητεῖς, ὦ Ἰουδαῖε, καὶ τὴν ἀπὸ τοῦ τῆς Χριστοῦ προρρήσεως, καὶ τὴν ἀπὸ τῆς τῶν προφητῶν καὶ τῆς τῶν πραγμάτων ἀποδείξεως μαρτυρίαν ὁρῶν σου καταψηφιζομένην; Ἀλλ᾽ οὐδὲν θαυμαστόν· τοιοῦτον γὰρ ὑμῶν τὸ ἔθνος ἄνωθεν ἀναίσχυντον καὶ φιλόνεικον, καὶ τοῖς φανεροῖς ἀεὶ μάχεσθαι μεμελετηκὸς πράγμασι.

Chrysostom's use of rhetorical questions and invective in his direct addresses to the Jews makes a mockery of Judaism. Judaism is made to seem outdated and wrong, and Jews appear stubborn in their persistent rejection of truth and goodness. Through his use of apostrophe, Chrysostom focused the minds of listeners on (his belief in) the superiority of Christianity.

Apostrophe also allowed preachers to explore and explain points of doctrine. Basil of Seleucia used it to emphasize the significance of the raising of Lazarus.[104] At the end of the homily on Lazarus he addresses Death directly (13), telling him his grief is well-founded because of Christ's death and resurrection. The character of Death is brought into the world of the fifth century not as a powerful monster but as a defeated and dejected figure. It is a strong message to the congregation that 'death no longer has dominion'.[105] Basil not only vivified the narrative, but emphasized the change in the nature of death after the incarnation through his use of apostrophe.

Romanos' contemporary Leontius of Constantinople uses direct address to flesh out the story of Christ's resurrection. His homily *On Palm Sunday* (CPG 7983) includes a lively dialogue between Martha and Jesus elaborated from the Gospel account (e.g. John 11:1–44). Martha is almost adamant that Jesus can do nothing for her brother because he has been dead for four days (322) and Jesus is somewhat annoyed at Martha's constant questioning

---

[103]   Translation taken from Harkins (1979), 140.
[104]   See Cunningham (1986), 161–84.
[105]   Romans 6:9.

and scepticism (342). Towards the end of the homily Leontius himself asks Jesus why he could not roll back the stone himself:

Why, Lord, did you not have the strength to do this yourself? You raise a corpse and you do not roll away a stone?

Τί γάρ, δέσποτα, αὐτὸς οὐκ ἰσχύεις τοῦτο ποιῆσαι; Νεκρὸν ἐγείρεις καὶ λίθον οὐ κυλίεις; (367–8)

Leontius then reports Jesus' response:

Yes, it is not out of weakness that I order [the stone to be moved], but from my own wisdom that I command the Jews, so that they might be informed not only by sight and smell that what happened is true and not an illusion and that I am the Lord of the dead and the living.

Ναί, οὐκ ἀπὸ ἀσθενείας κελεύω, ἀλλ᾽ ἀπὸ σοφίας ἰδίας ἐπιτάττω τοῖς Ἰουδαίοις, ὅπως μὴ μόνον τῇ ὄψει καὶ τῇ ὀσφρήσει πληροφορηθῶσιν, ὅτι ἀλήθεια καὶ οὐ φαντασία τὸ γινόμενον, καὶ ὅτι ἐγώ εἰμι ὁ νεκρῶν καὶ ζώντων κύριος. (373–6)

Leontius makes himself part of the story when he asks the character of Jesus for an explanation of his actions; he becomes a first-hand witness to a Gospel event and so makes the story lively and engaging.[106] Leontius vocalizes the doubt and queries of his congregation through his created persona and gives the theological response more weight by placing it in Jesus' mouth.

Apostrophe in Romanos

Like these homilists, Romanos uses direct address to facilitate his congregation's participation in the new creation.[107] In *On the Marriage at Cana*, Romanos addresses the character of Mary and she responds (VII.6.1–3, 7.2–3):

We entreat you, holy virgin: Did you know the nature of his miracles,
how your son was able to give wine freely, not having gathered the grapes,
not yet being a miracle-worker, as the godly John wrote?

Σὲ δυσωποῦμεν, παρθένε σεμνή·   ἐκ ποίων ἔγνως θαυμάτων αὐτοῦ
   ὡς δύναται ὁ υἱός σου   σταφυλὴν μὴ τρυγήσας τὸν οἶνον χαρίζεσθαι
οὔπω θαυματουργήσας   πρώην, ὡς Ἰωάννης   ὁ θεσπέσιος ἔγραψεν;

---

[106] See further in Allen and Datema (1991), 14–15.

[107] Barkhuizen (1986a), 20. Barkhuizen only includes narrative intrusions which address characters in the *kontakia*, and not direct addresses to the listeners. Whereas Block specifically refers to occasions when the narrator addresses the audience: Block (1982), 8. I have included both in my analysis.

'Listen friends,' she says, 'that you might all
<blockquote>understand and perceive the mystery.</blockquote>
See my son is already a miracle-worker even before this marvel ...'

Ἀκούσατε', φησίν, 'ὦ φίλοι,
<blockquote>συνετίσθητε πάντες καὶ γνῶτε μυστήριῦ·</blockquote>
εἶδον τὸν υἱόν μου   ἤδη θαυματουργοῦντα   καὶ πρὸ τούτου τοῦ θαύματος.'

Romanos' imaginative dialogue makes the congregation a character with him in the Gospel story: together they ask Mary a question. Romanos gives his exegesis a Marian pedigree while transforming his listeners into participants, into Mary's contemporaries and indeed interlocutors. This is also part of Romanos' enactment of sacred time. By making the biblical character of Mary address his audience, he can cast her as a contemporary figure and emphasize the change in the nature of time which has taken place as a result of the ultimate miracle: God's incarnation.

At the beginning of *On the Presentation in the Temple*, Romanos calls on his congregation to take part in the Gospel (IV.1.1–2):

Let us rush to the God-bearer, we who wish to see her son
brought before Symeon.

Τῇ θεοτόκῳ προδράμωμεν   οἱ βουλόμενοι
<blockquote>κατιδεῖν τὸν υἱὸν αὐτῆς</blockquote>
πρὸς Συμεὼν ἀπαγόμενον·

Mary is made a contemporary, local character; she lives around the corner from the church and Romanos urges the congregation to hurry or they might miss an important local event. As narrator, Romanos draws them into the story of which he is already a part.

On the Resurrection II is another such example.[108] Romanos places himself right in the action of the hymn and addresses Christ, Hades and the guards at the tomb about the resurrection.[109] His professed reason for this is to convert even those who hate Christ (XXV.1.6–7) and he does this by recreating himself as a sort of time-travelling and boundary-crossing journalist who secures first-hand testimonies from those who witnessed the resurrection. He wants to discover the inner workings of the resurrection: what actually happened, how it happened and what its effect was, is or will be. Through Romanos the interviewer, the congregation comes face

---

[108] Interestingly, it is not one which Barkhuizen identifies in his list.

[109] In Marjorie Carpenter's translation, the only complete English translation of the hymns, she puts the questioning of Hades into the mouth of Adam. See Carpenter (1970), 263. There is, however, nothing in the Greek text to suggest that it is not Romanos speaking.

to face with a whinging Hades who mourns his loss and complains about being mocked for something he could not have been expected to predict. It is, in fact, not unlike the speech given by Death in Basil of Seleucia's homily discussed above. In his lengthy speech Romanos' Hades details the effect of the resurrection upon him: the destruction of his kingdom and his own enslavement (stanza 7). He describes the resurrection of the prophets, whom Christ leads out of hell and who sing and dance as they leave (8, 10–11). Death is completely defeated and is a vivid and believable character in his defeat. He is a sore loser, a cheater who has been found out. Romanos brings this character to life through speeches.

Following his conversation with Death, Romanos then turns to the men who guarded the tomb. After some coaxing, they relate that the angel rolled away the stone (stanzas 16–17) and the women came to anoint Jesus' body (18). Having given this testimony they then try to convince Romanos not to believe it, saying they have been persuaded by money (20). But Romanos is not persuaded and rejoices in discovering the truth even from the mouths of liars (21). They are reluctant informers and, once again, very believable characters: their silence has been bought but such loyalty is short-lived; they tell the truth with only a little persuasion. This image of the true liar appears in a few of Romanos' hymns and emphasizes that God's truth will not remain hidden; God can use even the tongues of his enemies to get his message out. In this hymn Romanos' persona as well as character development draws the congregation into the events. We have seen how Romanos' self-construction contributes to the congregation's involvement in the events of the *kontakia*.

Yet most instances of apostrophe in Romanos' *kontakia* do not involve a dialogue between Romanos and the addressee, but are a rhetorical address without response from the character. The most extended apostrophe is that of *On Judas*, in which Romanos addresses both Christ and Judas, in the latter's case several times and over several strophes. Romanos' addresses to Judas are filled with hatred and disgust at his actions (XVII.5.1–5):

Unrighteous one, heartless, implacable, brigand, traitor, schemer!
What happened that you rejected him?
What did you see that you acted so foolishly? What did you suffer that you hated
   him so much?
Did he not name you as his friend?
Did he not call you brother, although he knew you had deceived him?

Ἄδικε, ἄστοργε, ἄσπονδε,   πειρατά, προδότα, πολυμήχανε,
   τί γέγονεν   ὅτι ἠθέτησας;
   τί ἰδὼν οὕτως ἠφρόνησας;   τί παθὼν οὕτως ἐμίσησας;

οὐκ αὐτοῦ   φίλον σε   ὠνόμασεν;
οὐκ αὐτὸς ἀδελφόν σε κέκληκε,   καίτοι εἰδὼς ὅτι δεδόλωσαι;

This is one of many such passages in this *kontakion*. They are designed to make his congregation feel Romanos' outrage and participate in it.[110] Judas is not given any opportunity to explain his actions; rather Romanos and the congregation act as judge over him, and strongly condemn him.[111] In this case, Romanos models what he sees as the correct response for the congregation to imitate.

Romanos also speaks directly to the congregation to call them to participate in Gospel events. In *On the Raising of Lazarus II*, he says (XV.18.1–3):

Let us all hate fleeting matter and let us now meet our saviour, Christ,
                                                                                who is hurrying to Bethany,
so that we might feast with him, with his friend Lazarus and the disciples,
and may we now be delivered from evils by their prayers.

Ὕλην ῥευστὴν μισήσωμεν πάντες   καὶ Χριστῷ τῷ σωτῆρι   ὑπαντήσωμεν νῦν
                                       ἐν Βηθανίᾳ σπεύδοντι,
ὅπως αὐτῷ συνεστιαθῶμεν   σὺν τῷ φίλῳ Λαζάρῳ καὶ ἀποστόλοις,
καὶ ταῖς αὐτῶν   ἱκεσίαις ῥυσθῶμεν τῶν πρώην κακῶν·

The journey to Bethany is not something that happened centuries ago, but a present reality. The 'feast' has two referents: the eucharist and, ultimately, the eschaton. We have seen that Romanos understands the eucharist as a participation in the crucifixion of Christ and in the eternal feast taking place in heaven. At the eucharist, humans glimpse eternity, when all humanity will come together to 'feast' eternally with Christ and Lazarus and the disciples. Through apostrophe, Romanos focuses his listeners' attention on their participation in Christ and its future consummation.

Conclusions

Romanos' hymns revolve around the conviction that the incarnation has brought about a decisive change in the world. Although the world is not yet the ultimate paradise God promises humanity, Romanos argues that the result of God becoming human is that the world is a fundamentally new place which Christians experience in a radical new temporality which anticipates heavenly joys. Time is time in its fullness, with biblical events, the incarnation and anticipation of heavenly perfection shaping Christian

[110]   Barkhuizen (1986a), 25–6.
[111]   Frank (2006b), 69.

life in radical ways. This understanding of the fullness of time is seen in a wide range of contemporary texts, including homiletics, liturgical practices and in Christian art and architecture. Christians experience it as they participate in divine reality in the liturgy in churches whose architecture, decorative schemes and discursively imagined space tie heaven to earth and make space and time a holy anticipation of paradise.

This new reality brings with it responsibilities for Christians. Romanos believes that Christians are called to participate in the life of Christ and to live out a Christ-like life in preparation for and in anticipation of the coming eschaton. He sees that the liturgy already acts out that participation through the eucharist and baptism and through the concept of the heavenly liturgy, in which the earthly liturgy takes part. Romanos emphasizes and re-enacts these modes of participation; he also uses rhetorical techniques to facilitate it: characterization, *ekphrasis* and apostrophe. These techniques make Gospel events vibrant and immediate, bringing them into the eternal present which anticipates the eschaton. Through the refrain and dialogue, the congregation takes on different roles, playing out the biblical narratives; Romanos creates characters (including his own persona) with whom the congregation can identify and whom they may be able to imitate. These characters enact proper Christian behaviour in the time before the second coming. Vivid description makes the congregation witness the events, and other sensory appeals demonstrate the proper use of the senses as a means of connection with God. By directly addressing characters in the narrative, Romanos once again acts out the change in time, making biblical events contemporary and contemporary characters biblical. The congregation is thus drawn into participation in the new creation, which Romanos sees as the responsibility of Christians: they are to act out their humanity which has been corrected and perfected in Christ; they thus anticipate eschatological reality.

On the Resurrection IV: Conclusions and Beyond

There is a vibrancy and urgency to Romanos' poetry and his creative engagement with biblical stories. Anticipation of the approaching end times and expectant hope in the general resurrection drive Romanos' theology and pastoral preaching and help to generate his exuberant imagery. He crafts his compositions to guide his listeners into faithful new creation living. He shows how God in Christ corrects human wrongs and perfects humanity in himself, and he insists that Christians are called to enact this renewed humanity. He explores the concept of recreation, explaining the impact of the incarnation of Christ on time and history. And he argues that there is a still greater miracle to come: the final consummation of God's promise in the return to paradise.

Romanos' theology is dramatic; it is performed, enacted, *lived*, in the *kontakia*. Through dramatic techniques, rhetorical devices, vivifying imagery, Romanos makes both the biblical narratives and God's call upon Christians come to life. He creates imaginative and engaging dialogues which help to perform the life of Christ and make participation in that life seem more possible. The performed stories in the *kontakia* are 'world-creating'.[1] They create a sacred space and spiritual temporality in which the lives of Romanos' audience can be transformed by the reality of the new creation. Romanos' *kontakia* function in part to help his listeners participate in Gospel stories, engage with theological ideas, identify with Christ-like models and ultimately enact the Christ-like life in anticipation of the eschaton.

We have seen how Romanos uses particular rhetorical techniques to give life to his theology, how he lets his imagination run wild with biblical narratives, dramatizing and expanding existing stories to explore their salvific significance. The beauty of Romanos' compositions reflects his sense of the beauty of creation, which has been remade in Christ at the incarnation.

To draw together several of the themes of this book, I offer an analysis of *On the Resurrection IV*. This *kontakion* is set down for the third Sunday after Easter, and opens with the story of the woman with the lost coin (Luke

---

[1] For an important account of the ways in which enacted concepts make worlds, see Goodman (1978).

15:8–10).[2] It is mostly concerned with the harrowing of hell. We will see that the theological concepts outlined in this book are once again important in this *kontakion*, although I do not claim to have captured Romanos' thought *in toto*, and the following analysis also points to more in Romanos that would be worth exploring.

Romanos begins with an allegorical interpretation of the Lucan reading: the woman represents Christ, who is the wisdom of God (XXVII.2.3–4); the nine safe coins represent the angelic hierarchy and the one lost coin is Adam (2.5–9). Romanos was probably influenced by a homily of Pseudo-Chrysostom in this interpretation,[3] and throughout this book we have seen his indebtedness to earlier traditions of homiletics and exegesis. But he characteristically has his own emphases, and in this instance he is more explicit than Ps-Chrysostom in his assertion that the woman represents Christ. Romanos has no trouble with a woman representing Christ, just as in other *kontakia* he presents the sinful woman, the haemorrhaging woman and the Samaritan woman as models of penitence, piety and faith.

The following stanza explores God's actions to find the lost 'coin', taking on the role of the second Adam (XXVII.3):

Conquered by love, he came into the world to seek out
                    the one who had wandered, his creature,
he who is without beginning and incomprehensible, son of God and our God,
both wisely and divinely, as God, he carries out the search for this man.
And being made flesh from his mother, whom he swept clean and sanctified,
and, as a lamp of light, he presents his body,
illuminating everything at once by the fire and oil of his divinity.
For fire and clay always make a lamp.
So thus from his divinity and his fleshliness,
Christ caused the light of the lamp to shine,
[Christ], the life and the resurrection.

Ὑπὸ στοργῆς ἐκνικηθείς,   ἦλθεν ἐν κόσμῳ ζητῆσαι
                                        τὸ πλανηθὲν αὐτοῦ κτίσμα
    ὁ ἄναρχος καὶ ἄφραστος   υἱός τε   τοῦ Θεοῦ καὶ Θεὸς ἡμῶν,
    καὶ σοφῶς καὶ θεϊκῶς   ὥσπερ Θεὸς   τούτου ποιεῖται τὴν ζήτησιν,
    καὶ σαρκοῦται ἐκ μητρὸς   ἣν †ἐσάρωσε† καὶ ἡγίασε,
    καὶ ὥσπερ λύχνον φωτὸς   προσφέρει τὴν σάρκα,
                                        τῷ πυρὶ καὶ τῷ ἐλαίῳ

---

[2] I cannot find anything to suggest that this was the Gospel reading set down for the day, but it seems unlikely that it was not, given the pains Romanos takes to weave it into the opening of his *kontakion*.

[3] PG 61, 781–4. See Grosdidier de Matons (1967), 572–74.

τῷ τῆς θεότητος   καταυγάσας τὰ σύμπαντα·
  πῦρ γὰρ ἀεὶ   καὶ πηλὸς λύχνον ποιεῖ·
  οὕτως οὖν ἔλαμψεν   ἐκ θεότητος   καὶ σαρκώσεως
  τὸ τοῦ λύχνου φῶς, Χριστός,
  ἡ ζωὴ καὶ ἀνάστασις.

Romanos weaves a web of imagery, drawing on, recalling and elucidating the doctrinal and salvific significance of the Lucan story. The woman swept her house clean in order to find the coin; Jesus swept clean the womb that housed him so that he might enter the world and find his precious lost one. The woman lights a lantern so that she can see clearly to find the coin; Jesus is himself the lighted lamp which enlightens the world and restores lost Adam. Christ's unique role in salvation history as 'second Adam' and perfect God and man provides the grammar for these analogies of similarity and difference.

Romanos strongly emphasizes Christ's two natures in this stanza, and their equal importance in human salvation. Language and imagery in lines 1 to 3 highlight the relationship of the Son to the Father and the divine nature of Christ. Romanos draws on doctrinal language about Christ and his lack of separation from God even at the incarnation. Words for God and divine are repeated throughout and even the reference to Mary, whose role in salvation Romanos often emphasizes, is made in terms of Christ's divine actions towards her: he cleansed and sanctified her by making her bear him. Whereas Romanos often accentuates Mary's virginity and purity (and will again later in this *kontakion*, stanza 13), here he has Christ 'sweep her clean', reinforcing that Christ perfects humanity in the incarnation.

Christ's flesh bookends lines 4 and 5: Christ's human nature is just as important for human salvation as his divine one. We have seen how this emphasis resonates with Chalcedonian christological formulations. From then on Romanos makes reference to divine and human natures through the metaphor of the lamp. Christ's humanity is presented as the clay, the earthy fabric of the lamp; it is his divinity which provides the fuel and the flame. The word for oil is perhaps also intended to recall the Holy Spirit, who descends upon the initiate thus anointed at baptism. Word pairs play an important role in this stanza, as a way of acting out the pairing of two natures in Christ. They are also inscribed into the *kontakion* through the refrain. And here, 'divinity' and 'fleshliness' map onto 'life' and 'resurrection' in that final line.

The metaphor continues in the following stanza (4):

Then he went up onto the cross, as the lamp onto the lampstand,
                    and he observed from there,

crouching in gloom and darkness, Adam, the first-created.
And he who is inseparable [from heaven] hurries,
                              travelling far in the flesh to [Adam],
not separated from his father's bosom, and still fulfilling the things that happened.
He took with him the gall and the vinegar, the nails and the spear,
in order that with the spear and the nails
he might wound Death straightaway and with the gall
he might make things bitter for the unjust Hades encountering him,
and cause him pain by the vinegar he drank,
he who is the Life and the Resurrection.

Τότε ἀνῆλθεν ἐν σταυρῷ   ὡς ἐν λυχνίᾳ ὁ λύχνος,   καὶ ἐθεώρει ἐκεῖθεν
    ἐν σκότει καθεζόμενον   καὶ ἐν γνόφῳ   τὸν Ἀδὰμ τὸν πρωτόπλαστον.
καὶ σπουδάζει πρὸς αὐτὸν   ἀποδημεῖν   διὰ σαρκὸς ὁ ἀχώριστος,
    ὁ τῶν κόλπων τοῦ πατρὸς   μὴ χωρισθεὶς καὶ πληρῶν τὰ γινόμενα.
    ἔλαβε μεθ' ἑαυτοῦ   χολήν τε καὶ ὄξος,
                              τούς τε ἥλους καὶ τὴν λόγχην,
ἵνα τῇ λόγχῃ μὲν   καὶ τοῖς ἥλοις τὸν Θάνατον
    τρώσῃ εὐθὺς   καὶ π[ικρά]νῃ τῇ χολῇ
    Ἅιδην τὸν ἄδικον   συναντήσαντα,   δριμ[υχθέν]τα δὲ[4]
    ὄξει ὅπερ ἔπιεν
    ἡ ζωὴ καὶ ἀνάστασις.

Christ is again the lamp in this stanza: the lamp raised on the lampstand, from Matthew 5:15,[5] which gives light to all. This is certainly an important resonance for Romanos, but Romanos also uses this image for a different purpose: Christ can now see further. Romanos' character of Christ has been seeking Adam, looking everywhere like the woman with the lost coin, and from his raised position on the lampstand – that is, the cross – he has a clearer vision and catches sight of his lost one. The death of Christ is the means by which Adam is redeemed, but the picture we have of that death is one removed from any sense of suffering. Instead, Romanos focuses on the loving God whose every action, every concern is for his lost creature, and for whom crucifixion is simply the means of restoring Adam to his bosom. Romanos' crucified Christ, in this example, draws both on Pauline themes and on the glorified and exalted Johannine Christ.

The lamp is also the second Adam: the contrast between light and dark in the first few lines makes this clear. The first Adam is shrouded in darkness, crouching in the gloom of hell, and it is the second Adam who will restore him to the light. Again, Romanos stresses the importance of Christ's two

---

[4] I have followed the reconstruction in the SC edition here: Grosdidier de Matons (1967), 582.
[5] And similar texts in other Gospels: Mark 4:21, Luke 8:16, Luke 11:33.

natures in this restoration. It is his flesh, combined with his inseparability from God, which enables the second Adam to redeem and 'enlighten' the first.

To do this, Christ uses the weapons of the crucifixion against Hades: Death's own weapons are turned upon him. The way Romanos uses the spear and the nails – as weapons to wound Hades – recalls imagery of Hades stabbed by the cross, iconography employed elsewhere by Romanos but also in contemporary homiletics and later Christian art.[6] Romanos also makes Christ into a poisonous dish for the hungry Hades: the gall and vinegar which he drank on the cross will give Death a stomach ache when he swallows Christ. We have seen images elsewhere of Christ as the healer, as the doctor who cures Adam of his gluttony-induced stomach aches. Here, Christ is the instigator of pain and suffering. Once more we see the twinned images of redemption and punishment which are part of Christ's correction of the sins of the world and perfection of humanity. Adam is redeemed partly through the punishment of Hades. And, as we saw in the previous stanza, Romanos uses word pairs to match the double description of Christ in the refrain: gall and vinegar, spear and nails, will be used by the Life and the resurrection to wound and give pain to Death.

Christ descends into hell and Romanos likens him to Jonah (5.4–5):

For, indeed, just like Jonah, he was also in the belly of the tomb,
having been carried into the grave just as he willed it,
                    but in the coffin [Christ] lay awake.

καὶ γὰρ [[καὶ]] δὴ ὡς Ἰωνᾶς
                    ἦν καὶ αὐτὸς [ἐν] κοιλίᾳ τοῦ μνήματος·
ἐν τάφῳ μὲν πορευθεὶς   καθ[ὼς] ἠβουλήθη,
                    ἐν σορῷ δὲ ἀγρυπνήσας·

As we have seen in our discussion of typology, antitype surpasses type, governed by the grammar of the divine plan of salvation: Christ intended that he should descend into the tomb, whereas Jonah was certainly unwilling. The typology holds nicely in line 5: Jonah was awake in the fish and Christ in the tomb. 'Lay awake' (*agrypnēsas*) is also related to the word Romanos uses for the night vigil in *On the Man Possessed*, suggesting that Christ kept a vigil in the tomb just as Jonah prayed to God from the belly of the fish and just as Romanos' congregation now keeps a vigil. Romanos' listeners are drawn into the tomb and the fish with both Christ and Jonah, and they

---

[6] On this image and its use in homiletics, hymnography and iconography, see Frazer (1974), 153–61.

perform the descent into hell as part of their enactment of Christ's life. Romanos emphasizes death through variation, using three different words for 'tomb' in two lines.

And it is in that tomb that the drama of the *kontakion* (and the drama of the salvation story) really takes place. Hades, heretically mistaking Jesus for a mere man in contrast to the orthodox picture of Christ presented earlier in the *kontakion*, speaks at the opening of the stanza (6):

'Quick! Let us be daring,' he says, 'for here is the body of a man
　　　　　　　　　　　　　　which has been carried into the tomb.
Let us imprison with locks the one who has come and deliver him up to decay.'
And straightaway as he said this, he ran quickly and took hold of the body.
But Jesus Christ, as if rousing himself from some sort of sleep,
violently binds him and pushes him down
　　　　　　　　　　　　　　　and he cries aloud to those in Hades:
'Everyone rise up and trample on Hades.
Come now to me, Adam, with Eve.
Do not be afraid as if you are liable for your judgement-debts,
for I have paid for everything, who am
the life and the resurrection.'

'Τάχος τολμήσωμεν', φησίν· 'σῶμα γὰρ ἀνθρώπου ἐστὶ
　　　　　　　　　　　　　　τὸ κομισθὲν ἐν τῷ τάφῳ·
τοῖς κλείθροις φυλακίσωμεν　τὸν ἐλθόντα　καὶ φθορᾷ παραδώσωμεν'·
καὶ εὐθὺς ταῦτα εἰπὼν　τρέχει ταχὺ　καὶ τῆς σαρκὸς ἐπελάβετο·
　Ἰησοῦς δὲ ὁ Χριστὸς　ὥσπερ ἐξ ὕπνου τινὸς ἐξανίσταται,
δεσμεῖ δὲ τοῦτον σφοδρῶς　καὶ τίθησι κάτω
　　　　　　　　　　　　　　καὶ κραυγάζει τοῖς ἐν Ἄιδου·
'Πάντες ἀνάστητε　καὶ τὸν Ἄιδην πατήσατε·
　δεῦρο Ἀδάμ　σὺν Εὔα νῦν πρὸς ἐμέ·
　μὴ δειλιάσητε　ὡς ὑπεύθυνοι　τοῖς ὀφλήμασι·
　πάντα γὰρ ἀπέδωκα,
　ἡ ζωὴ καὶ ἀνάστασις.'

Death has lost its sting: this is the message of much of the rest of the *kontakion*. Here Romanos makes Hades into a tragicomic villain, beaten into submission by the hero, Christ. Violence is associated with Christ, whom Romanos depicts as the leader of an uprising. The language of violence pervades this *kontakion* and, as here, is associated with the punishment of death. The loving God is fierce and vengeful in his treatment of the enemy of life, Hades, who has kept his creatures prisoner since they left paradise.

Romanos draws on imagery from everyday life to personalize the narrative for his listeners. Sin is figured by debts, as if monetary compensation

payments or fines meted out by an earthly judge. The restoration of humanity is a payment of those debts. Christ has paid off everything and Adam
and Eve have no more to fear.

In the following stanza Christ calls for humans to perform the destruction of Death, again through violence, but also through the ultimate speech
act which performs and creates the new dispensation (7):

'Come, mortals, strike the face of Hades shamelessly,
                               and trample on his neck,
enter crying aloud, "Hades and Death have been swallowed up."
For your sakes I have come, for I am the life and resurrection for all.
So everyone with joy now recite psalms and hymns:
"Where is your victory, O dishonoured Hades?
                          Where, Death, is your sting?
You lie powerless, Death, you have been condemned to death.
And you too Hades, you who have been skilfully bound.
You who were ruling are enslaved at the moment when you see
that he has arrived,
the Life and Resurrection."'

Ἀλλὰ ῥαπίσατε, θνητοί,   Ἅιδου τὰς ὄψεις ἀτίμως,
                               καὶ τὸν αὐχένα πατοῦντες
    εἰσέλθατε κραυγάζοντες· "κατεπόθη
                          καὶ ὁ Ἅιδης καὶ ὁ Θάνατος"·
δι' ὑμᾶς ἦλθον ἐγώ·   καὶ γάρ εἰμι   πάντων ζωὴ καὶ ἀνάστασις·
    ἀλλὰ πάντες σὺν χαρᾷ   εἴπατε νῦν τοὺς ψαλμοὺς καὶ τὰ ᾄσματα·
    "ποῦ ἐστι νῖκος τὸ σόν,   ὦ ἄτιμε Ἅιδη;
                          ποῦ σοῦ, Θάνατε, τὸ κέντρον;
κεῖσθε ἀδύνατοι·   Θάνατε, τεθανάτωσαι·
    Ἅιδης, καὶ σὺ   καταδέδεσαι δεινῶς·
    οἱ βασιλεύσαντες   ἐδουλώθητε   θεασάμενοι
    ὅτι παρεγένετο
    ἡ ζωὴ καὶ ἀνάστασις."'

Christ gives directions to 'mortals' as if they were waiting in the wings to
burst upon the stage. He wants them *enter*, crying out Hades' death (line 2),
and here 'crying out' has connotations of wild beasts baying or screeching,
emphasizing both that the raising of the dead is a frightening and unnatural
thing, and that the death of Death is an event which should cause frenzied
excitement in mortals. Romanos' Christ himself brings listeners into the
action of hell's destruction, using the inclusive category 'mortals' and calling
for spoken acts (easily performed by Romanos' listeners) as well as physical
ones. And in a dramatic reversal of the earlier image of Hades swallowing
poison, here Hades and Death are themselves swallowed up.

In response to his advent, Christ also wants mortals to sing psalms and hymns announcing the fulfilment of Hosea's prophecy (Hosea 13:14). The latter may also be a reference to the vigil in which the congregation is taking part, which involved group recitation and singing of psalms and songs. In this way, the liturgy, and the *kontakion* in particular, are performances of Christ's command which construct a new world for believers. The imaginative expansion of the Gospel story is a key means by which Romanos aims to create a transformed spiritual reality for his congregation.

I have altered the punctuation of the last few lines, which in both the SC and the Oxford editions are said by Christ alone. But they make more sense as a further directive from Christ to 'mortals'. The continued address to Hades and the third-person verbs referring to Christ support this reading. So Christ instructs humans in the singing of the *kontakion* which is the performance of their salvation.

These final lines deploy paradox to figure the post-incarnation life: death is put to death, the enslaving one is enslaved, and so on. After the impossible miracle of God becoming human, all reality, time and history are altered so that paradox performs the new paradise; it breaks through the tired conceptual categories of the old dispensation and encourages believers to imagine new worlds and new possibilities, to imagine themselves as free from the conceptual relations, social structures and all material negotiations that bind them to the old life and become liberated to participate in the new creation.

As I have argued, Romanos repeatedly aims to construct a new liturgical temporality through his *kontakia*. There is no sense in this passage that Christ is only speaking to those who were dead when he harrowed hell. 'Mortals' incorporates all time and the death of death is absolute and eternal. So although Romanos still awaits the second coming of Christ, he insists that the harrowing of Hades has forever emptied hell. This is evident in stanza 16 (1–5), the conclusion of Christ's long speech:

'Only so that you may not be ignorant of what you are placed under, O Hades:

                       not only will you give back
those whom you took and I have raised, whom I take with me as I go,
but, as you know, if any are escorted to you for the rest of time,

                           they will rise up,
since I will raise them all up together with the sound of a trumpet,
because you have dared to lay hold of the faultless son of the king.'

Μόνον ἵνα μὴ ἀγνοῆς   ἅπερ ὑπέστης, ὦ Ἅιδη·

                     οὐ μόνον γὰρ ἀποδώσεις

οὓς ἔλαβες καὶ ἤγειρα,   οὓς λαμβάνω
                              μετ' ἐμοῦ [[ὁ]] ἐξερχόμενος,
ἀλλὰ γὰρ †ὡς εἶδες† ἄν σοι   καὶ τοῦ λοιποῦ
                              παραπεμφθῶσιν, ἐγείρονται,
ἐπειδὴ πάντας ὁμοῦ   ἐξαναστήσω φωνῇ τῇ τῆς σάλπιγγος,
ὅτι ἐτόλμησας σὺ   υἱὸν βασιλέως   ἀναμάρτητον κρατῆσαι.

Christ details the destruction of Hades' power and realm. The present
actions of Christ are contrasted (using the same verb, line 2) with the past
actions of Hades. This is the final part of a long defence speech Romanos
gives Christ. In stanzas 8 and 9, Death feels he is under attack and complains that he has been treated unjustly. Romanos has him express his lack
of understanding: Christ is in the form of a man so why does he not obey
human rules? The following stanzas (10–16) are set out as a trial, with Hades
bringing a case against Christ. This hints at the wider cultural resonance
of the dialogues in Romanos' poetry, a background that includes homiletics, biblical commentary, question and answer literature, rhetorical class-
rooms and, as here, the law courts; it is certainly a cultural phenomenon
worthy of further exploration. Hades speaks in stanza 10 but is not allowed
to cross-examine: the following five strophes are all Christ's. In stanza 16
(line 6) Romanos says 'Hades was submerged' ("Αιδης ἦν ὑποβρύχιος); he
sank beneath the weight of Christ's arguments, banished to the waters of
chaos which is now, as in Genesis 1, a realm controlled by divine action. We
do not hear Death speak again. The gatekeepers of Hades flee and Christ
breaks through the gates of hell (16.7–10). All the action of the *kontakion*
up to this point has been in the dramatic speeches of Christ and Hades, and
now the dead arise and do as Christ had commanded them (stanza 17).

Romanos brings the *kontakion* to a close with the appearance of the angel
who rolls away the stone at the tomb: all the action has been taking place in
the tomb where Christ was laid. This angel queries Christ's need of him and
Christ explains (19.3–6):

But now learn my wise scheme. For I have given this as symbol
and sign to mortals, the raising of this stone from the tombs,
that in this hour the gates of Hades are not operating in the tombs as before,
but have been pulled up from the middle.

ἀλλὰ νῦν μάθετε μοῦ   τέχνην σοφήν·
                              τοῦτο γὰρ δέδωκα σύμβολον
καὶ σημεῖον τοῖς θνητοῖς   τούτου τοῦ λίθου ἐκ τάφων ἡ ἔπαρσις
ὡς ἐν τῇ ὥρᾳ αὐτῇ   αἱ πύλαι τοῦ Ἅιδου
                              ἀνεσπάσθησαν ἐκ [μέ]σου,

οὐ χρηματίζουσαι   ἐν τοῖς τάφοις ὡς πρότερον·

Dialogue often functions in late antique Christian literature as a means of explaining aspects of the biblical account of Jesus' life that could raise doctrinal problems.[7] We have seen Romanos employ it, for example, to discuss divine freedom, the nature of Christ's will, and the two natures of Christ. Here the problem seems to be the potential criticism that Jesus' divine power should have rendered the work of the angel superfluous. Romanos' solution is to make the angel a symbol of God's power and the stone's removal a sign that the enclosing gates of hell have been destroyed.[8]

For Romanos, in this *kontakion* as elsewhere, Easter is a triumphant celebration of God's power, demonstrated on that day by his victory over death.[9] That victory is brought about the second Adam, whose two natures, divine and human, enable him to die and yet destroy death. We have seen how Romanos emphasizes those two natures through rhetorical devices and dramatic characterization. The restoration of Adam is paired with punishment: violent imagery, focused on Hades, helps Romanos capture something of God's anger at his separation from humans and his passionate desire to restore humans to paradise. God's entry into the world in the person of Christ is the means of restoration and the beginning of something fundamentally new: a recreation of the old, broken world. Romanos uses typology to demonstrate the fulfilment of history in Christ and paradox as a figure of the changed reality. This change requires something of believing Christians, and Romanos gives the character of Christ the role of instructor. Christ speaks directly to listeners, bringing them on the journey and calling for their participation in death's destruction. And he himself gives them the hope of the final resurrection.

That universal resurrection stands at the heart of Romanos' theology and his imaginative, vibrant and engaging creation of biblical stories in his *kontakia*, and, at the conclusion of our analysis, we may appropriately leave him praying this prayer (20.2–5):

---

[7] See Kecskeméti (1993), 29–68.

[8] This explanation looks like the common type of Christian elaboration of a potentially difficult biblical passage, in the manner of explanations for Christ's agony in the garden: for example, Origen, *Against Celsus* II.25 and Didymus, *On the Trinity* III (PG 39, 908). I have not been able to find another instance of Romanos' explanation for the angel moving the stone. Grosdidier de Matons also notes he cannot find a similar explanation in patristic writings or contemporary homiletics: Grosdidier de Matons (1967), 599 n. 1.

[9] Although Romanos also uses images from the natural world to emphasize God's power. See stanza 18.

Therefore, as God, Christ, spare those who believe in your cross
and tomb and resurrection. And grant to us forgiveness of our faults.
And count us worthy, whenever the general awakening happens,
without fear to see your face and hear your voice.

διὸ τῶν δοξαζόντων σου

                   τὸν σταυρὸν καὶ τὴν ταφὴν καὶ ἀνάστασιν

ὡς θεὸς φεῖσαι, Χριστέ·   δὸς δὲ ἡμῖν   πλημμελημάτων συγχώρησιν

  καὶ ἀξίωσον ἡμᾶς,   ὅταν ἡ πάνδημος γένηται ἔγερσις,

  τὸ πρόσωπόν σου ἰδεῖν   μετὰ παρρησίας

                       καὶ ἀκοῦσαι τῆς φωνῆς σου.

Select Bibliography

Editions and Translations of Romanos

Complete Editions

Grosdidier de Matons, J. (ed. and trans.) (1964–81) *Romanos le Mélode: Hymnes.*
    5 vols. Sources chrétiennes 99, 110, 114, 128, 283. Paris.
Koder, J. (ed. and trans.) (2005) *Romanos Melodos: Die Hymnen.* 2 vols. Bibliothek
    der griechischen Literatur. Stuttgart.
Maas, P. and Trypanis, K. (eds) (1963) *Sancti Romani Melodi Cantica: Cantica
    Genuina.* Oxford.
Maisano, R. (ed. and trans.) (2002) *Cantici di Romano il Melodo.* 2 vols. Torino.

Complete English Translation

Carpenter, M. (trans.) (1970) *Kontakia of Romanos, Byzantine Melodist.* 2 vols.
    Columbia.

Partial English Translations

Lash, E. (trans.) (1995) *On the Life of Christ: Kontakia.* The Sacred Literature Series.
    San Francisco.
Schork, R. J. (trans.) (1995) *Sacred Song from the Byzantine Pulpit: Romanos the
    Melodist.* Gainesville.

Other Primary Texts and Translations

Aelius Theon. *Progymnasmata.* In Kennedy, George A. (trans.) (2003) *Progymnasmata:
    Greek Textbooks of Prose Composition and Rhetoric.* Writings from the Greco-
    Roman World. Atlanta, 1–72.
Ambrose. *On the Mysteries.* In Botte, B. (ed. and trans.) (1994) *Ambroise de Milan:
    Des sacrements, Des mysteres, Explication du symbole.* Sources chrétiennes 25.
    Paris.
Anonymous. *Early Byzantine* Kontakia. In Maas, P. (ed.) (1910b) *Frühbyzantinische
    Kirchenpoesie: Anonyme Hymnen des V.–VI. Jahrhunderts.* Bonn.
    In Trypanis, C. A. (ed.) (1968) *Fourteen Early Byzantine Cantica.* Vienna.

Anonymous. *Gospel of Nicodemus*. In Gounelle, R. and Izydorczyk, Z. (eds and trans) (1997) *L'Evangile de Nicodème: Introduction, traduction et notes*. Turnhout.

In Ehrman, B. and Plese, Z. (eds and trans) (2011) *The Apocryphal Gospels: Texts and Translations*. New York and Oxford, 465–89.

Anonymous. *Gospel of Pseudo-Matthew*. In Gijsel, J. and Beyers, R. (eds) (1997) *Libri de Nativitate Mariae, Volume I: Pseudo-Matthaei Evangelium Textus et Commentarius*. Turnhout.

In Elliott, J.K. and James, M.R. (trans) (1993) *The Apocryphal New Testament: A Collection of Apocryphal Christian Literature in an English Translation*. Oxford, 84–99.

Anonymous. *Life of Mary of Egypt*. In Migne, J.-P. (ed.) (1865) PG 87, 3697–726.

In Kouli, M. (trans.) (1996) 'The Life of St Mary of Egypt' in Talbot (ed.) *Holy Women of Byzantium: Ten Saints' Lives in English Translation*. Washington, DC, 65–93.

Anonymous. *Miracles of Artemios*. In Crisafulli, V.S. and Nesbitt, J.W. (eds and trans.) (1997) *The Miracles of St. Artemios*. Leiden.

Anonymous. *Sayings of the Desert Fathers*. In Guy, J.-C. (ed. and trans.) (1993) *Les apophtegmes des pères: Collection systématique, chapitres i–ix. Sources chrétiennes* 387. Paris.

In Migne, J.-P. (1864) *Patrologiae cursus completus. Series Graeca (MPG)* 65. Paris, 71–440.

In Ward, B. (trans.) (2003) *The Desert Fathers: Sayings of the Early Christian Monks*. London.

Anonymous. *Typikon of the Great Church*. In Mateos, J. (ed. and trans.) (1962) *Le Typicon de la Grande Église: MS Sainte-Croix n.40, Xe siècle. Introduction, texte critique, traduction et notes par Juan Mateos. Tome I: Le Cycle des douze mois*. 2 vols. Orientalia Christiana Analecta 1. Rome.

Aphthonius. *Progymnasmata*. In Rabe, H. (ed.) (1926) *Aphthonii Progymnasmata*. Rhetores Graeci 10. Leipzig.

Athanasius. *On the Incarnation of the Word*. In Kannengiesser, C. (ed. and trans.) (1973) *Sur l'incarnation du verbe. Sources chrétiennes* 199. Paris, 258–468.

Three Orations against the Arians. In Metzler, K. and Savvidis, K. (eds) (1998) *Athanasius: Werke, Band I. Die dogmatischen Schriften, Erster Teil, 2*. Berlin; New York, 109–75; 177–260; 305–81.

Epistles. In Migne, J.-P. (ed.) (1857) *Athanasii archiepiscopi Alexandrini opera omnia quae exstant. Patrologia Graeca* 25–6. Paris.

Barnabas. *Epistle of Barnabas*. In Ehrman, Bart D. (ed. and trans.) (2003) *The Apostolic Fathers, Volume II: Epistle of Barnabas. Papias and Quadratus. Epistle to Diognetus. The Shepherd of Hermas*. Loeb Classical Library 25. Cambridge, MA; London, 12–84.

Basil of Caesarea. *Epistles*. In Courtonne, Y. (ed.) (1957; 1961; 1966) *Saint Basile: Lettres*. 3 vols. Paris.

Basil of Seleucia. *Homily on Lazarus*. In Cunningham, M. (ed. and trans.) (1986) 'Basil of Seleucia's Homily on Lazarus: A New Edition', *Analecta Bollandiana* 104: 161–84.

Clement of Alexandria. *Paedagogus*. In Harl, M., Marrou, H. I., Mondésert, C. and Matray, C. (eds and trans) (1960) *Le Pédagogue*. Sources chrétiennes 70, 108, 158. Paris.

Cosmas Indicopleustes. *Christian Topography*. In Wolska-Conus, W. (ed. and trans.) (1968; 1970; 1973) *Cosmas Indicopleustès: Topographie chrétienne*. 3 vols. Sources chrétiennes 141, 159, 197. Paris.

Cyril of Alexandria. *Commentary on John*. In Pusey, P.E. (1872) *Sancti patris nostri Cyrilli archiepiscopi Alexandrini in D. Joannis evangelium*. 3 vols. Oxford.

Five Tomes against Nestorius. In Pusey, P.E. (trans.) (1881) *Five Tomes against Nestorius: Scholia on the Incarnation; Christ is One; Fragments against Diodore of Tarsus, Theodore of Mopsuestia, the Synousiasts*. Library of the Fathers of the Holy Catholic Church 47. Oxford.

Part translated in Russell, N. (2000) *Cyril of Alexandria*. The Early Church Fathers. New York.

Third Letter to Nestorius. In Migne, J.-P. (ed.) (1864) PG 77.105–21. Paris.

In McGuckin, J. (ed. and trans.) (2009) *We Believe in One Lord Jesus Christ*. Commentaries in Ancient Christian Doctrine. Downers Grove, 266–75.

Cyril of Jerusalem. *Mystagogical Lectures*. In Paris, P. and Piedagnel, A. (eds and trans) (1966) *Cyrille de Jérusalem: Catéchèses mystagogiques*. Sources chrétiennes 126. Paris.

Didymus. *On the Trinity*. In Hönscheid, J. (ed.) (1975) *Didymus der Blinde: De trinitate, Buch 1*. Beiträge zur klassischen Philologie 44. Meisenheim am Glan.

In Seiler, I. (ed.) (1975) *Didymus der Blinde: De trinitate, Buch 2, Kapitel 1–7*. Beiträge zur klassischen Philologie 52. Meisenheim am Glan.

Dionysius of Halicarnassus. *De Lysia*. In Radermacher, L. and Usener, H. (eds) (1899; repr. Stuttgart, 1965) *Dionysii Halicarnasei quae exstant*, Volume V. Leipzig.

Ps-Dionysius the Areopagite. *Ecclesiastical Hierarchy*. In Heil, G. and Ritter, A.M. (1991) *Corpus Dionysiacum, Volume II: Pseudo-Dionysius Areopagita: De coelesti hierarchia, De ecclesiastica hierarchia, De mystica theologia, Epistulae*. Patristische Texte und Studien 36. Berlin.

Ephraem Graecus. De Passionibus Animi; Sermo Paraeneticus. In Phrantzoles, K.G. (ed.) (1988; repr. 1995) Ὁσίου Ἐφραίμ τοῦ Σύρου ἔργα, Volume I. Thessalonica.

Ephrem the Syrian. *Commentary on Genesis*. In Tonneau, R.M. (ed. and trans.) (1955) *Sancti Ephraem Syri in Genesim et in Exodum commentarii*. CSCO 152–3, Scriptores Syri 71–2. Leuven.

Hymns on Nativity. In Beck, E. (ed. and trans.) (1958) *Des heiligen Ephraem des Syrers Hymnen de Nativitate (Epiphania)*. CSCO 186–7, Scriptores Syri 82–3. Leuven.

In McVey, K.E. (trans.) (1989) *Ephrem the Syrian: Hymns*. The Classics of Western Spirituality. New York, 61–217.

Hymns on Paradise. In Beck, E. (ed. and trans.) (1957) *Des heiligen Ephraem des Syrers Hymnen de Paradiso und Contra Julianum*. CSCO 174–5, Scriptores Syri 78–9. Leuven.

In Brock, S.P. (trans.) (1990) *Hymns on Paradise*. Crestwood, NY.

Hymns on the Resurrection. In Beck, E. (1964) *Des heiligen Ephraem des Syrers Paschahymnen (De azymis, De crucifixione, De resurrectione)*. CSCO 248–9, Scriptores Syri 108–9. Leuven.

Hymns on Virginity (1962) *Des heiligen Ephraem des Syrers Hymnen de Virginitate*. CSCO 223–4, Scriptores Syri 94–5. Leuven.

In McVey, K.E. (trans.) (1989) *Ephrem the Syrian: Hymns*. The Classics of Western Spirituality. New York, 261–468.

Nisibene Hymns. In Beck, E. (1961) *Des heiligen Ephraem des Syrers Carmina Nisibena, Volume I*. CSCO 218–19, Scriptores Syri 92–3. Leuven.

In Beck (1963) *Des heiligen Ephraem des Syrers Carmina Nisibena, Volume II*. CSCO 240–1, Scriptores Syri 102–3. Leuven.

On the Sinful Woman (attr.). Translated in Schaff, P. and Wace, H. (1890) *Gregory the Great (II), Ephraim Syrus, Aphrahat*. A Select Library of Nicene and Post-Nicene Fathers of the Christian Church. Second Series, XIII; New York.

Selected Translations. In Brock, S.P. and Kiraz, G.A. (trans.) (2006) *Ephrem the Syrian: Select Poems, with English Translation, Introduction and Notes by Sebastian P. Brock and George Anton Kiraz*. Provo, UT.

Eusebius. *Demonstrationis Evangeliae*. In Migne, J.-P. (ed.) (1857) *Eusebii Pamphili opera omnia quae exstant*. Patrologia Graeca 22. Paris, cols 9–794.

George Kedrenos. *Chronicle*. In Bekker, I. (ed.) (1838) *Georgius Cedrenus, Ioannis Scylitzae Ope*. Bonn.

Gregory of Nazianzus. *Theological Orations*. In Barbel, J. (ed.) (1963) *Gregor von Nazianz: Die fünf theologischen Reden*. Düsseldorf.

Epistles. In Gallay, P. (ed. and trans.) (1974) *Grégoire de Nazianze: Lettres théologiques*. Sources chrétiennes 208. Paris.

Gregory of Nyssa. *Antirrheticus adversus Apollinarium*. In Mueller, F. (ed.) (1958) *Gregorii Nysseni opera*. 3.1. Leiden, 127–233.

Life of Moses. In Daniélou, J. (ed. and trans.) (1968) *Grégoire de Nysse: La vie de Moïse*, 3rd edn. Sources chrétiennes 1. Paris.

In Malherbe, A.J. and Ferguson, E. (trans.) (1978) *Gregory of Nyssa: The Life of Moses*. New York.

Hermogenes. *Progymnasmata*. In Kennedy, G.A. (trans.) (2003) *Progymnasmata: Greek Textbooks of Prose Composition and Rhetoric*. Writings from the Greco-Roman World. Atlanta, 73–88.

Ignatius. *Letters*. In Camelot, P.T. (ed. and trans.) (1969) *Ignace d'Antioche. Polycarpe de Smyrne. Lettres. Martyre de Polycarpe*, 4th edn. Sources chrétiennes 10. Paris.

Irenaeus. *Against Heresies*. In Doutreleau, L. and Rousseau, A. (eds and trans.) (1965; 1969; 1974; 1982) *Irénée de Lyon: Contre les heresies. Sources chrétiennes* 100, 101, 152, 153, 263, 264, 293, 294. Paris.

    In Roberts, A. (ed. and trans.) (1979) *The Apostolic Fathers: Justin Martyr, Irenaeus.* The Ante-Nicene Fathers: Translations of the Writings of the Fathers down to AD 325, 1; Grand Rapids, MI.

    The Proof of Apostolic Preaching. In Rousseau, A. (ed. and trans.) (1995) *Irénée de Lyon: Démonstration de la prédication apostolique.* Sources chrétiennes 406. Paris.

John Chrysostom. *Ad populum Antiochenum.* In Migne, J.-P. (ed.) (1862) PG 49. Paris, 15–222.

    Catecheses ad Illuminandos/Baptismal Instructions (ed.) (1862) PG 49. Paris, 223–40.

    In Quasten, J. and Burghardt, W.J. (eds), Harkins P.W. (trans) (1963) *Baptismal Instructions.* Ancient Christian Writers: The Works of the Fathers in Translation 31. Westminster, MD.

    Discourses against Judaizing Christians. In Harkins, P.W. (trans.) (1979) *Discourses against Judaizing Christians.* Washington, DC.

    Homilia de Beato Philogono 6. In Migne, J.-P. (ed.) (1862) PG 48. Paris, 747–56.

    Homiliae in Epistolam Primam ad Corinthios (ed.) (1862) PG 61. Paris, 9–382.

    Homiliae in Ioannem (ed.) (1862) PG 59. Paris, 23–482.

    Homilia in Martyres (ed.) (1862) PG 50. Paris, 661–6.

    Homilia L in Mattheum (ed.) (1862) PG 58. Paris, 503–10.

    Sur le Sacerdoce. In Malingrey, A.M. (ed. and trans.) (1980) *Sur le sacerdoce: Dialogue et homélie.* Sources chrétiennes 272. Paris.

Justin Martyr. *Dialogue with Trypho.* In Goodspeed, E.J. (ed.) (1915) *Die ältesten Apologeten.* Göttingen.

Justinian. *Contra Monophysitas.* In Albertella, R., Amelotti, M. and Migliardi, L. (eds) (1973) *Drei dogmatische Schriften Iustinians,* 2nd edn. Legum Iustiniani imperatoris vocabularium. Subsidia 2. Milan.

    In Wesche, K.P. (trans.) (1991) *On the Person of Christ: The Christology of Emperor Justinian.* Crestwood, N., 27–107.

    Novella. In Kroll, W. and Schöll, R. (1895; repr. 1968) *Corpus iuris civilis,* Volume III. Berlin.

Leontius of Byzantium. *Homilies.* In Allen, P. and Datema, C. (eds) (1987) *Leontii Presbyteri Constantinopolitani Homiliae.* Corpus Christianorum Series Graeca. Leuven.

    (trans.) (1991) *Leontius, Presbyter of Constantinople: Fourteen Homilies.* Byzantina Australiensia. Brisbane.

Libanius. *Letters.* In Bradbury, S. (trans.) (2004) *Selected Letters of Libanius: From the Age of Constantius and Julian.* Translated Texts for Historians. Liverpool.

Lucretius. *De Rerum Natura*. In Martin, J. (ed.) (1963) *T. Lucreti Cari: De rerum natura libri sex*, 5th edn. Leipzig.

Malalas. *Chronicle*. In Thurn, H. (ed.) (2000) *Ioannis Malalae Chronographia*. Corpus fontium historiae Byzantinae. Series Berolinensis 35. Berlin.

In Jeffreys, E., Jeffreys, M. and Scott, R. (trans.) (1986) *The Chronicle of John Malalas*. Melbourne.

Maximus the Confessor. *Mystagogia*. In Cantarella, R. (ed.) (1931) *S. Massimo Confessore: La mistagogia ed altri scritti*. Florence.

Nestorius. *III Epistula Nestorium ad Celestinum*. In Loofs, F. (ed.) (1905) *Nestoriana*. Halle, 169–72.

Nicolaus the Sophist. *Progymnasmata*. In Felten, J. (ed.) (1913) *Nicolai progymnasmata. Rhetores Graeci* 11. Leipzig.

In Kennedy, G.A. (trans.) (2003) *Progymnasmata: Greek Textbooks of Prose Composition and Rhetoric*. Writings from the Greco-Roman World. Atlanta, 129–72.

Origen. *Against Celsus*. In Borret, M. (ed. and trans.) (1967; 1968; 1969) *Origène: Contre Celse*, 4 vols. Sources chrétiennes 132, 136, 147, 150. Paris.

Paul the Silentiary. *Description of Hagia Sophia*. In De Stefani, C. (ed.) (2011) *Paulus Silentiarius Descriptio Sanctae Sophiae Descriptio Ambonis*. Bibliotheca scriptorum Graecorum et Romanorum Teubneriana. Berlin; New York.

Part translated in Mango, C.A. (1972) *The Art of the Byzantine Empire, 312–1453: Sources and Documents*. Sources and Documents in the History of Art Series. Englewood Cliffs, NJ, 80–96.

Plato. *Timaeus, Alcibiades 1, Hipparchus, Philebus*. In Burnet, J. (ed.) (1902; repr. 1968) *Platonis opera*, Volume IV. Oxford.

Proclus of Constantinople. *Homilies*. In Constas, N. (ed. and trans.) (2003) *Proclus of Constantinople and the Cult of the Virgin in Late Antiquity: Homilies 1–5, Texts and Translations*. Supplements to Vigiliae Christianae. Leiden; Boston.

Procopius of Caesarea. *Buildings*. In Wirth, G. (ed.) (post J. Haury) (1964) *Procopii Caesariensis opera omnia*, Volume IV, Leipzig.

Pseudo-Chrysostom. *In Drachmam et In Illud: Homo Quidam Habebat Duos Filios*. In Migne, J.-P. (ed.) (1862) PG 61.781–4. Paris.

Socrates Scholasticus. *Ecclesiastical History*. In Maraval, P. and Périchon, P. (eds) (2004–7) *Socrate de Constantinople: Histoire ecclésiastique* (Livres I–VII). Paris.

Symeon of Thessaloniki. *De Sacra Precatione*. In Migne, J.-P. (ed.) (1866) PG 155, 535–670. Paris.

Tertullian. *On Baptism*. In Evans, E. (ed. and trans.) (1964) *Tertullian's Homily on Baptism*. London.

Theodore of Mopsuestia. *Catechetical Sermons*. In Tonneau, R. (trans.) (1949) *Les homélies catéchétiques: Reproduction phototypique du ms. Mingana Syr. 561 (Selly Oak Colleges' Library, Birmingham)*. Vatican City.

Commentary on the Eucharist. In Mingana, A. (ed. and trans.) (1933) *Commentary of Theodore of Mopsuestia on the Lord's Prayer and on the Sacraments of Baptism and the Eucharist*. Woodbrooke Studies: Christian Documents 6. Cambridge.

(ed. and trans.) (1963) *Le Typicon de la Grande Église: MS Sainte-Croix n.40, Xe siècle. Introduction, texte critique, traduction et notes par Juan Mateos. Tome II: Le Cycle des fêtes mobiles*. 2 vols. Orientalia Christiana Analecta 2. Rome.

Secondary Works

Alexander, P.J. (1985) *The Byzantine Apocalyptic Tradition*. Edited with an Introduction by Dorothy deF. Abrahamse. Berkeley.

Alexiou, M. (1974) *The Ritual Lament in Greek Tradition*. Cambridge.

(2002) *After Antiquity: Greek Language, Myth and Metaphor*. Ithaca, NY and London.

Allen, P. (1979) 'The "Justinianic" Plague', *Byzantion* 48: 5–20.

(1998) 'The Sixth-Century Greek Homily: A Re-assessment', in *Preacher and Audience: Studies in Early Christian and Byzantine Homiletics*, eds M. Cunningham and P. Allen. Leiden: 201–25.

(2011) 'Portrayals of Mary in Greek Homiletic Literature (6th–7th Centuries)', in *The Cult of the Mother of God in Byzantium: Texts and Images*, eds L. Brubaker and M. Cunningham. Oxford: 116–47.

Ameringer, T.E. (1921) *The Stylistic Influence of the Second Sophistic on the Panegyrical Sermons of St John Chrysostom: A Study in Greek Rhetoric*. Washington, DC.

Anderson, C.P. (2014) *Reclaiming Participation: Christ as God's Life for All*. Minneapolis.

Anson, J. (1974) 'The Female Transvestite in Early Monasticism: The Origin and Development of a Motif', *Viator* 5: 1–32.

Arentzen, T. (2013) '"Your Virginity Shines": The Attraction of the Virgin in the *Annunciation* Hymn by Romanos the Melodist', *Studia Patristica* 68: 125–32.

(2014) 'Virginity Recast: Romanos and the Mother of God', doctoral dissertation. Lund University.

Aslanov, C. (2011) 'Romanos the Melodist and Palestinian *Piyyut*: Sociolinguistic and Pragmatic Perspectives', in *Jews in Byzantium: Dialects of Minority and Majority Cultures*, eds R. Bonfil, R. Talgam, G.G. Stroumsa and O. Irshai. Leiden: 613–28.

Assis, E. (2007) 'The Alphabetic Acrostic in the Book of Lamentations', *The Catholic Biblical Quarterly* 69: 710–24.

Atanassova, A. (2008) 'Did Cyril of Alexandria Invent Mariology?', in *The Origins of the Cult of the Virgin Mary*, ed. C. Maunder. London; New York: 105–25.

Baldovin, J.F. (1987) *The Urban Character of Christian Worship: The Origins, Development, and Meaning of Stational Liturgy.* Orientalia Christiana Analecta. Rome.

Bandy, A.C. (1975) '*Addenda et Corrigenda* to M. Carpenter, *Kontakia* of Romanos, Byzantine Melodist, Volume I: On the Person of Christ, Vol. II: On the Christian Life. Volume I [Part 1]', *Byzantine Studies* 2.2: 139–82.

(1976) '*Addenda et Corrigenda* to M. Carpenter, *Kontakia* of Romanos, Byzantine Melodist, Volume I: On the Person of Christ, Vol. II: On the Christian Life. Volume I [Part 2]', *Byzantine Studies* 3.1: 64–113.

Barber, C. (1991) 'The Koimesis Church, Nicaea: The Limits of Representation on the Eve of Iconoclasm', *JOB* 41: 43–60.

Barkhuizen, J.H. (1986a) 'Narrative Apostrophe in the *Kontakia* of Romanos the Melodist, with Special Reference to his Hymn "On Judas"', *AClass* 29: 19–27.

(1986b) 'Romanos Melodos: Essay on the Poetics of his *Kontakion* "Resurrection of Christ" (Maas–Trypanis 24)', *ByzZ* 79: 17–28.

(1989) 'Romanos Melodos and the Composition of his Hymns: Prooimion and Final Strophe', *Hellenika* 40: 62–77.

(1990a) 'Romanos Melodos, *Kontakion 10 (OXF)*: "On the Sinful Woman"', *AClass* 33: 33–52.

(1990b) 'Romanos Melodos, On the Temptation of Joseph: A Study on his Use of Imagery', *APB* 1: 1–31.

(1990c) 'Romanos' Encomium on Joseph: Portrait of an Athlete', *JOB* 40: 91–106.

(1991a) 'An Analysis of the Form and Content of Prayer as a Liturgical Component in the Hymns of Romanos the Melodist', *Ekklesiastikos Pharos* 75.2: 91–102.

(1991b) 'Christ as Metaphor in the Hymns of Romanos the Melodist (Part 1)', *APB* 2: 1–15.

(1992) 'The "New Song" in Romanos the Melodist', *Hellenika* 42: 157–62.

(1993) 'Romanos Melodos, "On Repentance" (Oxf. 52: 8b SC)', *Ekklesiastikos Pharos, New Series* 4: 43–53.

(1994) 'Lazarus in the Tomb and the *Topos* of the *Lament of Hades*', *Ekklesiastikos Pharos, New Series* 5: 83–105.

(1995) 'Romanos Melodos: On Earthquakes and Fires', *JOB* 45: 1–18.

(1996) 'The Parable of the Prodigal Son as a Eucharistic Metaphor in Romanos Melodos' *Kontakion* 49 (Oxf.)', *AClass* 39: 39–54.

(1997) 'Romanos Melodos, Verse Homily "On the Leper": An Analysis', *Acta Patristica et Byzantina* 8: 26–41.

(2007) 'Romanos Melodos, "On the Massacre of the Innocents": A Perspective on *Ekphrasis* as a Method of Patristic Exegesis', *AClass* 50: 29–50.

(2008a) 'Romanos Melodos "On Dives and Lazarus": Preaching the New Testament', *Ekklesiastikos Pharos* 90: 251–71.

(2008b) 'Romanos the Melodist: "On Adam and Eve and the Nativity": Introduction with Annotated Translation', *APB* 19: 1–22.

Barnett, P. (1997) *The Second Epistle to the Corinthians*. The New International Commentary on the New Testament. Grand Rapids, MI.

Barrett, C.K. (1978) *The Gospel According to St. John: An Introduction with Commentary and Notes on the Greek Text*. 2nd edn. Philadelphia.

Bartsch, S. (2006) *The Mirror of the Self: Sexuality, Self-Knowledge, and the Gaze in the Early Roman Empire*. Chicago.

Baud-Bovy, S. (1938a) 'Sur un "Sacrifice d'Abraham" de Romanos et sur l'existence d'un théâtre religieux à Byzance', *Byzantion* 13: 321–34.

(1938b) 'Sur une prélude de Romanos', *Byzantion* 13: 217–26.

Baumstark, A. (1905) 'Syrische und hellenistische Dichtung', *Gottesminne* 3: 570–93.

Becker, A.H. (2006) 'The Dynamic Reception of Theodore of Mopsuestia in the Sixth Century: Greek, Syriac, and Latin', in *Greek Literature in Late Antiquity: Dynamism, Didacticism, Classicism*, ed. Scott Fitzgerald Johnson. Aldershot: 29–48.

Behr, J. (2000) *Asceticism and Anthropology in Irenaeus and Clement*. Oxford Early Christian Studies. Oxford; New York.

Best, E. (1987) *Second Corinthians*. Interpretation: A Bible Commentary for Teaching and Preaching. Atlanta.

Betz, H.D. (1979) 'Matthew iv.22f and Ancient Greek Theories of Vision', in *Text and Interpretation: Studies in the New Testament Presented to Matthew Black*, eds E. Best and R. McL. Wilson. Cambridge: 43–56.

Block, E. (1982) 'The Narrator Speaks: Apostrophe in Homer and Vergil', *TAPhA* 112: 7–22.

Bornet, R. (1966) *Les Commentaires byzantines de la divine liturgie du VIIe au XVe siècle*. Paris.

Borsook, E. (2000) 'Rhetoric or Reality: Mosaics as an Expression of a Metaphysical Idea', *Mitteilungen des Kunsthistorischen Institutes in Florenz* 44: 3–18.

Boss, S.J. (2007) 'The Title *Theotokos*', in *Mary: The Complete Resource*, ed. S.J. Boss. London; New York: 50–5.

Boyarin, D. (2007) 'Semantic Differences; or, "Judaism"/ "Christianity"', in *The Ways that Never Parted: Jews and Christians in Late Antiquity and the Early Middle Ages*, eds A.H. Becker and A.Y. Reed. Minneapolis: 65–85.

Bradbury, S. (2004) *Selected Letters of Libanius: From the Age of Constantius and Julian*. Translated Texts for Historians. Liverpool.

Brakke, D. (1995) *Athanasius and the Politics of Asceticism*. Oxford.

(2001) 'Jewish Flesh and Christian Spirit in Athanasius of Alexandria', *JECS* 9.4: 453–81.

Brock, S.P. (1982a) 'Clothing Metaphors as a Means of Theological Expression in Syriac Tradition', in *Typus, Symbol, Allegorie bei den östlichen Vätern und ihren Parallelen im Mittelalter*, ed. M. Schmidt. Regensburg: 11–38.

(1982b) 'From Antagonism to Assimilation: Syriac Attitudes to Greek Learning', in *East of Byzantium: Syria and Armenia in the Formative Period*, eds N.G. Garsoïan, T.F. Mathews and R.W. Thomson. Washington, DC: 17–34.

(1983) 'Dialogue Hymns of the Syriac Church', *Sobornost* 5.2: 35–45.

(1985) 'Syriac and Greek Hymnography: Problems of Origin', *Studia Patristica* 16: 77–81.

(1986) 'Two Syriac Verse Homilies on the Binding of Isaac', *Le Muséon* 99: 61–129.

(1987) 'Dramatic Dialogue Poems', in *Literary Genres in Syriac Literature: IV Symposium Syriacum 1984*, ed. H.J.W. Drijvers. Rome: 135–47.

(1989) 'From Ephrem to Romanos', *Studia Patristica* 20: 139–51.

(1991) 'Syriac Dispute Poems: The Various Types', in *Dispute Poems and Dialogues in the Ancient and Medieval Near East*, eds G.J. Reinink and H.L.J. Vanstiphout. Leuven: 109–19.

(1992) *The Luminous Eye: The Spiritual World Vision of Saint Ephrem*. Rev. edn. Cistercian Studies Series. Kalamazoo, MI.

(1994) 'Greek and Syriac in Late Antique Syria', in *Literacy and Power in the Ancient World*, eds A.K. Bowman and G. Woolf. Cambridge: 149–60.

(2001) 'The Dispute Poem: From Sumer to Syriac', *Journal of the Canadian Society for Syriac Studies* 1: 3–10.

(2002) 'The Dispute between the Cherub and the Thief', *Hugoye: Journal of Syriac Studies* 5.2: <http://syrcom.cua.edu/hugoye/Vol5No2/HV5N2Brock.html>.

Brown, P. and MacCormack, S. (1975) 'Artifices of Eternity', *New York Review of Books* 22.

Brümmer, V. (2005) *Atonement, Christology and the Trinity: Making Sense of Christian Doctrine*. Aldershot.

Buchan, T. (2007) 'Paradise as the Landscape of Salvation in Ephrem the Syrian', in *Partakers of the Divine Nature: The History and Development of Deification in the Christian Traditions*, eds M.J. Christensen and J.A. Wittung. Grand Rapids, MI: 146–59.

Byrne, B. (1996) *Romans*, ed. D.J. Harrington. Sacra Pagina 6. Collegeville, MN.

Byron, J. (2011) *Cain and Abel in Text and Tradition: Jewish and Christian Interpretations of the First Sibling Rivalry*. Themes in Biblical Narrative: Jewish and Christian Traditions. Leiden.

Cameron, A. (1985) *Procopius and the Sixth Century*. London.

(1989) 'Virginity as Metaphor: Women and the Rhetoric of Early Christianity', in *History as Text: The Writing of Ancient History*, ed. A. Cameron. London: 181–205.

(1990) 'Models of the Past in the Late Sixth Century: The Life of the Patriarch Eutychius', in *Reading the Past in Late Antiquity*, eds G. Clarke, B. Croke, A. Nobbs and R. Mortley. Rushcutters Bay: 205–23.

(1991a) *Christianity and the Rhetoric of Empire: The Development of Christian Discourse*. Berkeley.

(1991b) 'Disputations, Polemical Literature and the Formation of Opinion in the Early Byzantine Period', in *Dispute Poems and Dialogues in the Ancient and Mediaeval Near East*, eds G.J. Reinink and H.L.J. Vanstiphout. Leuven: 91–108.

(2004) 'The Cult of the Virgin in Late Antiquity: Religious Development and Myth-Making', in *The Church and Mary*, ed. R.N. Swanson. Studies in Church History 39. Woodbridge: 1–21.

(2007) 'Jews and Heretics: A Category Error?', in *The Ways that Never Parted: Jews and Christians in Late Antiquity and the Early Middle Ages*, eds A.H. Becker and A.Y. Reed. Minneapolis: 345–60.

(2014) *Dialoguing in Late Antiquity*. Hellenic Studies. Cambridge, MA.

Capelle, D.B. (1954) 'Typologie mariale chez les Pères et dans la liturgie', *Les questions liturgiques et paroissiales* 35: 109–21.

Cardman, F. (1982) 'The Rhetoric of Holy Places: Palestine in the Fourth Century', *Studia Patristica* 17.1: 18–25.

Carleton Paget, J. (2010) *Jews, Christians and Jewish Christians in Antiquity*. Winona Lake, IN.

Carpenter, M. (1932) 'The Paper that Romanos Swallowed', *Speculum* 7.1: 3–22.

(1936) 'Romanos and the Mystery Play of the East', *The University of Missouri Studies* 11.3: 21–51.

(1970) *Kontakia of Romanos, Byzantine Melodist*, 2 vols. Columbia.

Caseau, B. (1999) 'Christian Bodies: The Senses and Early Byzantine Christianity', in *Desire and Denial in Byzantium: Papers from the Thirty-first Spring Symposium of Byzantine Studies, Brighton, March 1997*, ed. E. James. Society for the Promotion of Byzantine Studies Publications 6. Aldershot: 101–9.

(2013) 'Experiencing the Sacred', in *Experiencing Byzantium*, eds C. Nesbitt and M. Jackson. Farnham: 59–77.

Champion, M.S. (2014) 'Fullness of Time: Temporalities of the Fifteenth-Century Low Countries', PhD dissertation. Queen Mary College, London.

Champion, M.W. (2006) 'Kosmas Indikopleustes and Narratives in Sixth-Century Liturgy and History', in *Byzantine Narrative: Papers in Honour of Roger Scott*, eds J. Burke, U. Betka, P. Buckley, K. Hay, R. Scott and A. Stephenson. Melbourne: 383–92.

(2014) *Explaining the Cosmos: Creation and Cultural Interaction in Late-Antique Gaza*. Oxford; New York.

Cohen, J. (1999) *Living Letters of the Law: Ideas of the Jew in Medieval Christianity*. Berkeley; London.

Cohen, T. (1978) 'Metaphor and the Cultivation of Intimacy', *Critical Inquiry* 5.1: 3–12.

Constas, N. (1995) 'Weaving the Body of God: Proclus of Constantinople, the *Theotokos*, and the Loom of the Flesh', *JECS* 3.2: 169–94.

(2003) *Proclus of Constantinople and the Cult of the Virgin in Late Antiquity: Homilies 1–5, Texts and Translations*. Supplements to Vigiliae Christianae. Leiden; Boston.

(2005) 'Review of Leena Mari Peltomaa, *The Image of the Virgin Mary in the Akathistos Hymn*', *St Vladimir's Theological Quarterly* 49.3: 355–8.

Cooper, L.H. and Denny-Brown, A. (eds) (2014) *The Arma Christi in Medieval and Early Modern Material Culture: With a Critical Edition of 'O Vernicle'.* Farnham.

Cunningham, M. (1986) 'Basil of Seleucia's Homily on Lazarus: A New Edition', *AB* 104: 161–84.

(1988) 'The Mother of God in Early Byzantine Homilies', *Sobornost* 10.2: 53–67.

(1990) 'Preaching and the Community', in *Church and People in Byzantium: Society for the Promotion of Byzantine Studies Twentieth Spring Symposium of Byzantine Studies, Manchester, 1986*, ed. R. Morris. Birmingham: 29–47.

(1995) 'Innovation or Mimesis in Byzantine Sermons?', in *Originality in Byzantine Literature, Art and Music*, ed. A.R. Littlewood. Oxford: 67–80.

(1996) 'The Sixth Century: A Turning-Point for Byzantine Homiletics?', in *The Sixth Century: End or Beginning?*, eds P. Allen and E. Jeffreys. Brisbane: 176–86.

(2003) 'Dramatic Device or Didactic Tool? The Function of Dialogue in Byzantine Preaching', in *Rhetoric in Byzantium: Papers from the Thirty-Fifth Spring Symposium of Byzantine Studies, Exeter College, University of Oxford, March 2001*, ed. E. Jeffreys. Aldershot: 101–13.

(2008) 'Homilies', in *The Oxford Handbook of Byzantine Studies*, eds E. Jeffreys, J.F. Haldon and R. Cormack. Oxford; New York: 872–81.

(2010) 'The Reception of Romanos in Middle Byzantine Homiletics and Hymnography', *DOP* 62: 251–60.

Daley, B. (1998) *On the Dormition of Mary: Early Patristic Homilies.* Crestwood, NY.

(2002a) 'Divine Transcendence and Human Transformation: Gregory of Nyssa's Anti-Apollinarian Christology', *Modern Theology* 18.4: 497–506.

(2002b) '"Heavenly Man" and "Eternal Christ": Apollinarius and Gregory of Nyssa on the Personal Identity of the Saviour', *JECS* 10.4: 469–88.

(2003) *The Hope of the Early Church: A Handbook of Patristic Eschatology.* Peabody, MA.

Dalimier, C. (2004) 'L'Usage scientifique de la métaphore chez Aristote', in *Skhèma/figura: Formes et figures chez les anciens: Rhétorique, philosophie, littérature*, eds M.S. Celentano, P. Chiron and M.-P. Noël. Paris: 127–41.

Daniélou, J. (1956) *The Bible and the Liturgy.* Notre Dame, IN.

Davidson, D. (1978) 'What Metaphors Mean', *Critical Inquiry* 5.1: 31–47.

Davis, S.J. (2002) 'Crossed Texts, Crossed Sex: Intertextuality and Gender in Christian Legends of Holy Women Disguised as Men', *JECS* 10.1: 1–31.

de Halleux, A. (1978) 'Héllenisme et syrianité de Romanos le Mélode', *Revue d'histoire ecclésiastique* 73: 632–41.

De Lange, N.R.M. (2005) 'Jews in the Age of Justinian', in *The Cambridge Companion to the Age of Justinian*, ed. M. Maas. Cambridge: 401–26.

Demus, O. (1948) *Byzantine Mosaic Decoration: Aspects of Monumental Art in Byzantium.* London.

Dobrov, G.W. (1994) 'A Dialogue with Death: Ritual Lament and the "Threnos Theotokou" of Romanos Melodos', *GRBS* 35.4: 385–405.

Dodd, C.H. (1968) *The Interpretation of the Fourth Gospel*. Cambridge.

Doig, A. (2008) *Liturgy and Architecture from the Early Church to the Middle Ages*. Aldershot.

Drewer, L. (1981) 'Fisherman and Fish Pond: From the Sea of Sin to the Living Waters', *The Art Bulletin* 63.4: 533–47.

Dunn, G.D. (1998) 'Tertullian and Rebekah: A Re-Reading of An "Anti-Jewish" Argument in Early Christian Literature', *VChr* 52.2: 119–45.

Dunn, J. (2007) *The New Perspective on Paul*. Grand Rapids, MI.

Duval, Y.M. (1973) *Le livre de Jonas dans la littérature chrétienne grecque et latine: Sources et influence du Commentaire sur Jonas de Saint Jérôme*. Paris.

Eriksen, U.H. (2013) 'Drama in the *Kontakia* of Romanos the Melodist: A Narratological Analysis of Four *Kontakia*', doctoral dissertation. Aarhus.

Fantino, J. (1998) 'Le Passage du premier Adam au second Adam comme expression du salut chez Irénée de Lyon', *VChr* 52.4: 418–29.

Ferreiro, A. and Oden, T.C. (eds) (2003) *The Twelve Prophets*. Ancient Christian Commentary on Scripture. Downers Grove, IL.

Frank, G. (2000) *The Memory of the Eyes: Pilgrims to Living Saints in Christian Late Antiquity*. The Transformation of the Classical Heritage. Berkeley.

— (2001) '"Taste and See": The Eucharist and the Eyes of Faith in the Fourth Century', *Church History* 70.4: 619–43.

— (2005) 'Dialogue and Deliberation: The Sensory Self in the Hymns of Romanos the Melodist', in *Religion and the Self in Antiquity*, eds D. Brakke, M.L. Satlow and S. Weitzman. Bloomington: 163–79.

— (2006a) '*Loca Sancta* Souvenirs and the Art of Memory', in *Pèlerinages et lieux saints dans l'antiquité et le moyen âge: Mélanges offerts à Pierre Maraval*, eds B. Caseau, J.-C. Cheynet and V. Déroche. Paris: 193–201.

— (2006b) 'Romanos and the Night Vigil in the Sixth Century', in *Byzantine Christianity*, ed. D. Krueger. Minneapolis: 59–78.

— (2013a) 'Memory and Forgetting in Romanos the Melodist's *On the Newly Baptized*', in *Between Person and Institutional Religion: Self, Doctrine, and Practice in Late Antique Eastern Christianity*, eds B. Bitton-Ashkelony and L. Perrone. Turnhout: 37–55.

— (2013b) 'Sensing Ascension in Early Byzantium', in *Experiencing Byzantium*, eds C. Nesbitt and M. Jackson. Farnham: 293–309.

Frankfurter, D. (2007) 'Beyond "Jewish Christianity": Continuing Religious Sub-Cultures of the Second and Third Centuries and Their Documents', in *The Ways that Never Parted: Jews and Christians in Late Antiquity and the Early Middle Ages*, eds A.H. Becker and A.Y. Reed. Minneapolis: 131–43.

Frazer, M.E. (1974) 'Hades Stabbed by the Cross of Christ', *Metropolitan Museum Journal* 9: 153–61.

Fredriksen, P. (2000) 'Allegory and Reading God's Book: Paul and Augustine on the Destiny of Israel', in *Interpretation and Allegory: Antiquity to the Modern Period*, ed. J. Whitman. Brill's Studies in Intellectual History 101. Leiden: 125–49.

(2007) 'What "Parting of the Ways"? Jews, Gentiles, and the Ancient Mediterranean City', in *The Ways That Never Parted: Jews and Christians in Late Antiquity and the Early Middle Ages*, eds A.H. Becker and A.Y. Reed. Minneapolis: 35–63.

Fredriksen, P. and Irshai, O. (2006) 'Christian Anti-Judaism: Polemics and Policies', in *The Cambridge History of Judaism*, ed. S.T. Katz. Cambridge: 977–1034.

Freedman, D. (1972) 'Subat Basti: A Robe of Splendor', *Journal of the Ancient Near Eastern Society of Columbia University* 4: 91–5.

Gador-Whyte, S. (2010) 'Emotional Preaching: Ekphrasis in the Kontakia of Romanos', Australasian Society for Classical Studies Conference, University of Western Australia, February 2010, Conference Proceedings: classics.uwa. edu.au/ascs31.

(2011) 'Self-Construction: "Auto-ethopoeia" in Romanos' Kontakia', *Cultural (Re) constructions, Melbourne Historical Journal* 39, special issue no. 2: 23–37.

(2013a) 'Changing Conceptions of Mary in Sixth-Century Byzantium: The *Kontakia* of Romanos the Melodist', in *Questions of Gender in Byzantine Society*, eds B. Neil and L. Garland. Farnham: 77–92.

(2013b) 'Playing with Genre: Romanos the Melodist and his *Kontakion*', in *Approaches to Genre in the Ancient World*, eds M. Borg and G. Miles. Newcastle upon Tyne: 159–75.

Gager, J.G. (1983) *The Origins of Anti-Semitism: Attitudes towards Judaism in Pagan and Christian Antiquity*. New York; Oxford.

Gerstel, S.E.J. (2010) 'The Layperson in Church', in *Byzantine Christianity*, ed. D. Krueger. Minneapolis: 103–23.

Glenthøj, J.B. (1997) *Cain and Abel in Syriac and Greek Writers (4th–6th Centuries)*. CSCO Subsidia 95. Leuven.

Goldhill, S. (2008) 'Introduction: Why Don't Christians Do Dialogue?', in *The End of Dialogue in Antiquity*, ed. S. Goldhill. Cambridge: 1–11.

Goodman, N. (1978) *Ways of Worldmaking*. Hassocks.

Gounelle, R. (2000) *La Descente du Christ aux enfers: Institutionnalisation d'une croyance*. Paris.

Grosdidier de Matons, J. (1977) *Romanos le Mélode et les origines de la poésie religieuse à Byzance*. Paris.

(1980) 'Kontakion et Canon: Piété populaire et liturgie officielle à Byzance', *Augustinianum* 20: 191–203.

(1980–1) 'Liturgie et hymnographie: Kontakion et canon', *DOP* 34: 31–43.

Grypeou, E. and Spurling, H. (2013) *The Book of Genesis in Late Antiquity: Encounters between Jewish and Christian Exegesis*. Leiden.

Gy, P.-M. (1967) 'La Question du système des lectures de la liturgie byzantine', *Miscellanea liturgica in onore di sua eminenza il Cardinale Giacomo Lercaro* 2: 251–61.

Haack, S. (1987–8) 'Surprising Noises: Rorty and Hesse on Metaphor', *PAS New Series* 88: 293–301.

Haas, C. (1997) *Alexandria in Late Antiquity: Topography and Social Conflict.* Ancient Society and History. Baltimore.

Hahn, C. (1997) 'Seeing and Believing: The Construction of Sanctity in Early-Medieval Saints' Shrines', *Speculum* 72.4: 1079–106.

Hall, L.J. (2004) *Roman Berytus: Beirut in Late Antiquity.* London; New York.

Hammond, C.E. and Brightman, F.E. (eds) (1965) *Liturgies, Eastern and Western.* Oxford.

Hannick, C. (1999) 'Exégèse, typologie et rhétorique dans l'hymnographie byzantine', *DOP* 53: 207–18.

Harrington, W.J. (1993) *Revelation*, ed. D.J. Harrington. Sacra Pagina 16. Collegeville, MN.

Harrison, V.E.F. (1988) 'Word as Icon in Greek Patristic Theology', *Sobornost* 10: 38–49.

(1992) *Grace and Human Freedom According to St. Gregory of Nyssa.* Lewiston; Lampeter.

(2008) 'Eve, the Mother of God, and Other Women', *The Ecumenical Review* 60.1–2: 71–81.

Harvey, S.A. (1998) 'St Ephrem on the Scent of Salvation', *JThS* 49.1: 109–28.

(1999) 'Embodiment in Time and Eternity: A Syriac Perspective', *St Vladimir's Theological Quarterly* 43: 105–30.

(2002) 'Why the Perfume Mattered: The Sinful Woman in Syriac Exegetical Tradition', in *In Dominico eloquio = In Lordly Eloquence: Essays in Patristic Exegesis in Honor of Robert L. Wilken*, eds P.M. Blowers, A. Christman, D. Hunter and R. Young. Grand Rapids, MI: 69–89.

(2006) *Scenting Salvation: Ancient Christianity and the Olfactory Imagination.* The Transformation of the Classical Heritage. Berkeley.

Hayward, R. (2009) 'What Did Cain Do Wrong? Jewish and Christian Exegesis of Genesis 4:3–6', in *The Exegetical Encounter between Jews and Christians in Late Antiquity*, eds H. Spurling and E. Grypeou. Jewish and Christian Perspectives Series. Leiden: 101–23.

Heath, M. (2004) 'John Chrysostom, Rhetoric and Galatians', *Biblical Interpretation* 12.4: 369–400.

Heil, J.P. (2005) *The Rhetorical Role of Scripture in 1 Corinthians.* Atlanta.

Hinterberger, M. (2010) 'Emotions in Byzantium', in *A Companion to Byzantium*, ed. E. James. Blackwell Companions to the Ancient World. Chichester: 123–34.

Hirsh, J.C. (1996) *The Boundaries of Faith: The Development and Transmission of Medieval Spirituality.* Leiden.

Hooker, M.D. (1990) *From Adam to Christ: Essays on Paul*. Cambridge.

Hovorun, C. (2008) *Will, Action, and Freedom: Christological Controversies in the Seventh Century*. Leiden.

Hunger, H. (1981) 'The Classical Tradition in Byzantine Literature: The Importance of Rhetoric', in *Byzantium and the Classical Tradition: University of Birmingham Thirteenth Spring Symposium of Byzantine Studies 1979*, eds M. Mullett and R. Scott. Birmingham: 35–47.

Hunt, H.M. (1998) 'The Tears of the Sinful Woman: A Theology of Redemption in the Homilies of St. Ephraim and His Followers', *Hugoye: Journal of Syriac Studies* 1.2: http://syrcom.cua.edu/Hugoye/Vol1No2/HV1N2Hunt.html.

Hunter, D.G. (1987) 'Resistance to the Virginal Ideal in Late-Fourth-Century Rome: The Case of Jovinian', *ThS* 48: 45–64.

(1989) '*On the Sin of Adam and Eve*: A Little-Known Defense of Marriage and Childbearing by Ambrosiaster', *HThR* 82.3: 283–99.

Jacobs, A.S. (2004) *Remains of the Jews: The Holy Land and Christian Empire in Late Antiquity*, eds D. Boyarin, V. Burrus, C. Fonrobert and R. Gregg. Divinations: Rereading Late Ancient Religion. Stanford.

James, E. (1991) 'Colour and the Byzantine Rainbow', *BMGS* 15: 66–94.

(1995) *Light and Colour in Byzantine Art*. Clarendon Studies in the History of Art. New York.

(2000) 'What Colours Were Byzantine Mosaics?', in *Medieval Mosaics: Light, Colour, Materials*, eds E. Borsook, F.G. Superbi and G. Pagliarulo. Milan: 35–46.

(2003) 'Colour and Meaning in Byzantium', *JECS* 11.2: 223–33.

(2004) 'Senses and Sensibility in Byzantium', *Art History* 27.4: 522–37.

James, E. and Webb, R. (1991) 'To Understand Ultimate Things and Enter Secret Places: *Ekphrasis* and Art in Byzantium', *Art History* 14: 1–17.

Jeffreys, E. (1990) 'Chronological Structures in the Chronicle', in *Studies in John Malalas*, eds E. Jeffreys, R. Scott with B. Croke. Byzantina Australiensia 6. Sydney: 111–66.

Jensen, R.M. (2000) *Understanding Early Christian Art*. London.

(2010) *Living Water: Images, Symbols, and Settings of Early Christian Baptism*. Leiden.

Kallistos, Bishop of Dioklea (1990) 'The Meaning of the Divine Liturgy for the Byzantine Worshipper', in *Church and People in Byzantium: Society for the Promotion of Byzantine Studies Twentieth Spring Symposium of Byzantine Studies, Manchester, 1986*, ed. R. Morris. Birmingham: 7–28.

Kazhdan, A. P. and Constable, G. (1982) *People and Power in Byzantium: An Introduction to Modern Byzantine Studies*. Washington, DC.

Kecskeméti, J. (1989) 'Exégèse chrysostomienne et exégèse engagée', *Studia Patristica* 22: 136–47.

(1993) 'Doctrine et drame dans la prédication grecque', *Euphrosyne* 21: 29–68.

Kessler, E. (2004) *Bound by the Bible: Jews, Christians, and the Sacrifice of Isaac*. Cambridge.

Knuuttila, S. (2004) *Emotions in Ancient and Medieval Philosophy*. Oxford.

Koder, J. (2010) 'Imperial Propaganda in the *Kontakia* of Romanos the Melode', *DOP* 62: 275–91.

Krueger, D. (2003) 'Writing and Redemption in the Hymns of Romanos the Melodist', *BMGS* 27: 2–44.

(2004) *Writing and Holiness: The Practice of Authorship in the Early Christian East*. Divinations: Rereading Late Antique Religion. Philadelphia.

(2005) 'Christian Piety and Practice in the Sixth Century', in *The Cambridge Companion to the Age of Justinian*, ed. M. Maas. Cambridge: 291–315.

(2006a) 'Romanos the Melodist and the Christian Self in Early Byzantium', in *Proceedings of the 21st International Congress of Byzantine Studies: London, 21–26 August 2006*, eds E. Jeffreys, F. K. Haarer and J. Gilliland. Aldershot: 255–74.

(2006b) 'The Practice of Christianity in Byzantium', in *Byzantine Christianity*, ed. D. Krueger. Minneapolis: 1–15.

(2010) 'Healing and the Scope of Religion in Byzantium: A Response to Miller and Crislip', in *Holistic Healing in Byzantium*, ed. J.T. Chirban. Brookline, MA: 119–30.

(2013) 'The Internal Lives of Biblical Figures in the Hymns of Romanos the Melodist', *Adamantius* 19: 290–302.

(2014) *Liturgical Subjects: Christian Ritual, Biblical Narrative, and the Formation of the Self in Byzantium*. Divinations: Rereading Late Antique Religion. Philadelphia.

Küng, H. (1987) *The Incarnation of God: An Introduction to Hegel's Theological Thought as Prolegomena to a Future Christology*, trans. J. Stephenson. Edinburgh.

Kustas, G.L. (1973) *Studies in Byzantine Rhetoric*. Analekta Vlatadon. Thessalonika.

La Piana, G. (1936) 'The Byzantine Theatre', *Speculum* 11.2: 171–211.

Ladouceur, P. (2006) 'Old Testament Prefigurations of the Mother of God', *St Vladimir's Theological Quarterly* 50.1–2: 5–57.

Lampe, G.W.H. (1961) *A Patristic Greek Lexicon*. Oxford; New York.

Lee, S.-I. (2012) *Jesus and Gospel Traditions in Bilingual Context: A Study in the Interdirectionality of Language*. Berlin; Boston.

Lingas, A. (1995) 'The Liturgical Place of the *Kontakion* in Constantinople', in *Liturgy, Architecture and Art of the Byzantine World: Papers of the XVIII International Byzantine Congress (Moscow, 8–15 August 1991) and Other Essays Dedicated to the Memory of Fr. John Meyendorff*, ed. C. C. Akentiev. St Petersburg: 50–7.

(2008) 'Music', in *The Oxford Handbook of Byzantine Studies*, eds E. Jeffreys, J.F. Haldon and R. Cormack. Oxford; New York: 915–35.

Loerke, W. (1984) '"Real Presence" in Early Christian Art', in *Monasticism and the Arts*, ed. T.G. Verdon. Syracuse: 29–51.

Louth, A. (2005) 'Christian Hymnography from Romanos the Melodist to John Damascene', *JECS* 57.3: 195–206.

Maas, P. (1910a) 'Das *Kontakion*', *ByzZ* 19: 285–306.

MacCormack, S. (1982) 'Christ and Empire, Time and Ceremonial in Sixth-Century Byzantium and Beyond', *Byzantion* 52: 287–309.

(1990) 'Loca Sancta: The Organisation of Sacred Topography in Late Antiquity', in *The Blessings of Pilgrimage*, ed. R. Ousterhout. Urbana: 7–40.

Macrides, R. and Magdalino, P. (1988) 'The Architecture of *Ekphrasis*: Construction and Context of Paul the Silentiary's Poem on Hagia Sophia', *BMGS* 12: 47–82.

Maguire, H. (1981) 'The Classical Tradition in the Byzantine *Ekphrasis*', in *Byzantium and the Classical Tradition*, eds M. Mullett and R. Scott. Birmingham: 94–102.

Maisano, R. (2010) 'Romanos's Use of Greek Patristic Sources', *DOP* 62: 261–73.

Mango, C.A. (1972) *The Art of the Byzantine Empire, 312–1453: Sources and Documents*. Sources and Documents in the History of Art Series. Englewood Cliffs, NJ.

(1980) *Byzantium: The Empire of New Rome*. London.

Marinis, V. (2010) 'Defining Liturgical Space', in *The Byzantine World*, ed. P. Stephenson. New York: 284–302.

Markus, R. A. (1994) 'How on Earth Could Places Become Holy? Origins of the Christian Idea of Holy Places', *JECS* 2.3: 257–71.

Maxwell, J. (2006) *Christianization and Communication in Late Antiquity: John Chrysostom and his Congregation in Antioch*. Cambridge; New York.

McGuckin, J. (1994) *St. Cyril of Alexandria: The Christological Controversy: Its History, Theology, and Texts*. Leiden.

(2001) 'The Paradox of the Virgin-*Theotokos*: Evangelism and Imperial Politics in the Fifth-Century Byzantine World', *Maria* 2.1: 8–25.

(2008) 'Poetry and Hymnography (2): The Greek World', in *The Oxford Handbook of Early Christian Studies*, eds S.A. Harvey and D.G. Hunter. Oxford; New York: 641–56.

McLeod, F.G. (2012) 'The Significance of Constantinople II's Alteration of Chalcedon's Formula about Christ's Natures "Coinciding in One *Prosôpon*"', *Irish Theological Quarterly* 77: 365–84.

Merton, T. (1965) *Seasons of Celebration*. New York.

Meyendorff, J. (1990) 'Christian Marriage in Byzantium: The Canonical and Liturgical Tradition', *DOP* 44: 99–107.

Meyendorff, P. (1985) 'Eastern Liturgical Theology', in *Christian Spirituality: Origins to the Twelfth Century*, eds B. McGinn, J. Meyendorff and J. Leclercq. New York: 350–63.

Millar, F. (2009) 'Linguistic Co-existence in Constantinople: Greek and Latin (and Syriac) in the Acts of the Synod of 536 C.E.', *JRS* 99: 92–103.

Moleas, W. (2004) *The Development of the Greek Language*. London.

Muir, L.R. (1995) *The Biblical Drama of Medieval Europe*. Cambridge; New York.

Mulard, C. (2011) 'La Pensée symbolique de Romanos le Mélode', doctoral dissertation. Université de Strasbourg.

Murray, R. (1971) 'Mary, the Second Eve in the Early Syriac Fathers', *Eastern Churches Review* 3.4: 372–84.

(2006) *Symbols of Church and Kingdom: A Study in Early Syriac Tradition*. 2nd rev. edn. London.

Nelson, R.S. (2000) 'To Say and to See: *Ekphrasis* and Vision in Byzantium', in *Visuality before and beyond the Renaissance: Seeing as Others Saw*, ed. R.S. Nelson. Cambridge: 143–68.

Nilsson, I. (2005) 'Narrating Images in Byzantine Literature: The Ekphraseis of Konstantinos Manasses', *JOB* 55: 121–46.

(2006) 'Discovering Literariness in the Past: Literature vs History in the Synopsis Chronike of Konstantinos Manasses', in *L'Écriture de la mémoire: La littérarité de l'historiographie. Actes du IIIe colloque international philologique 'ERMHNEIA', Nicosie, 6-7-8 mai 2004*, eds P. Odorico, P.A. Agapitos and M. Hinterberger. Dossiers byzantins 6, Centre d'études byzantines, néo-helléniques et sud-est européennes, École des Hautes Études en Sciences Sociales. Paris: 15–31.

Nussbaum, M.C. (1994) *The Therapy of Desire: Theory and Practice in Hellenistic Ethics*. Princeton.

Osborn, E.F. (2001) *Irenaeus of Lyons*. Cambridge; New York.

Palmer, L.R. (1996) *The Greek Language*. Norman, OK.

Papoutsakis, M. (2007) 'The Making of a Syriac Fable: From Ephrem to Romanos', *Le Muséon* 120: 29–75.

Peltomaa, L.M. (2001) *The Image of the Virgin Mary in the Akathistos Hymn*. The Medieval Mediterranean. Leiden; Boston.

Perczel, I. (2006) 'Finding a Place for the *Erotapokriseis* of Pseudo-Caesarius: A New Document of Sixth-Century Palestinian Origenism', *Palestinian Christianity, ARAM Periodical* 18: 49–83.

Perry, T. and Kendall, D. (2013) *The Blessed Virgin Mary*. Grand Rapids, MI.

Petersen, W.L. (1983) 'Romanos and the Diatessaron: Readings and Method', *NTS* 29: 484–507.

(1985a) 'The Dependence of Romanos the Melodist upon the Syrian Ephrem: Its Importance for the Origin of the *Kontakion*', *VChr* 39.2: 171–87.

(1985b) *The Diatessaron and Ephrem Syrus as Sources of Romanos the Melodist*. CSCO 475 (Subsidia 74). Louvain.

Peterson, E. (1993) 'A Theology of Dress', *Communio* 20.3: 558–68.

Price, R.M. (2004) 'Marian Piety and Nestorian Controversy', in *The Church and Mary*, ed. R.N. Swanson. Studies in Church History 39. Woodbridge: 31–8.

(2007) '*Theotokos*: The Title and its Significance in Doctrine and Devotion', in *Mary: The Complete Resource*, ed. S.J. Boss. London; New York: 56–73.

(2008) 'The *Theotokos* and the Council of Ephesus', in *The Origins of the Cult of the Virgin Mary*, ed. C. Maunder. London; New York: 89–103.

(2009) *The Acts of the Council of Constantinople of 553, with Related Texts on the Three Chapters Controversy*. Liverpool.

Rapp, C. (2007) 'Holy Texts, Holy Men, and Holy Scribes: Aspects of Scriptural Holiness in Late Antiquity', in *The Early Christian Book*, eds W.E. Klingshirn and L. Safran. Washington, DC: 194–222.

Reichmuth, R.J. (1975) *Typology in the Genuine Kontakia of Romanos the Melodist.* Ann Arbor, MI.

Robinson, G. (1993) *Let Us Be Like the Nations: A Commentary on the Books of 1 and 2 Samuel.* Grand Rapids, MI.

Rollinson, P. (1981) *Classical Theories of Allegory and Christian Culture: With an Appendix on Primary Greek Sources by Patricia Matsen.* Pittsburgh.

Rosenqvist, J.O. (2007) *Die byzantinische Literatur: Vom 6. Jahrhundert bis zum Fall Konstantinopels 1453*, trans. J.O. Rosenqvist and D. Reinsch. Berlin.

Rubin, B. (1961) 'Der Antichrist und die "Apokalypse" des Prokopios von Kaisareia', *Zeitschriften der Deutschen Morgenländischen Gesellschaft* 110: 55–63.

Rutgers, L.V. (2003) 'Justinian's Novella 146: Between Jews and Christians', in *Jewish Culture and Society under the Christian Roman Empire*, eds R.L. Kalmin and S. Schwartz. Leuven: 385–407.

Sandwell, I. (2007) *Religious Identity in Late Antiquity: Greeks, Jews, and Christians in Antioch.* Cambridge.

Savage, T.B. (1996) *Power Through Weakness: Paul's Understanding of the Christian Ministry in 2 Corinthians.* New York.

Schirmann, J. (1953) 'Hebrew Liturgical Poetry and Christian Hymnography', *Jewish Quarterly Review* 44.2: 123–61.

Schork, R.J. (1957) 'The Sources of the Christological Hymns of Romanos the Melodist', PhD dissertation. Oxford.

   (1960) 'The Medical Motif in the Kontakia of Romanos the Melodist', *Traditio* 16: 354–63.

   (1962) 'Typology in the Kontakia of Romanos', *Studia Patristica* 6: 211–20.

   (1966) 'Dramatic Dimension in Byzantine Hymns', *Studia Patristica* 8: 271–9.

   (1975) 'Romanos, *On Joseph I*, Stanza α: Text and Type', *Byzantion* 45: 131–44.

   (1995) *Sacred Song from the Byzantine Pulpit: Romanos the Melodist.* Gainesville.

Schouler, B. (2005) 'L'Éthopée chez Libanios ou l'évasion esthétique', in *ΗΘΟΠΟΙΙΑ: La Représentation de caractères entre fiction scolaire et réalité vivante à l'époque impériale et tardive*, eds E. Amato and J. Schamp. Salerno: 79–92.

Schulz, H.-J. (1986) *The Byzantine Liturgy: Symbolic Structure and Faith Expression.* New York.

Scott, R. (1985) 'Malalas, The Secret History and Justinian's Propaganda', *DOP* 39: 99–109.

   (2009) 'Byzantine Chronicles', *The Medieval Chronicle* 6: 31–57.

   (2010) 'From Propaganda to History to Literature: The Byzantine Stories of Theodosius' Apple and Marcian's Eagles', in *History as Literature in Byzantium*, ed. R. Macrides. Farnham: 115–31.

Ševčenko, I. (1980) 'A Shadow Outline of Virtue: The Classical Heritage of Greek Christian Literature (Second to Seventh Centuries)', in *Age of Spirituality: A Symposium*, ed. K. Weitzmann. New York: 53–73.

Shepardson, C.C. (2008) *Anti-Judaism and Christian Orthodoxy: Ephrem's Hymns in Fourth-Century Syria*. Washington, DC.

Shoemaker, S.J. (2007) 'Marian Liturgies and Devotion in Early Christianity', in *Mary: The Complete Resource*, ed. S.J. Boss. London; New York: 130–45.

  (2008) 'The Cult of the Virgin in the Fourth Century: A Fresh Look at Some Old and New Sources', in *The Origins of the Cult of the Virgin Mary*, ed. C. Maunder. London; New York: 71–87.

Smith, J.W. (2004) *Passion and Paradise: Human and Divine Emotion in the Thought of Gregory of Nyssa*. New York.

Smitmans, A. (1966) *Das Weinwunder von Kana: Die Auslegung von Jo 2, 1–11 bei den Vätern und heute*. Beiträge zur Geschichte der biblischen Exegese. Tübingen.

Sorabji, R. (2000) *Emotion and Peace of Mind: From Stoic Agitation to Christian Temptation*. Oxford.

Soskice, J.M. (1985) *Metaphor and Religious Language*. Oxford.

Starowieyski, M. (1989) 'Le titre Θεοτόκος avant le concile d'Ephèse', *Studia Patristica* 19: 236–42.

Steenberg, M.C. (2008) *Irenaeus on Creation: The Cosmic Christ and the Saga of Redemption*. Supplements to Vigiliae Christianae 91. Leiden.

  (2009) *Of God and Man: Theology as Anthropology from Irenaeus to Athanasius*. London.

Stevenson, J. (1966) *Creeds, Councils and Controversies: Documents Illustrative of the History of the Church A.D. 337–461*. London.

Taft, R.F. (1977) 'How Liturgies Grow: The Evolution of the Byzantine "Divine Liturgy"', *OCP* 43: 355–78.

  (1991) 'Asmatike Akolouthia', *Oxford Dictionary of Byzantium*. Oxford.

  (1995) 'Church and Liturgy in Byzantium: The Formation of the Byzantine Synthesis', in *Liturgy, Architecture and Art of the Byzantine World: Papers of the XVIII International Byzantine Congress (Moscow, 8–15 August 1991) and Other Essays Dedicated to the Memory of Fr. John Meyendorff*, ed. C.C. Akentiev. St Petersburg: 13–29.

  (1998) 'Women at Church in Byzantium: Where, When – and Why?', *DOP* 52: 27–87.

  (2006) *Through Their Own Eyes: Liturgy as the Byzantines Saw It*. Berkeley.

  (2008) 'Liturgy', in *The Oxford Handbook of Byzantine Studies*, eds E. Jeffreys, J.F. Haldon and R. Cormack. Oxford; New York: 599–610.

Taylor, D.G.K. (2002) 'Bilingualism and Diglossia in Late Antique Syria and Mesopotamia', in *Bilingualism in Ancient Society: Language, Contact and the Written Word*, eds J.N. Adams, M. Janse and S. Swain. Oxford: 298–331.

Theokritoff, E. (2003a) 'The Orthodox Services of Holy Week: The Jews and the New Sion', *Sobornost* 25.1: 25–50.

(2003b) 'The Orthodox Services of Holy Week: The Jews and the New Sion (Notes)', *Sobornost* 25.2: 74–8.

Tomadakis, N.B. (1974) 'Romanus Melodus and the Greek Tragedians', in *Serta Turyniana: Studies in Greek Literature and Palaeography in Honor of Alexander Turyn*, eds A. Turyn, J.L. Heller and J.K. Newman. Urbana, IL: 401–9.

Topping, E.C. (1976) 'St. Romanos the Melodos and his First Nativity *Kontakion*', *Greek Orthodox Theological Review* 21.3: 231–50.

(1978) 'On Earthquakes and Fires: Romanos' Encomium to Justinian', *ByzZ* 71: 22–35.

Torrance, A. (2013) *Repentance in Late Antiquity: Eastern Asceticism and the Framing of the Christian Life c.400–650 CE*. Oxford.

Upson-Saia, K. (2006) 'Caught in a Compromising Position: The Biblical Exegesis and Characterization of Biblical Protagonists in the Syriac Dialogue Hymns', *Hugoye: Journal of Syriac Studies* 9.2: <http://syrcom.cua.edu/hugoye/Vol9No2/HV9N2UpsonSaia.html>.

Van Bekkum, W.J. (1993) 'Anti-Christian Polemics in Hebrew Liturgical Poetry (*PIYYUT*) of the Sixth and Seventh Centuries', in *Early Christian Poetry: A Collection of Essays*, eds J. den Boeft and A. Hilhorst. Leiden: 297–308.

van Esbroeck, M. (1968) 'La lettre de l'empereur Justinien sur l'annonciation et la Noël en 561', *AB* 86: 351–71.

Varghese, A. (2006) 'Kaiserkritik in Two *Kontakia* of Romanos', in *Byzantine Narrative*, eds J. Burke, U. Betka, P. Buckley, K. Hay, R. Scott and A. Stephenson. Melbourne: 393–403.

Vasiliev, A. (1942–3) 'Medieval Ideas of the End of the World: East and West', *Byzantion* 16: 462–502.

Waldman, N. (1989) 'The Image of Clothing, Covering and Overpowering', *Journal of the Ancient Near Eastern Society of Columbia University* 19: 161–70.

Wallace, H.N. (2009) *Psalms*, ed. J. Jarick. Readings: A New Biblical Commentary. Sheffield.

Watts, E.J. (2006) *City and School in Late-Antique Athens and Alexandria*. Berkeley; London.

Webb, R. (1997) 'Imagination and the Arousal of Emotion in Greco-Roman Rhetoric', in *The Passions in Roman Thought and Literature*, eds S. Morton Braund and C. Gill. Cambridge: 112–27.

(1999a) 'The Aesthetics of Sacred Space: Narrative, Metaphor, and Motion in "Ekphraseis" of Church Buildings', *DOP* 53: 59–74.

(1999b) '*Ekphrasis* Ancient and Modern: The Invention of a Genre', *Word and Image* 15.1: 7–18.

(2007) 'Accomplishing the Picture: Ekphrasis, Mimesis and Martyrdom in Asterios of Amaseia', in *Art and Text in Byzantine Culture*, ed. E. James. Cambridge: 13–32.

(2009) *Ekphrasis, Imagination and Persuasion in Ancient Rhetorical Theory and Practice*. Aldershot.

Weinandy, T.G. (2003) 'Cyril and the Mystery of the Incarnation', in *The Theology of St Cyril of Alexandria: A Critical Appreciation*, eds T.G. Weinandy and D.A. Keating. London; New York: 23–54.

Weitzmann, K. (1974) '"Loca Sancta" and the Representational Arts of Palestine', *DOP* 28: 31–55.

Wellesz, E. (1949) *A History of Byzantine Music and Hymnography*. Oxford.

Wessel, S. (1999) 'Nestorius, Mary and Controversy, in Cyril of Alexandria's *Homily IV* (*De Maria deipara in Nestorium*, CPG 5284)', *Annuarium Historiae Conciliorum* 31: 1–49.

Whitaker, E.C. (2003) *Documents of the Baptismal Liturgy*. Revised and expanded by Maxwell E. Johnson. 3rd edn. London.

White, H. (1980) 'The Value of Narrativity in the Representation of Reality', *Critical Inquiry* 7.1: 5–27.

Wilken, R.L. (1966) 'Exegesis and the History of Theology: Reflections on the Adam–Christ Typology in Cyril of Alexandria', *Church History* 35.2: 139–56.

(1971) *Judaism and the Early Christian Mind: A Study of Cyril of Alexandria's Exegesis and Theology*. New Haven.

(1983) *John Chrysostom and the Jews: Rhetoric and Reality in the Late 4th Century*. The Transformation of the Classical Heritage. Berkeley.

(2003) 'Cyril of Alexandria as Interpreter of the Old Testament', in *The Theology of St Cyril of Alexandria: A Critical Appreciation*, eds T.G. Weinandy and D.A. Keating. London; New York: 1–21.

Wright, D.F. (2004) 'From "God-Bearer" to "Mother of God" in the Later Fathers', in *The Church and Mary*, ed. R.N. Swanson. Studies in Church History 39. Woodbridge: 22–30.

Wybrew, H. (1990) *The Orthodox Liturgy: The Development of the Eucharistic Liturgy in the Byzantine Rite*. Crestwood, NY.

Yahalom, J. (1987) 'Piyyut as Poetry', in *The Synagogue in Late Antiquity*, ed. L.I. Levine. Philadelphia: 111–26.

Yarnold, E. (2000) *Cyril of Jerusalem*. The Early Church Fathers. London.

Young, F.M. (1979) 'The God of the Greeks and the Nature of Religious Language', in *Early Christian Literature and the Classical Intellectual Tradition*, eds W.R. Schoedel and R.L. Wilken. Paris: 45–74.

(1994) 'Typology', in *Crossing the Boundaries: Essays in Biblical Interpretation in Honour of Michael D. Goulder*, eds S.E. Porter, P. Joyce and D.E. Orton. Leiden: 29–48.

(2003) '*Theotokos*: Mary and the Pattern of Fall and Redemption in the Theology of Cyril of Alexandria', in *The Theology of St Cyril of Alexandria: A Critical Appreciation*, eds T.G. Weinandy and D.A. Keating. London; New York: 55–74.

(2013) *God's Presence: A Contemporary Recapitulation of Early Christianity.* Cambridge.

Young, F.M. and Teal, A. (2010) *From Nicaea to Chalcedon: A Guide to the Literature and its Background.* 2nd edn. London.

Yuval, I.J. (2006) *Two Nations in Your Womb: Perceptions of Jews and Christians in Late Antiquity and the Middle Ages*, trans. B. Harshav and J. Chipman. Berkeley; London.

Zanker, G. (1981) 'Enargeia in the Ancient Criticism of Poetry', *Rheinisches Museum* 124: 297–311.

Index of Biblical Passages

General Index

Aaron, biblical priest: 63, 128, 179
    rod of: 128, 130, 131
Abel, biblical figure: 42, 45, 47, 184–5
Abraham, biblical patriarch: 50, 103, 126, 153,
    173–4; *see kontakia*, XLI. *On Abraham
    and Isaac*
acrostics: 10, 13, 14, 43
Adam, biblical patriarch: 33–5, 37, 40, 132,
    135–6, 139, 166
    blindness of: 88, 91, 152–3
    Christ, comparison to: 55–80, 83–4; *see also*
        Jesus Christ, as second Adam
    clothing and nakedness: 84–7
    first creation: 106
    gluttony of: 133
    hunger: 96, 133
    ill health of: 97–9, 101
    as iron: 76
    as lost coin: 196
    restoration to paradise: 60
    resurrection, after: 132, 198, 200–1, 204
    senses: 91–4, 120
    thirst: 95
Akathistos hymn: 104
alliteration: 2, 3, 31, 36, 45, 110, 115, 117, 119,
    129, 168, 185
anaphora: 29, 32
Anastasios, hymnographer: 13
anti-Judaism: 48–51, 136–45; *see also under*
    creation, second; *kontakia*, XX. *On the
    Passion of Christ*
antistrophe: 31, 32
Aphthonius: 39
Apollinarius: 57
apostrophe (direct address): 22, 25–7, 53
    and second coming: 147, 188–93, 194
        early and contemporary uses: 188–90
        in Romanos: 190–3
architecture *see* second coming, art and
    architecture
Arianism: 30
art/artists *see under* second coming, art and
    architecture
asmatike akolouthia: 15, 16
assonance: 2, 31, 32, 45, 110, 115, 119, 129

Athanasius: 54, 56, 61, 100
    On the Incarnation of the Word: 56–7
    Three Orations against the Arians: 56
audience *see* congregation/audience

Balaam, biblical figure: 63
baptism: 5, 13, 41, 74, 91, 102, 108, 127, 143,
    160, 197
    of Christ: 41, 84, 87, 106, 108, 114, 150, 159,
        178–9; *see also kontakia*, V. *On the
        Baptism of Christ*
    and second coming, liturgy of: 150, 159, 160
    of sinful woman: 167–8
Basil of Caesarea: 104
Basil of Seleucia: 170–1
    On Lazarus: 170–1, 189, 192
    On the Man Possessed: 13
Belial *see under* Satan/the devil
Benjamin, biblical figure: 121
Berytus (Beirut): 7–9
Bethlehem: 88, 95, 116, 152
    as metaphor for birth of incarnate God: 82
Blachernae: 15
blindness *see under* metaphor
Brock, Sebastian: 84

Caiaphas: 19, 28–9, 42, 45
Cain, biblical figure: 42, 45, 47
Cappadocians: 22, 54, 100
Chalcedon, Council of (451): 22, 24
characterization (*ethopoeia*): 5, 32–3, 53
    apostrophe, link to: 188
    in earlier homiletics: 170–1
    and second coming: 147, 169, 172–9, 180,
        194
    self-characterization of Romanos: 174–8,
        192, 194
Cherubikon (Cherubic hymn): 158
Christ *see* Jesus Christ
Chrysostom, John: 144, 148, 157, 158, 161
    Homilia de beato Philogono 6: 148
    Homilia in epistolam primam ad Corinthios:
        154–5
    Homilia in Ioannem: 158
    In epistulam ad Hebraeos: 157

Made in the USA
Coppell, TX
01 October 2023